LONG LIVE THE NEW FLESH

6 PLAYS FROM THE DIGITAL FRONTIER

EDITED BY DAVID OWEN

PLAYWRIGHTS CANADA PRESS

TORONTO

First edition: July 2021
Printed and bound in Canada by Imprimerie Gauvin, Gatineau

Jacket design by Leon Aureus
Jacket photo of Freya Björg Olafson © Hugh Conacher

Playwrights Canada Press
202-269 Richmond St. w., Toronto, ON M5V 1X1
416.703.0013 | info@playwrightscanada.com | www.playwrightscanada.com

LIBRARY AND ARCHIVES CANADA CATALOGUING IN PUBLICATION
Title: Long live the new flesh : 6 plays from the digital frontier / edited by David Owen.
Names: Owen, David, 1970- editor.
Identifiers: Canadiana 20210205598 | ISBN 9780369102508 (softcover)
Subjects: LCSH: Canadian drama—21st century. | CSH: Canadian drama (English)—21st century.
Classification: LCC PS8315.1 .L66 2021 | DDC C812/.608—dc23

Playwrights Canada Press operates on Mississaugas of the Credit, Wendat, Anishinaabe, Métis, and Haudenosaunee land. It always was and always will be Indigenous land.

We acknowledge the financial support of the Canada Council for the Arts, the Ontario Arts Council (OAC), Ontario Creates, and the Government of Canada for our publishing activities.

Canada Council for the Arts | Conseil des arts du Canada

ONTARIO ARTS COUNCIL
CONSEIL DES ARTS DE L'ONTARIO
an Ontario government agency
un organisme du gouvernement de l'Ontario

Canada

ONTARIO CREATES | ONTARIO CRÉATIF

This collection is dedicated to all the brave artistic experimenters who courageously forge ahead into unknown territory and to the equally brave audiences who follow them there.

CONTENTS

INTRODUCTION

DAVID OWEN

"Long live the new flesh" is the last line spoken in the 1983 classic Canadian sci-fi/horror film, *Videodrome*, written and directed by David Cronenberg. In it, the character of Brian O'Blivion says, "The television screen is the retina of the mind's eye. Therefore, the television screen is part of the physical structure of the brain. Therefore, whatever appears on the television screen emerges as raw experience for those who watch it. Therefore, television is reality, and reality is less than television." I chose this title from the '80s because now in 2021 our relationships formed over social media are often as important, if not more, than our face-to-face encounters. Holograms appear on live stages, our physical spaces are augmented by fictional characters from the universes of Pokémon and Harry Potter (among others), our entertainment experiences are sprinkled with "meaningful choices" that seemingly impact the narrative outcome. Perception of ourselves and others is shaped by a constant stream of curated lives and lifestyles fed to us through screens. We see ourselves through our screens. *Send pics or it didn't happen*. The idea of blurring the line between reality and the virtual was thrilling and dangerous back in the time of Cronenberg's classic but is innocuously common now, almost forty years later. Long live the new flesh . . . A fitting title for this collection of six plays from the digital frontier during the time of COVID. A time when traditional theatres have been faced with the choice to move their programming online, mediated through screens, or go dark.

Personally, I see the promise of digital performance as a strange realization of Artaud's Body without Organs, a virtual Theatre of Cruelty where the physical participant (spect-actor) is either reimagined in an alternative or augmented reality, projected into a virtual space through an avatar, or virtually present through telepresence. It is an extension of William Gibson's (and Herbert Blau's after him) consensual hallucination of "data bodies flying through cyberspace" (*Neuromancer*) or inversely, enhanced bodies in augmented environments achieved through digital means. Post-human performance for cyborg audience members. To paraphrase Blau from "Virtually Yours: Presence, Liveness, Lessness" in Reinelt and Roach's *Critical Theory and Performance* (2007), the cyber-body is an index for the promise of the real but absent body. Taken further, the idea of the cyber-body can be expanded to include the promise of a cultural or national identity absented or even fabricated to support dominant ideologies in virtual spaces.

Gibson's vision of cyberspace as a consensual hallucination dates to back to 1984, around the same time as the release of *Videodrome*. Today, due to digital technology, this consensual hallucination defines the new contract between performers and spect-actors, framing a renegotiated suspension of disbelief in contemporary performance. Even the concept of narrative has exploded into six variations thanks to Jesper Juul's work on videogames. It is no wonder, then, that the playwrights and ensembles represented by the texts within this anthology grappled with the challenge to capture these "plays" in written form. In many cases decisions had to be made and novel strategies created to convey the visual, aural, and social media elements essential to these unique pieces. Through their examples, these six plays lay a groundwork for future digital performance texts to build from. Just like experimentation in music during the twentieth century pushed musical notation into new territories, these plays forced us to question and re-examine theatrical notation as well. For example, how should a playwright describe text message exchanges between future audience members and fictional characters that occur days before the performance date? How might a playwright attempt to convey the impact of seeing composite video images and live actors simultaneously on stage in a stage direction? How could a playwright/performer describe in words the act of literally erasing her body in front of an audience, replacing/reconstructing it with a distorted online persona, and then pulling up a stool to take questions from the audience? These were just some of the questions that arose while putting together this anthology.

This collection launches with a fun sci-fi thriller that is environmental theatre, live-action-roleplay, and B-movie zombie apocalypse rolled into one. *Alien Contagion: Rise of the Zombie Syndrome* may seem out of place in a digital performance collection, but the narrative follows an algorithmic structure similar to narrative rich videogames, including multiple possible endings. The story is conveyed and enhanced through video feeds and the use of smartphones to translate, locate, and communicate. This piece is an excellent example of how contemporary artists and audiences are blowing the doors off traditional notions of theatre, performance, and the audience's involvement with the story.

Freya Björg Olafson's one-performer show, *AVATAR*, follows. This piece explores online identity, identity creation and destruction, and navigating that struggle for identity using movement, blue screens, and audience interaction.

This piece is an intimate experience between audience and performer made strange through digital media. It is difficult to describe this play succinctly in a few words. Among several compelling and diverse sections, this play allows its audience to witness the performer literally erase their body before their eyes, and then reconstruct themselves as an "enhanced" online persona, creating a viscerally felt comment on curated online bodies and impossible beauty expectations. This is a powerful piece that seamlessly combines movement, humour, audience interaction, and technological wizardry.

The third play of the collection may seem more like a traditional play in that it features a compelling narrative story in the style of a film noir. However, *Helen Lawrence* is not just a play nor is it a film, but both simultaneously. The scenes are performed live and are visible to the audience while the film is composited and projected on a massive downstage scrim filling the proscenium arch. The actors not performing in the current scene are moving the cameras and setting up for the following scene. It is not only a technical marvel but also an excellent noir story exploring last-century Vancouver's colourful underbelly, striking a perfect balance between engaging storytelling and spectacle.

Town Choir by Theatre Replacement is the most non-linear performance in this collection. It features text by four writers, each in a different part of Canada: Prince George, Winnipeg, Montreal, and Canning, Nova Scotia. During the performance, the writers send their words simultaneously in real time through a series of text messages to a choir in Vancouver where the audience awaits. The choir sings selections of the texts in four-part harmony as they arrive through the text feeds and are shown scrolling by on four multimedia screens. The subject matter of the written material streamed into the space is at times quotidian, sometimes intimate, at other times touching and inquisitive. This is a delightfully evocative piece of performance art using voice, visuals, and digital communication.

The fifth play in the collection is the beautiful and moving *Muse* by Barbra French. This play uses video mapping, projections, and sound modulation to tell the compelling story of Grace, a young, institutionalized woman who finds her voice through music. The way technology is used in this piece reminds me of the expressionist play *Machinal*, by Sophie Treadwell, in the way it uses sound and light to communicate her mental and physical environment. The harsh reality of her situation is contrasted starkly by the lush imagery and sound of the inner life of Grace, punctuated further by Grace's joyful moments of direct interaction with the audience. This play can be seen as an example of neo-expressionism in how the technical tools allow the audience into Grace's inner emotional journey, carrying us through her dreamlike reality.

The final play of the collection is *You Are Very Star* by Electric Company Theatre. This is an ambitious and complex story that spans several time periods transporting the audience both backward and forward in time. This "transmedia exploration" uses the iconic H.R. MacMillan Space Centre in Vancouver as its backdrop, both in the narrative of the play and a site of exploration and interactivity for the audience. This piece involves several innovative elements that deserve note. First, the play features a robust online presence, an online portal, where audience members are asked questions. In the days leading up to the performance, a character from the play texts and engages in enigmatic exchanges with audience members via their cellphones, prior to experiencing the main performance. At the performance, between the acts, audience members are sent on a form of scavenger hunt throughout the Space Centre to various stations. These stations involve tasks that provide clues about the overarching narrative and also allows the audience to play and explore the Space Centre itself. And third, the performance takes place in the viewing dome of the Space Centre, featuring both live and filmed elements. An important part of the narrative timeline has to do with the year the projection technology in the planetarium was changed from analogue to digital. The unifying idea of the play is the tension between the analogue and the digital, and the concept of singularity. The scale of this play is immense, reaching audiences virtually through digital means and physically through the site-specific location, as the journey of the story takes audiences through both time and space.

Considering the highly innovative and inspiring work being created in this country, an anthology of Canadian digital performance plays like this one is definitely overdue! Thank you to Playwrights Canada Press for sharing this vision with me and making this anthology (and its accompanying essay anthology) possible. This collection is meant to be an important resource and inspiration for theatre creators and instructors across Canada, and abroad. Let this serve as the first of many collections to record the Canadian performance perspective in relation to the new vistas of creative opportunities provided through digital means and to demonstrate how digital technology is reshaping our definition and expectations from performance. I hope you find this collection as inspiring as I do.

ALIEN CONTAGION: RISE OF THE ZOMBIE SYNDROME

STORY BY TYLER CLARKE,
FINN GHOSH-LEUDKE,
AND ANDY THOMPSON

PLAY WRITTEN BY ANDY THOMPSON

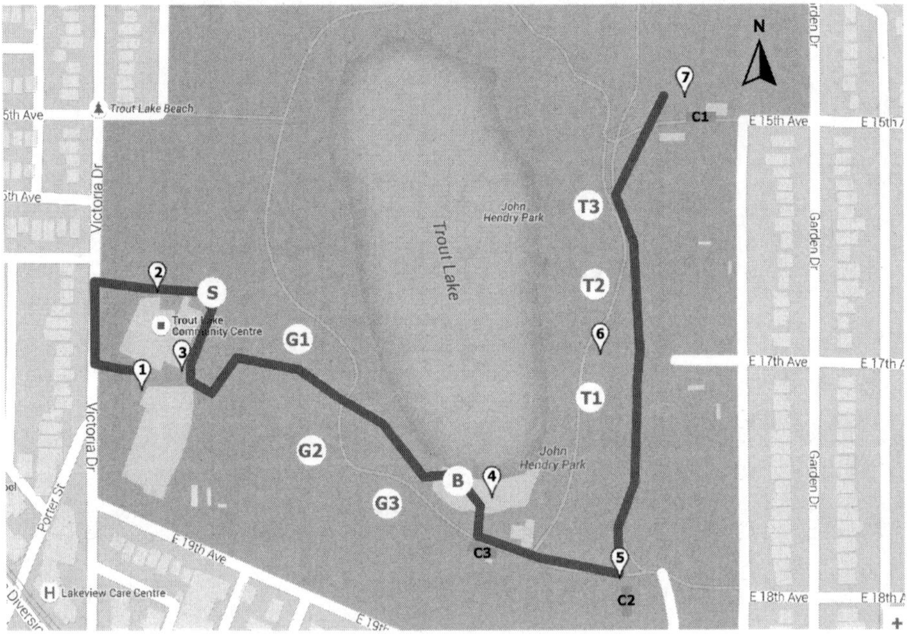

LEGEND

Numerals = Site Numbers
S = Stairwell Zombie Areas
G = Garbage Zombie Areas
B = Beach Zombie Areas
T = Tree Zombie Areas
C = Shipping Container Placement

PLAYWRIGHT'S NOTE

This script was written as an interactive, roving, smartphone-enabled, site-specific play that took place in Vancouver's Trout Lake Community Centre and neighbouring John Hendry Park. The show involved small groups of audience members travelling on a circuit of seven sites. There were five performances a night along this circuit, departing at half-hour intervals.

This play is part scripted, part improvised. The improvised areas are indicated with "improv." While these sections are meant to provide the structure in and out of the scripted sections of the story, other improvisation may occur. The audience group, in the "lead role," should be empowered to make decisions as to what to do, where to go, and how to interact with the performers wherever possible and within reason.

Each audience group will be competing for points and high score. The points system has not been detailed herein. That is an entirely different matter for production.

There are three possible endings. Only one of the endings (Ending 2 in this script) is the correct or winning scenario. The other two endings are different versions of audience failure. Audience decisions determine which ending takes place in any given performance. The script indicates when to skip ahead to other pages based on audience decision-making at the final site.

Detailed production notes related to the audience role assignments are on the last page of this script.

The Virtual Stage acknowledges the financial support of the province of British Columbia. Special thanks also goes to Choco Eyes for the zombie and alien contact lenses, Trout Lake Community Centre, and the Vancouver Board of Parks and Recreation for hosting our undead production with so much vitality and enthusiasm. I would also like to extend my thanks to Massimo Rocchetta, Kristin Mattock, Jennifer McLean, and Meghan Byrne from the drama departments at Killarney Secondary School, Lord Byng Secondary School, and Magee Secondary School for allowing us to integrate their talented and extremely hard-working students into our production as zombies.

Lastly, I would also like to offer my sincere and immense gratitude to the extremely creative and talented Tyler Clarke and Finn Ghosh-Leudke, my story co-writers, for so enthusiastically and playfully crafting with me the plot and characters upon which this script is based.

Andy Thompson
Vancouver, BC, Canada
October 2018

Alien Contagion: Rise of the Zombie Syndrome was produced by The Virtual Stage, running from October 6 to November 1, 2015, at Trout Lake in Vancouver. It was the fourth instalment in a series of five annual *Zombie Syndrome* productions between 2012 and 2016. Visit www.thevirtualstage.org/zombies2015 for more information.

Conceived, written, directed, and produced by Andy Thompson
Story by Tyler Clarke, Finn Ghosh-Leudke, and Andy Thompson

Starring, in order of appearance:
Ron Chartier: Site 1, Blotsky
Josephine Gray: Site 1, Private Black
Eva Butterly: Site 2, Lucy Peterson
Jennifer Hughes: Site 3, Anderson
Jared Hubicka: Sites 3 and 4, Hoffstead
Sinead Grewcock: Site 3, Entity
Lukas Bell: Site 4, Taylor
Odile Brooks: Site 4, McCain
Darcy Millar: Site 4, Williams
Marina Pasqua: Site 5, Dubois
Tyler Clarke: Site 5, Johnson
Jake Anthony: Site 6, Man in Black
Nailya Red: Site 6, Woman in Black
Amelia MacKenzie-Gray-Hyre: Sites 6 and 7, Patty the Hacker
Rowan Jang: Site 7, Khufu

Zombie performers: Boston Bjork, Leo Bui, Daniel Chan, Kelly Chan, Erika Dawe, Mark Dizon, Jennifer Henry-Warnock, Chanamon Klaimongkol, Lauren Lee, Kayleigh Ley, Michelle Lin, Caitlin Mak, Maria Mendez, Kristen Miller, Justin Mo, David Ochieng, Matthew Ogilvie, Chase Prior, Alina Qiu, Hansel Rehberger, Austin Sarballon, Kristy Tran, Nathan Tran, Aaron Tsang, Ashley Tsang, Anna Webster, Rosie Weir, Colleen Wrench, and Michelle Zheng

Production Manager: Tee Crane
Stage Manager: Josephine Gray
Technical Director: Michael Brooks
Alien Design: Kyle Huculak
Lead Makeup Design: Elizabeth McLeod
Lead Makeup Artists: Lanny Brown, Candice Harvey, Elizabeth McLeod, Mary Phan, and Jenny Ruth
Assistant Makeup Artists: Madoka Baumann, Samantha Faith, Benjamin Fieschi-Rose, Kaeko Fujiyama, Madi Hamilton, Meghan Judge, Monica Kurowska, Molly Mackay-Smith, Nikki McCormack, Kayla Rowand, Jessica Sampson, Wakana Shimamura, Sydney Thornton, and Marisse (Emmy) Winder
Entity Makeup: Lily Barrett
Set Designers: Duncan MacCallum and Darcy Millar
Costume Design: Natalie Collins
Site Management: Michael Brooks, Natalie Collins, Tee Crane, Josephine Gray, and Giovanni Zarata
Media Relations: Murray Paterson Marketing Group (MPMG)
Media Relations Account Manager: Sarah Ghosh (MPMG)
Box Office and Website Design: Adam Jones
Additional Crew: Benjamin Fieschi-Rose, Janmie Gunawardina, and Josh Lerner

CHARACTERS

Blotsky
Private Black
Lucy Peterson
Anderson
Hoffstead
Entity
Taylor
McCain
Williams
Dubois
Johnson
Man in Black
Woman in Black
Patty the Hacker
Khufu
Zombies

. . . and, of course, the audience!

Photo illustration by Andy Thompson; alien design by Kyle Huculak.

SITE 1: ORIENTATION AND BRIEFING

BLOTSKY meets the group at the rendezvous point. He has the front-of-house report and hollers the last names of those who have made reservations.

BLOTSKY: *(example)* Smith. Johnson. Patterson. Waxman. Jones. There should be seventeen of you in all. Is everyone here?

Improv as required. Then, when the front-of-house check is done:

Follow me.

He moves them to Site 1. When they arrive to a secret area with an animated NASA logo on one wall:

Line up. Right here. My name's Sergeant Blotsky. I work for NASA. Thank you for answering the call to duty. Private Black here has some paperwork for you to review and sign. Please look it over carefully and sign it if you wish to proceed with your mission.

Improv the necessary front-of-house matters.

BLACK distributes waivers and pens, facilitating the signing process. Wristbands are also distributed.

As you sign your paperwork, listen closely. If we even remotely suspect any of you of being under the influence of drugs or alcohol, of causing a disruption or putting the mission, the public, or your fellow agents in jeopardy, you will be subject to immediate ejection from the mission. And there are no refunds. The stakes are simply too high. Is that understood?

(improv) Good.

> BLACK *collects the waivers.*

When you have completed signing the paperwork, please return it to Private Black and put the coloured wristband on your wrist.

> *Once they do that:*

Before you proceed, look around you. This is your team. As a team, you will require a unique team name for the record. Select a name now. You have sixty seconds.

> *Improv. Once they have selected a name:*

Have you selected a name? *(reiterate the name)*? Private Black, please note for the record that this team is called *(reiterate name and improv for any comedic potential)*. Throughout the mission your intelligence will be assessed and a score will be awarded based on how well you use your wits and initiative, think on your feet, and execute the tasks at hand. You will then be able to compare your team's success with others. So, *(name)*, don't screw up. All right. Private Black, you may distribute their ID tags.

(to group) You're the best of the best. All experts in your respective fields. What you are about to receive is your identification tag. Put it on and wear it at all times during your mission.

> *Private* BLACK *hands out an* ID *tag to each audience member. See the notes at the end of script for more detail.*

Anybody who has a blue dot on their ID tag will need a smartphone. Look at your tag. Do you have a blue dot? If so, raise your hands. Okay, you people need smartphones. If you don't have a smartphone, you need to switch your area of expertise with someone who does. Do that now.

> *Improv: a moment of checking for blue dots and* ID *tag swapping, if necessary.*

Now, which one of you is the navigator? You? You'll be in charge of GPS. Who's the electrician? You? You're very important on this mission. The undead thrive in the dark and hate the light. Your flashlight is like a weapon. Don't lose it. On that topic, people: Your tags, as well as any and all items you might acquire on your mission, are government property. You got it?!? We need everything back when you are finished. They are not souvenirs. Understood?

A PowerPoint presentation starts up.

All right. Here is the situation. *(a UFO at night)* An unidentified flying object recently appeared on military radar and was shot down. It crashed somewhere nearby but, for some reason, we can't find it. Every single person who has gone to look for it has either vanished or resurfaced *(a zombie)* as a walking corpse. The craft must have either vaporized or concealed itself with some sort of cloaking device. Fortunately, in the past twenty-four hours we discovered the dead body of the UFO's alien pilot. *(a dead alien)* It was in a house not far from here. Apparently, it died after raiding the kitchen and pigging out on chocolate. *(toxic chocolate)* Possible toxic allergic reaction. Plus, this was at the scene. *(a cube fragment)*

BLOTSKY gingerly produces the cube fragment (Cube Piece 1) as seen in the video.

Who is your chemist? Here. Take a look at this. Handle it carefully. The alien being wasn't the only one at the scene when we arrived. Next to the dead alien's body was an unconscious young girl. *(a young girl)* She has since awoken, but she's not the same. *(close up of alien eye)* Her eyes are discoloured and she's behaving erratically and not talking to us. Our working hypothesis is that the dying alien being somehow took possession of the young girl's body. We need to establish communication with it. But we don't know how. There is one person we believe can help. *(photo of Lucy PETERSON)* Her name is Lucy Peterson. She's a bit of a freak. A paranoid alien and UFO enthusiast. Claims to be an alien abductee. Even runs a support group for people who have been "taken by the ships." Interestingly, she lives nearby. We've been running surveillance on her for a while now. This is what we've got on her. Who's your profiler? Here's her file. Look it over.

Improv as the profiler is handed a file on Lucy PETERSON.

She runs a website. *(screenshot of the website, including its link and PETERSON's face—but not the phone number)*. According to her site, she predicted that aliens would be landing in the area at this time. She claims to have intimate knowledge of their methods of communication. And their agenda. We need you to contact her, set up a meeting, and figure out how to communicate with the alien Entity.

("Find the UFO*")* You must then find the downed alien spacecraft as soon as possible and quell this mysterious and bizarre zombie outbreak before it gets out of hand. *(zombies with a red circle and a line across: i.e., "No Zombies")* Understood?

The PowerPoint presentation ends, returning to the NASA *logo once again.*

Okay, so you're the experts. Who's your actor?

Improv to the actor.

You? We heard your performance in *My Fair Lady* was second to none. Good work. And who's communications? You? Got your phone ready? You'll need to call Lucy Peterson. Set up a meeting. It's important to note that she hates the government. You'll need to act your way into her good books. She runs a support group for alien abductees. Maybe work that angle. Okay. Over to you. You're the experts. You should know what you need to do. Right?

Audience action: BLOTSKY *coaxes them, as required, to visit Lucy* PETERSON*'s website and call the number that will be displayed on that site. The actor should act like an alien abductee and ask to meet her.*

Communications: Private Black here has speakers to hook into your phone. Private Black, hook this person up. Actor, it's up to you.

The phone call is pumped through portable speakers. The phone rings.

PETERSON: *(on phone)* Hello?

Improv: The actor should try to set up a meeting. They will need to earn PETERSON*'s trust. Eventually . . .*

(on phone) You've been abducted? We should meet. Do you know where Trout Lake Community Centre is? Are you anywhere nearby? *(improv)* What a remarkable coincidence. You know what they say: Pay attention to coincidences. I think I might like you. Let's meet. Meet me at the north side of the Trout Lake Community Centre in three minutes. Can you do that? I'm the one with the red umbrella.

End of phone call.

BLOTSKY: Well done.

(into earpiece) Mission control, this is Sergeant Blotsky. The team has contacted the target and is moving in. Rendezvous in three minutes. North side of Trout Lake Community Centre.

(to audience) All right. Let's go. Don't draw attention to yourselves. Act casual.

They head south to Trout Lake Community Centre.

Keep on the lookout. There have been reports of walkers everywhere in these woods.

Improv. Then they arrive at Trout Lake Community Centre. They meet NASA Scientist Susan ANDERSON.

ANDERSON: Blotsky.

BLOTSKY: Anderson.

ANDERSON: *(looking at audience)* Is this them?

BLOTSKY: The best of the best. In the flesh.

ANDERSON: Thank you so much for coming. We're in a bit of a situation here.

BLOTSKY: Who's your scout?

BLOTSKY hands over a pair of binoculars.

Here, take these. You know how to work these, don't you? You're a professional. Do you see anyone with a red umbrella? *(improv)* Well done! Lucy Peterson is right over there.

ANDERSON: Good. All right, people, listen up. She is highly suspicious of anyone she thinks might be a government spy. Who's the actor? *(improv)* All right. It's all on you.

ANDERSON pulls out a piece of paper with an image on it.

We think this symbol is the key. Try to figure out what it means. The rest of you, you can go on in as well, but act normal. Got it? Casual. When you're done with Peterson, I'll be around the corner. I'll take you to the Entity.

BLOTSKY: Good luck, agents.

BLOTSKY and ANDERSON take cover.

SITE 2: TROUT LAKE COMMUNITY CENTRE

The audience arrives.

Audience challenge: The actor needs to act like an alien abductee. The rest of the people need to act normally. Ideally, the actor will provide a good cover story as to why there are so many of them.

They are greeted by Lucy PETERSON. The following scene has a high degree of improv and the performer playing Lucy PETERSON will need to roll with whatever the audience throws her way. In essence, the PETERSON text below could be considered "talking points." The audience should show initiative and take control at this site.

PETERSON: You're the one who called? Wait a second. Who are all these people? This is weird. *(improv; once she's satisfied with their story)* Okay. Not here. This way. In here.

She takes them inside a daycare playground area. Once they are inside:

You can never be too sure. Not here! They might be watching!

She does a check of the area and hops into a covered gazebo.

Over here! *(once they're inside)* So, have you been abducted by aliens? All of you? Or just one of you? What happened? *(improv; after audience explains for a bit)* In all my years I've never heard an account such as that. Truly bizarre. Well, as you no doubt saw from my site, I've been abducted by aliens. Several times. What kind of UFO did you encounter? Do any of these look familiar?

She produces a chart depicting all categories, shapes and sizes of UFOs. Improv as the audience looks it over.

This one? You pick this one? That's part of the royal fleet! The fleet of the Overlord: Lord Khufu! He's coming, you know. If he hasn't already arrived. You must be very special. So, tell me—this is very important—do you have any *tangible evidence* of your visit? I'm collecting evidence. What do you have? *(improv)*

Improv: When the actor asks what the symbol might mean, PETERSON's eyes lock onto it. She is triggered into a state of shock, trauma, and panic. Out of the blue, she starts spouting phrases in Latin.

Finis adest Tellurem! Parare evacuatione! Humanum genus est cessandum! *["The end of the planet Earth is here! Prepare for evacuation! The human race must be stopped!"]*

After a few moments, she collapses. Then rouses.

(coming to) What happened?

A beat.

That image . . . Don't show it to me again. It's their symbol. The ancient alien species that's been studying my biology all of these years. Latin. Phrases in Latin flooded my mind when I saw that image. During one of my visits to the ships, I could hear them talking to one another. In my head. They're psychic. They don't actually communicate verbally. But I could hear them. It's hard to explain. But there was a phrase they said whenever they greeted one another, I'll never forget it. In English it was, "Nothing comes from nothing." I think it's their salute, or their greeting. But they said it in Latin. When aliens communicate with humans, for whatever reason, they speak Latin. Don't ask me why. "Nothing comes from nothing." I don't feel well. I must rest. Before I do, I feel compelled to give you something.

She produces another cube piece: Cube Piece 2.

This is very precious to me. It is not of this Earth. I was told that I would know what to do with it when the time comes. I am sensing that the time has come. Here. Take it.

She hands it to the audience—the chemist should be the handler of these cube pieces.

Go. Go now. I need space. Remember: "Nothing comes from nothing" in Latin. Will you remember? Go.

Improv: audience must leave now.

Once outside, the audience is met by ANDERSON.

ANDERSON: This way. Before she notices. Follow me. Quick. This way.

As they travel, they encounter some zombies in a stairwell!

We put the ones in here that we think might be worth saving. Don't ask me why.

A beat.

Follow me.

She hustles them around the corner.

Gather around. Okay, what happened? What did she say? *(improv)*

ANDERSON *should get them to reinforce what they need to remember.*

"Nothing comes from nothing"? Latin? Interesting. Do you have a linguistics expert? You speak Latin, right? *(improv)* Of course you do. If not, I'm sure you can use Google Translate. And what about a psychologist? You? All right. We need you two to work together. I will take you to the Entity. And the two of you will be the ones to do the talking. Understood? *(improv)* Okay. This way. Let's go.

SITE 3: ALIEN INTERROGATION

Improv: ANDERSON *guides them to a tent, prepping the audience with regard to the situation and how to stay safe near the* ENTITY. *Then:*

ANDERSON: All right. Here we are. Don't get too close; you could get exposed.

(to HOFFSTEAD*)* Anything?

HOFFSTEAD: No change. Won't talk to us.

ANDERSON: Open it.

HOFFSTEAD *opens the tent wall, revealing a girl in restraints (the same one with the alien eyes from the slide show).*

We tried everything. But it just won't talk to us. You're the experts. What should we do?

Audience challenge: figure out how to say "nothing comes from nothing" to the alien in Latin ("Ex nihilo nihil fit"). This is like the key to unlock the scene that follows. The two actors playing ANDERSON *and* HOFFSTEAD *will have to moderate and control the improv so it doesn't go off the rails. Once the* ENTITY *(in the girl) is satisfied with the proper greeting and courtesy, it speaks.*

ENTITY: *(ritualistically)* Ex nihilo nihil fit.

A beat, then:

You speak English. We can speak in English, if we must, humans. But it won't be for long. When we are finished our mission, the human race will be extinguished, appropriately having eaten itself into oblivion. You eat the planet. Now you eat yourselves. Poetic justice. You humans, with your wars and your addiction to fossil fuels. You are destroying the Earth. We have been trying to warn you for decades now, but your leaders would never listen. Your society. It's unsustainable. Have you not noticed the so-called natural disasters that are increasing? The floods? The earthquakes? The rising temperatures? And poisoned oceans? All man-made. There is nothing "natural" about them. Selfish, humans! Selfish! Not surprisingly, the planet recently called out for assistance. In pain. And we have responded to that call. There is nothing you can do, humans. My craft, though it crashed, is equipped with enough biological material to destroy you human parasites all across the globe.

The ENTITY *buckles in pain.*

My father will not be happy that I have received this treatment. My craft shot down. My body expired. And now this. Confined in this ugly form. I cannot maintain the connection for long. I cannot believe your military shot down my ship! There will be consequences. My father is very powerful. We are royalty. I am second in line to the throne. You have no idea who you are dealing with! The Earth needs to survive. You do not. So. You wanted communication. What is it that you want to know?

Audience challenge: In the following improv segment the audience must indicate they wish to find the ENTITY*'s* UFO*. Once the audience makes this kind of reference . . .*

You wish to find my craft? Very well. I will help you. Under one condition.

Photo by Andy Thompson; alien design by Kyle Huculak.

A beat.

My connection to this human form will remain stable for only a few more hours. Listen very carefully. When I am away from my craft, it broadcasts its location to my body so that we may be united at a moment's notice. The problem is, my body has died. However, I believe your military is detaining my corpse at a medical facility. Is this true?

ANDERSON: *(hesitantly)* It's true.

ENTITY: Good. Listen closely. In my body, my *real* body—not this one—there is a microchip implanted in my chest cavity. You will need to surgically remove it. Your military technicians should be able to decode the chip to determine the coordinates of my craft. But you will not be able to open it without the key. The key is a cube. You must locate all the pieces of this cube, assemble them, and insert it into the cube-shaped cavity along the edge of my craft. A service hatch will then open. Inside the hatch is a button. *(said strangely) Press that button.* Do you understand? That will summon my father. I will die without your help.

A beat.

Did you get all of that? Do you have a note taker? You? You're the note taker? Have you been taking notes?

Improv as the note taker struggles with recording the instructions. The ENTITY *might repeat them reluctantly if needed, giving the note taker a bit of a hard time, for example, "You're going to make me repeat all of that?"*

I only managed to salvage this piece of the key.

It hands them Cube Piece 3.

Assemble the pieces, form the cube, and the key will be ready. Remember. *(again, said strangely) Press that button.* You must trust me. Go now. I do not have much time.

HOFFSTEAD: All right, people. This way.

The curtain is closed.

You heard what it said. You need to locate the craft and press the button. Wait a minute. On the other hand, we have absolutely no reason to trust that thing. It wants you to find its ship and start pressing buttons?! For all we know, pressing that button will complete its mission to wipe us out! I don't know what to tell ya. We're going to have to trust your judgment to take the correct action once you get there. All right, everyone. This way.

He leads the audience out.

SITE 3-4: TRAVEL THROUGH THE GARBAGE ZONE

HOFFSTEAD: Like the Entity said, we do have its body. I will take you there now. However. The alien genetic material is not something we're entirely comfortable with at this point. People are falling ill. Therefore you all need to be thoroughly decontaminated prior to entering the facility. Unfortunately, the decontamination area is located on the other side of these woods. The area is not entirely secure and contains potential biohazards, so stay sharp. And most importantly: Always stay together. It's entirely possible that you could be spooked and it's important not to scatter. Ever. You got me? From this point on to the end of your journey: *Stick together as a group.* Is that understood? *(improv as he gets them to agree)* Good. All right. Follow me. Flashlights on, people.

En route, HOFFSTEAD *improvises with the audience about the dangers of the park and the need to stay vigilant. Some possible text:*

Stay alert. This is a hotspot. Stick together. I hate walking through here. Gives me the creeps.

Zombies appear along the path near some garbage cans (indicated as "Garbage Zombies" on the map). They leap out from behind trees and bushes, freaking everyone out. This is an interactive experience with the audience challenged to push the zombies back by shining flashlights in their faces.

Oh, sweet Jesus. Hurry up, people. Let's get outta here! Keep moving. I've gotcha covered. Shine a light in its face. They hate that. Let's go.

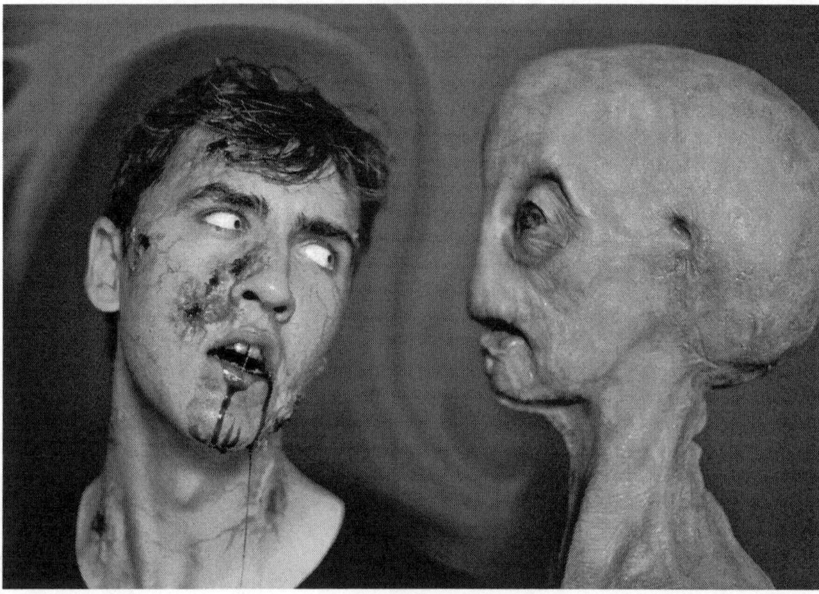

Photo of Rowan Jang by Andy Thompson; alien design by Kyle Huculak.

SITE 4[A]: THE PREP AREA

The audience arrives at the concession stand. TAYLOR *is waiting for them.*

TAYLOR: Is this them?

HOFFSTEAD: This is them.

(to crowd) Everyone, stay sharp. Thank you for your service to the human race. Godspeed and good luck.

HOFFSTEAD exits.

TAYLOR: Everybody listen up. What you are about to be exposed to is a deceased alien life form that we don't know anything about. We need to take precautions to ensure that you don't get infected, fall ill, and compromise the mission or the safety of your colleagues. The alien Entity fell ill eating chocolate so we think it's best if you ingest this serum that we have concocted. It's an inoculation against the viral agents we have thus far detected in the alien being. So, if you know what's good for you, drink up.

Improv as the audience is given hot cocoa.

MCCAIN: This way, please.

MCCAIN hands them a drink.

Line up against the wall. This way, please.

MCCAIN hands them a drink.

Line up against the wall. This way, please.

MCCAIN hands them a drink.

Line up against the wall.

And so on . . .

Once they are all lined up along the east side of the concession building, TAYLOR and MCCAIN start to scan the audience with a flashlight and Geiger counter.

TAYLOR: Have you come in contact with the undead or any alien beings within the past twenty-four hours?

Repeat. This continues for a while. Then suddenly they get a strange reading from one particular audience member.

I'm getting some strange readings from this one.

MCCAIN: Let's see.

TAYLOR: Have you come in contact with the undead or any alien beings within the past twenty-four hours?

Improv.

MCCAIN: I don't trust them.

TAYLOR: Neither do I.

An idea comes to him:

We heard there's a psychic in your group.

MCCAIN: Who's the psychic? *(improv)* You?

TAYLOR: Good. We need you to use your psychic powers to read this person's mind. Should we trust them?

Improv. If the psychic says they can be trusted:

MCCAIN: You're lucky.

If the psychic says they cannot be trusted, or is lying:

I knew it.

TAYLOR: I'm sorry, but for the safety of everyone here we're going to need you to wear this.

Improv as TAYLOR *and* MCCAIN *get the infected person to wear scrubs, a mask, and gloves.*

All right, let's head out.

MCCAIN: This way, people. Let's go.

SITE 4[B]: DECONTAMINATION

The audience is led to a decontamination area at the beach. They are met by WILLIAMS.

WILLIAMS: All right, everyone. Line up here. A single straight line. Line up.

Once they're lined up, they are processed. This involves each audience member passing through a decontamination area in which they are blasted with fog and bright lights.

Okay. Single file. One at a time through here.

The following three lines can happen on top of one another as the crowd is processed.

Go ahead. Wait. Go ahead. Wait. Go ahead. Wait . . .

MCCAIN: *(fogging them one at a time)* This way. Hold. Proceed. This way. Hold. Proceed. This way. Hold. Proceed . . .

TAYLOR: *(escorting them to the beach)* This way. Stand here. This way. Stand here. This way. Stand here . . .

After the ritual, MCCAIN *addresses the audience.*

MCCAIN: All right, people. The neurotoxin that you have just been subjected to should protect you—somewhat—from any alien viruses that you may become exposed to in your journey ahead. However, it offers no protection whatsoever from the walkers that have been detected in the area. Now. If any of you are pregnant, have high-blood pressure, or heart disease we will need to—

Suddenly zombies emerge from the sand and charge the audience.

TAYLOR: Oh my god!

MCCAIN: Holy crap! We gotta get outta here!

Walkers grab MCCAIN *and* TAYLOR. *A bloodthirsty swarm ensues. Some zombies continue to pursue the audience.*

WILLIAMS: Follow me, people! We can't wait for them. They're gone. Follow me! Stick together!

Improv. WILLIAMS *quickly ushers the audience to Site 5.*

SITE 5: THE ALIEN AUTOPSY

They arrive at the shipping container. WILLIAMS *ushers the entire audience inside.*

WILLIAMS: They're coming! Quickly! Get in! Get in!

DUBOIS: What the hell is going on?

WILLIAMS: We got ambushed! They're headed right this way!

DUBOIS: What's that on your hand?

WILLIAMS *looks at his bloodied hand.*

WILLIAMS: What? This? Nothing.

DUBOIS: You've been bit!

WILLIAMS: No no no . . .

DUBOIS: I'm sorry.

WILLIAMS: Please! No! I'm fine! Wait!

DUBOIS *shoves him outside and slams the door, leaving* WILLIAMS *vulnerable and outside.*

WILLIAMS *bangs on the container door.*

Hey, you can't leave me out here! You've gotta let me in!

A surveillance camera set up shows all the gory action. Zombies attack and swarm WILLIAMS.

DUBOIS: Everyone quiet! We can't let them know we're in here!

When the walkers are finished with WILLIAMS, *there is not much left of him, just a bloodied haz-mat suit and an awful mess. The zombies slowly dissipate on screen.*

I had no choice.

DUBOIS *sees the arm of a zombie trying to get inside.*

Getting out is gonna be fun. Let's just hope they wander off. Who's your muscle? *(improv)* This door stays closed at all times. And make sure to keep a safe distance. Are you *(audience group name)*? We've heard all about you. It's an honour to be working with you. This situation is a bit of a mess. This is what we're dealing with.

She pulls a curtain, revealing a NASA *medical facility. On the table is a small, dead alien. It is greyish green in colour and approximately four feet in height. A genetics analyst,* JOHNSON, *in surgical scrubs, works near a small operating table in the middle of the lab.*

Come on in.

The audience is invited to walk completely around the corpse. Computer monitors and other technical gear are at the far end.

JOHNSON: Never seen anything like it. Definitely not human. A scan showed that something's inside it. So, I started cutting it open—

DUBOIS: But we realized we should wait until the experts get here. Didn't we?

JOHNSON: My bad. Sorry.

JOHNSON *goes back to work on the computers.*

DUBOIS: Cause of death appears to be some sort of blunt force trauma to the internal organs. Do you have a biologist? *(improv)* Come take a look. No lungs. No liver either. There is a circulatory system of sorts. There's a heart—but what it pumps isn't like any kind of blood we've ever seen before. What do you think? *(improv)* The being was found not far from here, next to a girl who was acting very strangely. They said she was possessed. I understand you may have spoken with her, or "it" recently. Is that correct?

Improv as the audience replies.

I understand that you received some instructions as to how to proceed with the deceased? What are you supposed to do?

Improv as the audience is prompted to share what they learned in the Alien Interrogation scene. They then must surgically remove the microchip from the alien ENTITY*'s corpse.*

DUBOIS *and* JOHNSON *remind the audience, as required, of the tasks: surgically remove the chip from the corpse and provide the chip to the military to extract the* UFO*'s coordinates.*

Improv: the cast may have to recap the tasks to assist with audience action and comprehension. Then:

DUBOIS: All right. Let's do this. Who's your surgeon? *(improv)* You? I think it's time to scrub up. Johnson? Gloves.

JOHNSON: I'm on it. Here.

JOHNSON *preps the surgeon with gloves.*

So how long have you been a surgeon? *(improv)*

As JOHNSON *preps the surgeon,* DUBOIS *produces Cube Piece 4, the final puzzle piece. It might be on some sort of necklace.*

DUBOIS: We found this at the scene. Not sure what to make of it. Do you have any idea?

Improv. The audience may even want to assemble the cube as the surgeon gloves up. When the surgeon is ready:

JOHNSON: The surgeon is ready.

DUBOIS: Okay. The table is yours, Doctor.

Improv as the doctor in the audience tries to find the microchip in the alien's guts. At this point the scene transforms into an experience in which the audience is very hands on. The doctor should find an alien microchip prop inside the alien's chest.

You found it? Great. Let me see. *(examines it)* It's a standard microchip. Do you have an engineer? *(improv)* You're an engineer? Take a look at this. What do you think? *(improv)* I totally agree. It's suspiciously so. Johnson?

JOHNSON: Yeah?

DUBOIS: Run this. Let's see what it says.

JOHNSON: You got it.

JOHNSON pops it in an analyzer. Suddenly GPS coordinates pop onto the radar screen: 49.257050, -123.059870

DUBOIS and JOHNSON talk over one another for the next two lines:

DUBOIS: It's a set of coordinates! Who's your navigator? *(improv)* The ship's gotta be at these coordinates. You know what to do. *(improv, for example, "You have a smartphone, right? Let's get those coordinates in your map and see what the location is.")*

JOHNSON: This is Ground Zero to Mission Control. Mission Control, we have coordinates that have been extracted from the deceased. They are 49 point 257050 and negative 123 point 059870. The team is heading there now.

DUBOIS: Not quite yet, Johnson.

JOHNSON: Stand by, Mission Control.

Improv as the GPS gets loaded. When the location is found on the audience's smartphone:

DUBOIS: You get the coordinates? Where's the UFO? Let's see? *(improv)* That's just north of here.

JOHNSON: Mission Control, the coordinates have been locked. The team is heading there now.

DUBOIS: Now? They can't go there now. There are zombies right outside! How the hell are they gonna get out? And that ship? It might be a trap. We don't know anything about it! Everyone who's come close to finding it is gone. It could be emitting radiation. Biological warfare. Or worse.

JOHNSON: If they don't fix this, the entire human race could be wiped out.

DUBOIS: How are we gonna get outta here? Those things could be anywhere. Don't see any now, but the place is crawling. What are we gonna do? Anyone have a gun? We're not armed. We're scientists. Muscle, you up for this? *(improv)* Okay, people, muscle and I are gonna get you all outta here. Navigator, stick with me. Let me see that map. *(improv)* Okay. We'll round this corner and then head north in that direction. Are you all with me?!? Okay, people. Be brave. Follow me. And whatever happens, *stick together!* All right, muscle! Open the door in three, two . . . Are you all ready? We're gonna open this door. In three, two . . . ONE!

Improv. When DUBOIS gets them outside:

All right, navigator. It's all up to you to get your team there. Be careful!

She heads back.

SITE 6: THE MAN IN BLACK

As the audience travels north, they have to navigate through a horde of zombies, which they find nipping at their heels. Then:

A mysterious and somewhat creepy MAN IN BLACK *appears. A quiet* WOMAN IN BLACK *is at his side.*

MAN IN BLACK: Where are you folks all headed? *(improv)* Sure are a lot of you. *(improv)* Not very safe out here at night. Can I join you? *(improv, then no matter what they say)* Thanks.

Improv as they walk north. At one point they hear a zombie in a tree.

My mother always taught me never to talk to strangers. But you all seem like a nice bunch of folks. Yeah. Nice. So, where are we going? It's really kind of you to allow me into your group. Being in a group gives you a sense of belonging, of family. Yeah. Are you family? You all related? You don't look related. But looks can be deceiving. Never judge a book by its cover. Just its title and genre. Just a little joke there. Do you get it? It's humour. Do you like humour? I like humour. It's a little cold out here, don't you find? Important to dress warmly. Walk softly. And carry a big stick. Or a gun. More humour. Taking something that's expected and then adding a twist. Something unusual. Walk softly and carry a big gun. Now, that would be unusual. Right? Yeah. Unless you wanted to kill someone.

There's a sound from a nearby tree. He stops suddenly.

Whoa. Do you hear that? That doesn't sound too good. I think we should keep walking.

More walking.

Hey, friends, can I talk to you all for a second? Everybody. Gather around. Yeah. I have to ask you something.

The MAN IN BLACK *takes off his glasses. He has the same freaky eyes as the* ENTITY.

Have you seen a little guy? A little greyish green fella? He's a friend of mine. About four foot eight? Big black eyes? Sweetest smile you've ever seen?

More zombies suddenly appear behind them.

Oh, dear. What's over there? More of those things. Such a nuisance! You all go ahead without me. It was a pleasure talking with you all.

The MAN IN BLACK *and the* WOMAN IN BLACK *strangely collapse, as if someone hit their off switches. Their lifeless bodies lay in the grass in the most awkward positions.*

A nerdy lady, PATTY THE HACKER, *emerges from the woods.*

PATTY THE HACKER: Whoa. That dude was *definitely* not human.

The zombies pounce on the MAN IN BLACK.

Follow me, you guys. I don't know how long they'll be happy munching *just* on him. This way!

She leads them north. As they walk:

You must be the crack team of scientists they were talking so much about. My name's Patty. I've been listening to the chatter on the airwaves. Got my own ham radio set up. I've been listening to everything that's been going on. The Canadian military is so dumb! They think they've encrypted their communication, but it's so easy to crack! Anyway. Enough with the small talk! More walking. Less talking. I heard the coordinates on the radio. It's just up here. Right? Who's on GPS for you guys? It's this way, right?

Improv: they study the coordinates and continue walking.

Eventually they come upon a UFO *in a field!*

Whoa! There it is! Up ahead! Let's go, you guys! Oh my god! A real UFO!

SITE 7: THE CRASHED UFO

They arrive at the UFO *at* GPS *coordinates 49.257050, -123.059870.*

PATTY THE HACKER: Holy crap! I can't believe you found the UFO! Amazing! People have been dying to find this. And I mean that literally. They're all dead! Holeeeee! Will you check this out! Amazing! This is history in the making! It's like *Close Encounters* meets *28 Days Later* out here.

Improv: we allow an experiential minute for the audience to have UFO *investigation. During this time, they might figure out how to put the cube in the slot. However, if they need prompting.*

So, hey, in my eavesdropping I heard there are these cube things. Maybe they're a fuel cell of some sort. Did you get anything like that? *(looking at the receptacle)* I wonder what this is for.

Improv: if needed, PATTY *guides them in assembling the cube and figuring out that they need to put it in the* UFO*'s ignition. Eventually:*

You're going to put it in? Okay, who's going to do it? If anyone is going to touch something from outer space, I think it should be your astronaut. Who's your astronaut? Okay, you're going to put it in. You ready? Let's count it down, people! In three . . . two . . . one . . .

When they pop the cube in the hole, the UFO *starts. At least, it tries to. A loud start-up sound whines from within the craft. It lights up. It smokes. It shakes. Then, nothing.*

Except . . .

A small hatch pops open. In the hatch there is a button.

Oh my god, what's this? Some sort of button! Did the Entity tell you anything about a button? Listen. I know you're the experts and everything, but seriously, these aliens have come to wipe us out. As far as they're concerned, we're a virus. And these zombies are the cure! Obviously, the alien crashed. Maybe it didn't get a chance to complete its mission. And pushing this button is the last thing that

Illustration by Andy Thompson; alien design by Kyle Huculak.

you—or any human for that matter—will ever do in the history of humanity! On the other hand, it said it was dying. Maybe it was telling the truth and needs help. And this button is merely a benign homing beacon of sorts. But it's risky either way. Who's your strategist? *(improv)* You? All right. From what I hear you are the wisest, most cunning and intelligent person in this group. *(improv)* By all means, listen to what these lesser mortals have to say. But ultimately, you must make the choice for your group. What is your choice? Push the button? Or don't push the button?

They don't *press the button—skip ahead to Ending 3, page 38.*

They do *press the button—continue reading.*

Okay! We're gonna press the button!

The button is pressed. The UFO *suddenly tries to come to life. It shakes. It smokes. A loud start-up sound is heard. Then, nothing.*

Silence.

Well, that was anticlimactic—

Sudden dramatic music. A lighting shift. And a massive alien figure emerges out of the darkness: KHUFU, *the Alien Overlord. His lips do not move as his voice booms from seemingly everywhere.*

KHUFU: Humans!

Dramatic music.

PATTY THE HACKER: I think I just peed my pants.

KHUFU: Ex nihilo nihil fit. Allow me, if you will, to communicate with your minds directly. Who among your ranks is the leader?

Improv.

Come to me. Closer.

Improv as the leader is prodded to approach KHUFU.

KHUFU *speaks in a terrifying tone as if the person is about to be executed.*

You. You!

A tense moment as he holds the person's aura in his hands, then:

Thank you! You pressed the button and we are now able to locate and recover my son. We came to your planet at the request of Earth itself. Your species has been less than kind to its host. Much like renting a hotel room and leaving a terrible mess for the chambermaid. Very selfish. Very rude. We came here to cleanse the Earth of humans, but with this gesture of intelligence and compassion that you have shown for my son, I will let you live. Under one condition. One of you must be sacrificed as a gift to my species. To be ritualistically skewered, cooked, and eaten at the royal table. Which among you is the judge? *(improv)* Of course. Come here. Judge: You have had opportunity to assess the integrity of all of your companions. It is you and you alone that must judge: Which one will you allow us to kill, so that the others may live? *(improv)*

They do *press the button and the judge* refuses *to sacrifice anyone—skip ahead to Ending 2, page 37.*

They do *press the button and the judge* offers *to sacrifice someone—read Ending 1, page 36.*

ENDING 1

Improv: the judge suggests a fellow audience member should be sacrificed.

KHUFU: This one? You wish that this one dies?

Music. Dark music.

I am afraid that is the wrong answer, judge. You see, this mentality that someone must suffer in order for another to benefit is the very basis of your species' own flawed logic. If someone tells you to jump off a bridge, do you do it? If a bully tells you to give him your lunch money, do you do it? *(improv)* No. You mustn't. You must stand up to evil. You humans have not yet learned that it is only by giving that you will receive. Indeed, you are lowly species and far too unevolved to be permitted to remain on Earth. Your entire race must die.

Dramatic music.

I am very sorry.

He gestures for the extinction event to commence, then exits.

PATTY THE HACKER: *(to the judge, sarcastically)* Way to go.

Blackout. End of show voiceover and music.

The end.

ENDING 2

Improv: the judge refuses to allow anyone to be sacrificed.

KHUFU: You refuse to obey? Why? *(improv)* Well, I must inform you that you have behaved exactly in accordance with a being of commendable wisdom and compassion. I know that our people may appear frightening. But we are in fact a very peaceful race. We are the Watchers of the Earth. And your answer, Judge, is exactly what we had hoped your race could be capable of on this planet. My question was a test.

Music. Hopeful music.

And you passed. We will not harm you. You are ready. There is hope for the Earth. May the Creator be with you in peace, harmony, and joy. And thank you, once again, for saving my son. That was very kind.

PATTY THE HACKER: *(to judge)* You totally saved our butts, man! Way to go!

Blackout. End of show voiceover and music.

The end.

ENDING 3

PATTY THE HACKER: Okay. Let's just leave this thing alone.

Sudden dramatic music. A lighting shift. And a massive alien figure emerges out of the darkness: KHUFU, the Alien Overlord. His lips do not move as his voice booms from seemingly everywhere.

KHUFU: Humans!

Dramatic music.

PATTY THE HACKER: I think I just peed my pants.

KHUFU: Ex nihilo nihil fit. Allow me, if you will, to communicate with your minds directly. Who among your ranks is the leader?

Improv.

Come to me. Closer.

Improv as the leader is prodded to approach KHUFU.

KHUFU speaks in a terrifying tone as if the person is about to be executed.

You. You!

A tense moment as he holds the person's aura in his hands, then:

Why didn't you press the button? Time and time again the human race disappoints. It was a button. It wasn't that complicated. Pressing the button would have enabled a tracking device to locate my son. But you didn't have the heart. And now my son . . . has died! Do you realize what you have done through your deliberate inaction? You are a terrible leader. An embarrassment. And the rest of you are complicit in this crime! You should all be ashamed of yourselves! What do you have to say for yourselves? *(improv)* I don't want to hear it! The instructions were extremely simple. And you failed. Who is your judge? *(improv)* You? Come here. Judge. Are you fit to be remain as stewards of the planet? How do you judge your species?

Improv as the judge is challenged to defend the human race.

Dramatic music.

Well, I will tell you our judgment. The verdict is that you are a petty, selfish, fearful, violent, and stupid people. And not pressing that button was an act of war! You think you're on the top of the food chain? Well, from an interplanetary perspective, let's just say you're chicken feed.

Dramatic death of the species music.

And you all must die! Goodbye, humans!

He exits. Blackout. End of show voiceover and music.

The end.

PRODUCTION NOTES

The following is a breakdown of the sites and actions for each audience role assignment:

Assignment	**Site**	**Action & Props** *(for production purposes)*
1. Surgeon	Site 5	Removes the microchip
2. Engineer	Site 5	Analyzes the microchip
3. Navigator*	Site 5–6	Navigates from Site 5 to Site 7
4. Chemist	Sites 1, 2, 3, & 5	Manages cube pieces
5. Biologist	Site 5	Examines the dead alien
6. Actor	Site 1–2	Talks to Lucy Peterson
7. Electrician	Site 1 & 3–4	Manages flashlights and lighting
8. Muscle	Site 5	Guards the door
9. Communications*	Site 1	Calls Lucy Peterson
10. Linguist*	Site 2–3	Google Translates (Latin–English)
11. Psychologist	Site 2–3	Reasons with the Entity
12. Profiler	Site 1	Profiles Lucy Peterson, gets hard file

* Needs smartphone or access to a smartphone.

13. Note Taker	Site 3	Takes notes of the Entity's instructions
14. Strategist	Site 7	Makes decision: to push or not to push the button
15. Leader	Site 7	Leads talks with Khufu
16. Judge	Site 7	Decides which person gets sacrificed, if any
17. Scout	Site 1	Scouts Lucy Peterson
18. Psychic	Site 4	Assesses if a colleague is lying or not
19. Astronaut	Site 7	Turns on the UFO

AVATAR

FREYA BJÖRG OLAFSON

INTRODUCTION

The *AVATAR* performance is part of a series of artworks that explore methods of creating, validating, and disseminating individual identity through web cameras and the Internet. The series was inspired by the mantra "I post, therefore I am,"* whereby people validate their existence by documenting their lives through social media, personal web pages, blogs, and vlogs. The *AVATAR* series manifested in a sixty-minute performance, fourteen paintings (11" x 14"), five drawings (8" x 10"), a gallery performance streamed online through chatroulette.com, and four short single-channel video works.

This script documents the sixty-minute solo performance that is effectively a duet with technology employing live video feeds and projections on stage to magnify, manipulate, and broadcast persona and image. The structure of the performance is based on popular vlog formats. *AVATAR* includes the introductory "My First Vlog," the continuously in demand "Makeup Tutorial," the self-reflexive "How to Make a Good Vlog," alongside the ever-prevalent "Documentation of Body Processes and Changes," a format that extends the temporal limitations of a classic makeup tutorial video to cover longer-term transformations such as weight loss and muscle gain. Near the end of the work, *AVATAR* explores the "Shout Out to My Subscribers" vlog format, which is often presented in tandem with a "Get to Know Me" vlog. Most of the text spoken throughout *AVATAR*—excluding the Q & A at the end—was derived from vlogs posted online between 2007 and 2009.

Remixing the performance is invited; footnotes are provided for sections of the performance that would benefit from the inclusion of emergent texts/vlogs and software or video content relevant to the cultural climate at the time of production. Descriptions of the original video and audio work, as well as some links to original source material, are provided as entry points for integrating the visual aesthetics of the Internet, social-media platforms, and cyberspaces

* Pit Schultz, "The Producer as Poweruser," in *Engineering Culture: On the Author as (Digital) Producer*, ed. Geoff Cox, Joasia Krysa (New York: Autonomedia, 2005).

into remixes of *AVATAR*. While the *AVATAR* script contains footnotes for the creative engagement of readers, performers, and remixers, it is requested that the stage directions found in the script be thoroughly explored as they remain integral to the work.

AVATAR was initially created using the software Quartz Composer. The performance was later updated to run through the software Isadora, made by TroikaTronix.*

* To create a remix of *AVATAR*, the software QLab or OBS (Open Broadcaster Software), which is free, could also be used. Other suitable software for consideration: Vuo, TouchDesigner, Max/MSP/Jitter, and/or Processing.

AVATAR was first produced in 2009 by Winnipeg's Contemporary Dancers and the núna (now) Festival in Winnipeg, Manitoba, with the following creative team:

Performance, Audio, Video, Quartz Composer, and Isadora: Freya Björg Olafson
Lighting Design: Hugh Conacher
Costume Design: Norma Lachance

Following the premiere, the sixty-minute solo performance undertook national and international touring, including performances in five states, seven provinces in Canada, Iceland, Germany, Greece, as well as three cities in Ecuador. In July 2010 the *AVATAR* performance received the Buddies in Bad Times Vanguard Award for Risk and Innovation at the SummerWorks Theatre Festival in Toronto.

The development of the *AVATAR* series was generously supported by the Canada Council for the Arts, Manitoba Arts Council, Winnipeg Arts Council, and Video Pool Media Arts Centre. The series began at Studio 303 (Montreal) during a workshop lead by 2boys.tv. Subsequently, the *AVATAR* series benefited from residency support at PAF—Performing Arts Forum (Saint-Erme-Outre-et-Ramecourt, France), SÍM–The Association of Icelandic Visual Artists (Reykjavik, Iceland), Plug In ICA—Summer Institute (Winnipeg, Manitoba), and La B.A.R.N. with Tedd Robinson of 10 Gates Dancing Inc. (Ontario).

The publication of this script was made possible with script assistance from Jillian Groening, Andraea Sartison, and Penny Olafson; Q & A transcription by Jillian Groening; and support from York University and the Manitoba Association of Playwrights.

CHARACTERS

Performer: Everyone is a performer online.

AVATAR: By the end of the work the Performer has become an Avatar, an augmented version of themselves represented digitally. At once both vain and apologetic for their presence, they really just want to know, "Can you see me?"

Speaker: A middle-aged person who offers tips on how to present oneself online.

GreenTeaGirlie: A fake persona who created vlogs and stirred up controversy online in 2007.

Hannah: A five-year-old who offers a makeup tutorial, confirming that everybody online is an expert and has knowledge to share. Learn from them!

Computer: Sometimes the machine calls you in to wake you up and break the hyper focus of screen absorption.

Internet User: They are looking hard at themselves—too hard in fact.

Viewer: Spectators gathering in fabricated virtual spaces, like theatres—some seek connection, others troll for sport.

NOTES

Performer(s): They begin the work in all black, gender-neutral clothing and black orthopedic SAS shoes. Layers of clothing are removed throughout the duration of the performance and by the end of the work the Performer is clad in nude underwear. Vocal effects, makeup, a wig, and bluescreen body paint are used to varying degrees during the performance. These identity-altering methods destabilize the appearance of the Performer and support the mutability of identity on stage.

Setting: *AVATAR* occurs on the Internet. The performance is embedded in the Performer's desktop, which is mirrored to the projection screen on stage. The

Performer broadcasts to the web from their home; their bathroom and bedroom materialize on stage virtually through live chroma-keying.

Pre-set Stage: The stage is set with a white rectangular dance floor that matches the size of a projection screen located upstage of the white floor. The projector is positioned behind the projection screen to minimize shadows from the Performer. This configuration gives the appearance of a giant laptop sitting open on stage, with the dance floor as keyboard and projection surface as laptop screen. On the white floor, downstage front, is a small rolling table upon which sits a laptop. The laptop is open, facing toward the projection screen, as is the built-in web camera.* A rolling stool that has three legs and a bike seat is placed upstage of the table. Throughout the work, what the Performer sees on their laptop screen is what the viewers see on the projection screen. As the audience enters, the iconic Apple screensaver "Flurry" plays on the screen as if the laptop is asleep.†

* Originally, this work was performed using an external standard definition camera connected to a laptop with FireWire. Later *AVATAR* was upgraded to use an external HD web camera connected with USB; depending on the quality, a built-in laptop web camera could suffice.

† The "Flurry" screensaver can be found here: https://www.youtube.com/watch?v=bxJhrLADNiU.

SCENE 1: MY FIRST VLOG*

An audio track begins with a simple loop of three notes played on a digital keyboard accompanied by sounds of slowed down stomping, augmented to the point of ambiguity.

On the projection screen, the laptop wakes from screensaver mode. A photo booth app is open and the web camera on the laptop facing the projection screen is turned on; this camera placement creates a video feedback effect within the photo booth application window. The effect

---

* The monologue in Scene 1 is from a YouTube user named GreenTeaGirlie, whose first vlog—a ten-second video uploaded in late March 2007—gained massive ratings and appeared on YouTube's daily Most Viewed section with 170,000 hits on the first day. The video, featuring the user introducing herself, became one of the most watched videos on YouTube at the time with approximately 278,803 views. The drastic uptick in viewership sparked debate surrounding her identity, much of which arose due to GreenTeaGirlie appearing online less than one year after YouTube's biggest sensation to date, lonelygirl15. lonelygirl15 was later revealed to be a fake presence created as part of a web series shared through the vlog format. Although no new content has been uploaded since 2012, GreenTeaGirlie's YouTube channel holds seventy-eight hundred subscribers as of January 2021. When initially crafting this scene, phrases searched included "I'm New" and "My First Vlog."

establishes for the viewer that the projection screen and the screen of the laptop located downstage share a computer desktop.

Slow stomping sounds shift to slowed down clapping as the PERFORMER *enters.*

The PERFORMER *enters the stage with falling motions. They stumble and fight against gravity as their hair falls across their face. They pass close to the upstage screen.*

Distorted, slowed down laughter is heard. The digital keyboard sound loops evolve as the following pre-recorded text is heard over the speakers.

GREENTEAGIRLIE:* Hey, everyone. How is everyone doing? It's GreenTeaGirlie; I hope everyone is doing well.

The PERFORMER *begins stumbling toward the laptop downstage centre. without looking up at the viewers they slowly raise their hand to wave hello.*

I, first of all, would like to apologize for how long it has taken me to do a video.

The PERFORMER *opens their arms to signify "I dunno" alongside the text above. In response to the text below their arm gestures continue into abstraction, occasionally touching their messy hair.*

I been really busy and when we did try to do one in the past couple of days, the computer hasn't been working, the sound hasn't been working, so it's been nearly impossible, so I do apologize.

Increasingly, their falling takes up more space as they stumble forward and backward on their way toward the laptop.

As well as, I would like to apologize for my sick hair; I feel really gross right now, and I know it's unnecessary to say, but, I just do not feel cute, so I do apologize; my hair is kind of up in this little bun here, and, but, we just really needed to do another video 'cause I feel it has been so long, so I do apologize.

* Original source: https://www.youtube.com/watch?v=czTL7yvg_bA.

The vocal pitch shifts lower as the voice repeats the line: "I would like to apologize for my sick hair; I feel really gross right now, and I know it's unnecessary to say, but, I just do not feel cute . . . " The vocal pitch shifts even lower as the voice repeats the line a second time.

The PERFORMER *sits on the stool in front of the web camera and takes three photos using the photo booth app. In the first photo they hide behind their messy hair without looking at the camera. The subsequent two photos progressively show more of their face, and by the last image they look directly at the camera.*

There is no text layered over the soundscape while the three photos are taken.

Now what I would like you guys to do is rate my outfit, and see what you guys think of it. I am actually quite the fashion freak.

Echoes of the following text, which becomes quieter and quieter with each repeat: "quite the fashion freak, quite the fashion freak, quite the fashion freak."

The PERFORMER *walks upstage during the sound echoes, away from the laptop and web camera, in order to take a picture with more of their body in the frame. They face straight into the camera, pulling on the bottom of their shirt, as if to show it off.*

I didn't know if this shirt . . .

Flash! A photo is taken and appears on screen.

The PERFORMER *goes back to the laptop to look at the photo and to set up another. The* PERFORMER *steps away from the laptop to take the photo. This time their pose is awkward, presenting the back of their body to the camera.*

. . . kinda comes out, goes with the pants, 'cause they are kinda capris, but I didn't know if they went with the whole combination, with my shoes . . .

Flash! A photo is taken and appears on screen.

The PERFORMER *swiftly goes back to the laptop and sets up for another photo.*

. . . but my favourite thing is my shoes, so that's what my favourite part is but . . .

This time when the PERFORMER *runs upstage, they take on a confident, model-like pose.*

Flash! A photo is taken and appears on screen.

The PERFORMER *runs back to the laptop and adds an effect using the photo booth app to distort their image. They set up for another photo and run upstage.*

. . . I just don't wanna look pregnant in my shirt, I don't wanna look like I am having a baby . . .

The PERFORMER *creates a wide shape with open arms. This generates a unique result as the photo booth distortion filter creates an elongated body effect.*

Flash! A photo is taken and appears on screen.

The PERFORMER *runs back to the laptop and changes the effect,* preps for the next photo, and runs upstage to pose.*

The text repeats right away, pitched lower and playing slower.

. . . I just don't wanna look pregnant in my shirt, I don't wanna look like I am having a baby . . .

The PERFORMER *poses sideways to the camera.*

Flash! A photo is taken and appears on screen.

The PERFORMER *rushes back to the laptop for one last effect change.*

---

* Explore potential effects/filters for the photos. Different ones were used each performance.

So, I didn't know if that worked. Let me know.

The PERFORMER *runs upstage and times out a jump with the camera.*

Flash! The last photo is taken and appears on screen.

The PERFORMER *comes back to the laptop and sits down on the stool. Their head is down and their hair is in their face.*

A video slideshow of images from the PERFORMER*'s photo booth app starts to play. Gradually, the video switches from a slideshow of images from the* PERFORMER*'s photo booth app to various YouTube users' photo booth video slideshows that appeared online in 2007/2008 when the following search terms were used: "A year of me and my mac," "Photo Booth," and "slideshow."**

While the slideshow video plays, the following GREENTEAGIRLIE *text is heard.*

The background audio loops continue.

Number one, I love shoes. I love shoes so much, I collect them—I have seventy-five pairs of shoes. Some of you could have more than me but I do love shoes. I hope to have maybe two hundred pair one day.†

This bit of text is repeated at different pitches, starting at different times: "Number one, I love shoes. I love shoes so much, I collect them—I have seventy-five pairs of shoes."

* The first iPhone came out in 2007. At that time, the Photo Booth application on Apple computers was commonly used for taking selfies with a web camera rather than with a cellphone. For a contemporary staging of *AVATAR*, consider gathering footage, images, or slideshows from the apps currently used for taking and sharing selfies. Gather images from the performer, friends, and folks online. This content can then be compiled into a video slideshow and presented in the *AVATAR* remix. When content is used from online sources, use video effects, speed it up, and layer the images in order to make them less discernible. The duration of the slideshow is approximately one to a maximum of two minutes.

† Original source: https://www.youtube.com/watch?v=qtGqFnYRbEs&t=24s.

While seated on the stool the PERFORMER *gently slips off their shoes without using their hands.*

Gradually the following statements are heard:

Second, number two, is that I have been stuck on the top of a roller coaster . . . Number three, which, number three is I am scared of heights . . . Number four . . .

Vocals shift into being pitched too slow and low to be heard.

The PERFORMER *drifts off to sleep. Their head droops lower and lower. As they almost fall off the stool, they are jolted awake and quickly close the slideshow video on their desktop. The* PERFORMER *opens up QuickTime to record a vlog using their web camera. The* PERFORMER*'s hair is in their face. They do not make eye contact with the camera, nor with the viewers, as they speak the following monologue.*

PERFORMER:* Well, um, this is my first video, it's kind of just for me. I guess I am just here to tell the world who I am and what's going on with me, I guess, and, yeah, so, um, this is my intro. It's like, one thirty in the morning for me here, so just a little out of it, I guess I would say. And . . . ah . . . I guess I am kinda lonely too. That's why I am making these videos. Like, I just started college; I am in my third week here. It's Friday† night . . . Yay—why aren't I out partying or something? I guess I am not your average college student. So, I just sit here, watch videos. So, um, yeah, I guess this is the beginning of my videos. I'll try and post more, just about how I feel and what I have to say. So, feel free to subscribe or, whatever, post comments. I know I am pretty pathetic right now, um, hopefully, my next videos will be better. I guess this is it, welcome to my world.

The PERFORMER *quits the QuickTime video recording. Unexpectedly, icons on the* PERFORMER*'s desktop start moving, like a ghost has taken over the computer and is arranging the files and folders into letters and*

* This selection of text originates from a vlog that, at the time of the *AVATAR* performance creation, had under five views. This video can no longer be found online. Consider finding new text for this section through the search terms "I'm New" and "My First Vlog." Look for a vlog with few views. Editing lonelygirl15's first vlog could be suitable to explore in this section. YouTube's search algorithms have changed significantly since 2008, and I recommend using a different search engine and specifying time frames for your search.

† This should change according to the day the work is performed.

shapes on the desktop. This ghost in the machine movement mesmerizes the PERFORMER*. They push keys on their laptop keyboard in an effort to regain control of the computer. This action only prompts error sounds, signifying a shift into the next scene.*

SCENE 2: CVS [COMPUTER VISION SYNDROME]

This scene is approximately five and a half minutes long and features a complex accumulative layering of sound and video alongside improvised movement. The completed video work was tightly edited with fifteen to twenty layers of video.

The moving files and folders on the desktop-projector screen are overlaid by pre-recorded chroma-keyed footage of the PERFORMER *captured with a camera view from above.* In this pre-recorded footage, played in slow motion, the* PERFORMER *attempts to embed their 3D body into the left*

* Explore the possibility of a live web camera from above the stage for this scene, and consider using luma key or other tools instead of chroma key to manipulate the playback of the live footage.

side of the flat 2D desktop screen. The address www.______________. com/desktopdancers briefly appears on screen.

On stage the PERFORMER *walks away from the computer with their back toward the projection screen. Their movement is contorted and bound by gravity as they begin to work their way into and out of the floor. The movement of the* PERFORMER *on stage is initially slow.*

Gradually, new soloists join the performer's footage on screen. * *These dancers are mostly on the right side of the screen. They look out at the viewers, seductively drawing them in through their gaze. Their movement is slowed down and seems to skim the surface of the screen as their limbs at times block the screen-captured computer desktop behind them. This awareness of virtual spatiality is heightened by the pre-recorded footage of the* PERFORMER *working to penetrate the screen surface, their viewed-from-above body moving with sinking, grounded sensibilities. The desktop dancers fade in and out with new soloists appearing on the right side of the screen every twenty seconds or so.*

On stage the PERFORMER *mimics some of their onscreen movement captured on the pre-recorded footage. As the chroma-key dancers appear the* PERFORMER*'s arms push parts of their body into new shapes, forcefully conforming to match some of the seductive images on the screen behind them. The* PERFORMER *oscillates between dancing with their projected image and forcefully replicating the seductive desktop dancers' movements on stage. As though trying to change gears, and believing that the computer is voice activated, the* PERFORMER *speaks the following words sparingly, loudly, in any order, with repetition as they move.*

PERFORMER: Escape, ALT, Delete, Control, Function, Shift, Prompt, Option, Command . . .

The desktop screen capture behind the PERFORMER *changes from the dancing files and folders to a web browser opening and initiating web searches about two minutes into this scene. As more browser tabs are opened, the*

---

* This chroma-key footage of dancers came from various desktop stripper applications available for PC computers between 2007 and 2009. The following links are examples of similar footage associated with the search terms "green screen," "chroma key," "blue screen," "sexy," "desktop," "dance," and/or "dancer": https://www.youtube.com/watch?v=5n2Li7mVHQ8 and https://www.youtube.com/watch?v=jNHl2Fnq8ic.

*screen capture footage speeds up and YouTube becomes the primary search engine. The browser tabs contain both audio and video that play simultaneously.** *The order of the browser tabs keeps changing, with each tab in view for only a few seconds. Only the* PERFORMER*'s chroma-key footage is overlaid. Up to six layers of the* PERFORMER*'s slowed down footage accumulates over the rapid YouTube searches / open browser tabs.*

On stage the PERFORMER *oscillates between dancing with their projected image and dancing autonomously.*

Desktop dancers reappear on the left side of the screen about three and a half minutes into the scene. Gradually, they replicate and flood the screen; the footage is slowed down, sped up, and edited abruptly in an effort to destabilize the seductive quality of the dancers' movements. Any near nudity on screen was omitted by fragmenting the dancer's body and revealing the screen-captured desktop below rather than covering it up with a censor bar.

The PERFORMER *continues to oscillate between dancing with their projected image, dancing autonomously, and forcefully replicating the seductive desktop dancers' movement. Tension builds.*

Occasionally the text "click the link on the right" or simply "click the link" boldly flashes across the screen, beckoning both the PERFORMER *and viewers to respond. As the screen becomes populated with chroma-keyed dancers, the YouTube browser tabs screen capture behind the dancers starts to glitch in and out. Initially, it strobes to reveal a black screen behind the dancers; later the strobe reveals the* NTSC *video test pattern, or television static. The cacophony of the layered sound and visual overload of the strobing video, combined with the contorted weighted movement of the* PERFORMER *becomes unbearable to witness.*

At the peak of the chaos, around four and a half minutes in, each dancer fades away and the sound layers disappear. Roughly thirty seconds later footage of a simulated computer crash appears beneath any remaining dancers. The footage layers both the classic Windows "blue screen of

* The videos playing in the web browser tabs are associated to the search terms "muscle gain," "body progress," "body changes," "weight loss," "body journal," "belly," "posing," "flexing," "body," etc. Most videos featured subjects with their head cut out of the camera framing.

death" and the Apple "spinning wheel of death." Occasionally, the computer crash footage strobes in and out, alternately revealing the NTSC video test pattern, or television static in a video layer below. The following computer voice is heard during this simulated computer crash:*

COMPUTER:† Attention citizens, this is the computer. Remember, attention is mandatory. All praise the computer. Next new story not found . . . memory corrupt . . . x-o-four-three-seven-seven-x . . . next new story not found . . . x-o-four-three-seven-seven-x . . .

Echo effects and repeating sounds: "Next new story not found . . . memory corrupt . . . x-o-four-three-seven-seven-x . . . next new story not found . . . x-o-four-three-seven-seven-x."

The text "click the link," "click the link" flashes periodically overtop of all the video layers. Sequentially, any remaining onscreen dancers disappear till only one chroma-key video of the PERFORMER remains on screen near the end of the computer crash.

On stage, during the computer crash, the PERFORMER's feet seem stuck; they reach their arm toward the laptop. They yell the following word repeatedly as though the laptop might respond to voice commands:

PERFORMER: Escape, Escape, Escape . . .

Tension builds in their body as they attempt to make their way to the laptop downstage centre a few steps at a time. Once at the laptop table, they push buttons on the keyboard to generate well-known computer error sounds and invalid key noises. Consequently, the computer fails.

The screen on stage goes black. All sound cuts out.

The PERFORMER sits on the stool.

---

* Footage of computer crashes or errors featuring the "blue screen of death" and the "spinning wheel of death" were found online using those search terms. For example: https://www.youtube.com/watch?v=I8hxk3gCWWo.

† Explore the text-to-speech function on a computer or in a browser app to find a digitized voice. Another generative site for exploration is artificial intelligence applications such as Descript's Lyrebird, which can be used to create artificial voices for any section of the work.

SCENE 3: BATHROOM

In this scene, the PERFORMER *sets up the live web camera and paints a makeshift wall in order to create a virtual domestic space. The scene is approximately five minutes in length, depending on how long it takes to paint the rectangle on the wall.**

Throughout this scene a simple audio loop plays softly.

The PERFORMER *sits on the stool located upstage of the laptop table, which is in the middle of the white floor downstage front. The following text is heard over the speakers:*

SPEAKER:† Number one: test out your webcam in advance to make sure it is operating properly.

Sitting at the laptop, the PERFORMER *adjusts the camera.*

---

* In some venues, a raw plywood wall roughly eight feet square was used, while in others the wall was either white or black (e.g., white cube gallery vs. black-box theatre). Typically, the wall is placed stage left of the screen.

† Original source for Speaker: https://www.youtube.com/watch?v=HIq9mT2qAAQ.

Number two: make sure that your microphone is in the optimal location.

The PERFORMER *moves the laptop table so that it is directly in front of the wall.*

Number three: use a solid colour backdrop behind you.

The PERFORMER *fine tunes their live web camera viewing angle and then retrieves paint and a paintbrush from behind the wall. As they paint the wall, the video projection on the large screen upstage reveals that the paint creates a chroma-key effect.* As the* PERFORMER *paints the wall, the composite image reveals tile flooring, a sink, then a bathtub, and finally a toilet. By the end of this scene, the* PERFORMER *is virtually standing inside a bathroom. The wall now features a painted blue rectangle. The performer sets the paint down and stands in the centre of the camera frame.*

Place your head and upper torso in the frame. Keep eye contact with the camera.

As the line above is heard over the sound system, the PERFORMER *settles onto the stool with their shoulders and face situated in the camera frame.*

* Blue paint was used for the live chroma-keying—green paint also works well.

SCENE 4: MAKEUP TUTORIAL

The text for this scene is from five-year-old HANNAH, *who created a makeup tutorial that was posted online in 2008. The* PERFORMER *lip-synchs intentionally in and out of sync* with Hannah's pre-recorded instructions. The* PERFORMER *stares into the camera (pictured above) throughout the tutorial, and by the end they have been transformed with exaggerated makeup. This scene takes place in the same chroma-key bathroom revealed in Scene 3.*

HANNAH:[†] Hi guys, I'm Hannah and I'm gonna do a look today that's very pretty. Now, the first thing we're gonna do is, open up, um, powder, this is what it looks like.

The PERFORMER *shows the makeup to the camera.*

I'm gonna put it all over my face . . .

The PERFORMER *pretends to powder their face.*

---

* This performance choice mimics the many videos that are posted with sound that is out of sync.

† Original source for Hannah: https://www.youtube.com/watch?v=IDmEMwdIb44.

And when you're done with that, you, get this, bottom eyeshadow, see the bottom, yup, and, just gonna get, a little bit on the brush, that's all, and then just place it all over your eyes . . .

The PERFORMER *uses white face paint to make their eyelids white.*

And when you are done with that, you get, this blush, and just, get it, on the, cheeks . . .

The PERFORMER *uses red face paint to create a little red circle in the middle of their now white eyelids.*

And, ah, um, now we gonna get mascara, just normal mascara, we gonna get it, just . . .

The PERFORMER *uses a thin paint brush to outline the creases of their eyelids in black.*

'Kay, when we are done with that . . .

The PERFORMER *adds black dots in the centre of the red dots on their white outlined eyelids. The* PERFORMER*'s eyelids have now become painted eyes.*

You just get this lip gloss. It's sparkly, very sparkly.

The PERFORMER *paints their lips white and pulls their hair back with clips.*

Then . . . and ahh . . . that's my look!

The PERFORMER *pulls a blond wig out of their laptop table and places it on their head.*

SPEAKER:* Take a long, hard look at yourself in the mirror. Look at yourself as others would, then modify your facial expressions by adding that simple feature that nearly every person forgets: a smile.

---

* Original sources for the Speaker: https://www.youtube.com/watch?v=tAGWhnpcYlA and https://www.youtube.com/watch?v=boNSHrbT_po.

The PERFORMER *begins to paint a big red circle around the outside of their lips.*

A warm and genuine smile tells me you are a happy person.

The PERFORMER *outlines the red circle with a black eyeliner pencil.*

Practise your smile until it's natural and automatic.

The PERFORMER *adds vertical black lines on their white lips, so their lips become teeth, and they now have an outrageously exaggerated mouth.*

Number one: Be focused.

The PERFORMER *adjusts their wig, their costume, and then touches up their makeup.*

Number two: Be yourself. This is not a movie or a sitcom and you are not an actor putting on a show. Let the real you shine through.

The PERFORMER *gets up from the stool, bringing their face in close to the web camera. This fills the projection screen with a close-up image of their face. The screen fades to black, and now the* PERFORMER, *without a camera to perform for, awkwardly looks up and acknowledges the live audience.*

Number three: Be honest. Tell the truth in all your statements and examples and . . . number four: Be professional. Don't include your workout at the gym or your latest dance routine.

SCENE 5: CLOSED EYES

In this scene, the PERFORMER*'s eyes remain closed in order to show the new set of eyes painted on their eyelids.* The overall arc of this roughly four- to five-minute scene remains consistent despite the improvisational movement.*

Loops from some of the SPEAKER*'s instructions heard in the previous scene are layered with synthesizer-sounding loops to create a disorientating sound score.*

With their fake eyes fixed on the audience, the PERFORMER *steps onto the white flooring. They keep transferring their weight, showing discomfort with the spotlight. They briefly rest their hands on their hips, then draw one hand up to touch their wig, and almost really smile. They then switch arms to repeat the same gesture and facial expression. The* PERFORMER *fidgets awkwardly—their hands move across their torso,*

* Generally, the Performer can peek to see the floor and the viewers will not notice. This scene requires spatial awareness and the minimal addition of facial expressions in order to allow the face paint to be seen clearly. The movement in this scene is improvised, calling for variation in tempo, pacing, and repetition, as well as subtlety in expression.

*settling on crossed arms for a moment. The focus throughout this opening is the strongly painted fake smile.**

Unable to settle their hands anywhere on their body, the PERFORMER *continues to fidget. As tension builds, they increasingly conceal their face and retreat from the audience. In order to check their appearance, they shift their focus to the laptop and go to turn on the camera. Their face now appears as a close-up on the big screen. They make micro-adjustments to their hair and makeup on camera, boosting their confidence. They turn the camera off before returning to the white floor.*

The now-confident PERFORMER *points directly at the audience and scans the room. Slowly they withdraw their hand, abruptly flip their hair, and raise their heels off the floor. Holding this body posture, they travel on the balls of their feet as if wearing heels as they move across the diagonal toward one side of the white floor. They drop their heels, stick out their pelvis, and move their now stiff arms like a doll, using their gesturing hand to crack their doll neck, which then makes their head and arms move incongruously. They realign their pelvis, pop their heels, and again walk on the balls of their feet to the other side of the stage.*

Impulsively, the PERFORMER *crumbles like a collapsing puppet. Standing upright momentarily, the* PERFORMER *shifts through varied slow-motion facial expressions.*[†] *First, the* PERFORMER *moves into a crying facial expression with crossed arms and flexed muscles. Their facial expression deepens as the* PERFORMER *pulls up into wide, flexed arms. They execute a quick spin, finishing with their arms above their head, akin to the dying swan pose from* Swan Lake, *while conveying a pleasant expression on their face. They break their pose and run to the farthest downstage corner in an attempt to exit the square white dance floor. As though there is a force field, they are bounced back to the centre of the stage where they stand shocked with their real eyes wide open.*

*The phone number 1-800-*AVA-STAR *scrolls across the projection screen.*

* Note to performers: be careful not to crack a real smile as it overrides the illusion.

† These facial expressions need to be explored regarding how they affect the face paint and should be performed as though in slow motion.

The PERFORMER *stops their movements and stands with their real eyes open in a moment of disbelief. Stunned at seeing the audience with their real eyes, they try to leave the white floor, first stage left, then stage right, but they cannot pass the invisible barrier delineated by the edge of the white floor. They try the back of the stage, which has the projection screen barrier.*

A flash of light is emitted on stage.

The PERFORMER *turns around with their real eyes wide open. They melt into the ground and re-form, assuming a provocative pose on the floor and returning to having their fake eyes on view. This pose is held as the following text is heard over the sound system:*

SPEAKER:* Be focused . . . Be professional . . .

The sound of a tape rewinding is heard.

During the reversed audio sound, the PERFORMER *rolls out of their suggestive shape to come to standing; they keep their head down and slowly pull their arms in tight to their body. When their arms can come in no farther, they use gravity to break the pulling-in motion. We hear their breath. They release all tension and take a series of steps in order to get to the corner of the white floor opposite the painted blue screen. The* PERFORMER*'s arm is extended and their hand full of tension as it makes its way, as though it has a life of its own, toward the front of their neck. The* PERFORMER*'s real eyes remain closed until their hand gets very near to grabbing their neck. At the last second of this strangling gesture, their real eyes open and they stare at the palm of their hand in shock. While looking at their hand, they walk back to stand facing the large screen upstage.*

Flash!

Digital sounds loop with layered recordings of an old Speak & Spell† *saying, "Wrong. Try again," as well as various letters of the alphabet.*

* Original source for Speaker: https://www.youtube.com/watch?v=boNSHrbT_po.

† Speak & Spell is an electronic hand-held computer produced by Texas Instruments. Popular in the 1970s and '80s, the toys were one of the earliest computerized learning systems that used a speech synthesizer to assist children with spelling.

The PERFORMER *comes to the centre of the white floor and cycles through various emotional states in slow motion. They come forward with crying motions and their eyes closed; their hands touch their head. They begin to massage their head and then compress their skull; this tension causes them to rise up and balance on the balls of their feet. This rising action opens their eyes, and they purse their lips to hide their fake teeth. Their real eyes dart at the audience. They break the tension and drop into crying expressions again with fake eyes revealed and an exaggerated down-turned mouth.* The performer melts toward the floor. They gather their composure and take a pose on the floor. Upon getting up from the floor, they motion heartbeat gestures with wide open arms. This gesture takes them across the stage. Interspersed with the heart-beating gestures, the* PERFORMER *dances with pleasure and the awareness that they are being watched; they carry a newfound confidence about being witnessed in movement.*

This dance is interrupted by an incoming video call.

A phone starts ringing and the looped sounds drop out. The phone ringing pans across the available speakers. This phone ring sounds familiar.†

---

* Note to performers: explore closing the fake eyes by wincing.

† This familiar phone ring could be the sound of a Skype call, a Facebook Messenger call, a Whatsapp call, or a custom ring tone.

SCENE 6: A/S/L [AGE/SEX/LOCATION]

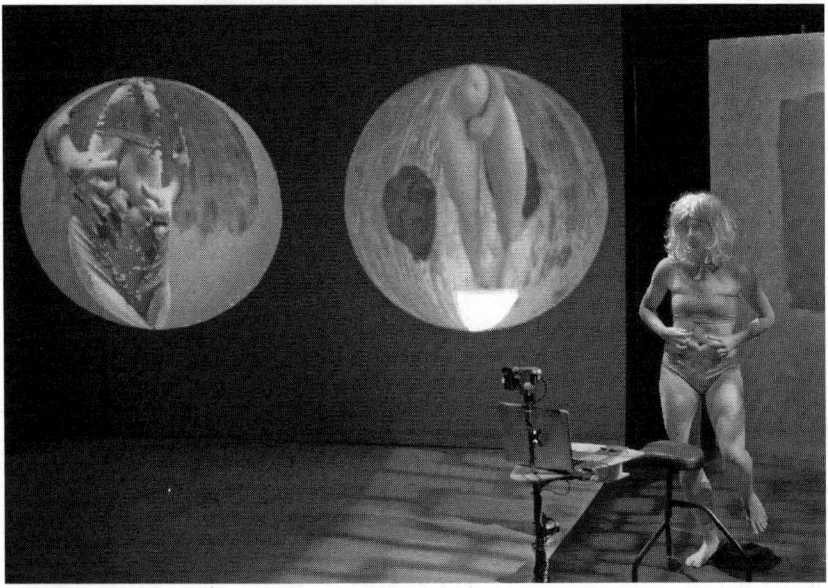

This is a video call duet. Both roles are enacted by the PERFORMER. *The* PERFORMER*'s voice is pre-recorded and pans across the available speakers.*

PITCHED HIGH: Hello, are you there?

PITCHED LOW: Can you see me? Ring . . . Ring . . . Hello? Are you there?

PITCHED HIGH: Are you there?

PITCHED LOW: I can't see you . . . Are you watching? Hello? . . . Ring . . . ring . . . Hello, are you there?

PITCHED HIGH: Hello, are you there? Can you see me? Are you there? Are you watching?

PITCHED LOW: Are you there? I can't see you . . . Are you watching?

The PERFORMER *still has their real eyes closed and can't tell where the voices are coming from. They move across the white floor trying to decipher the source of the voices. Their movement becomes restricted and self-conscious, again revealing that they are aware of being seen. The* PERFORMER *crosses in front of the projection screen and situates themself in front of the camera, which still faces the chroma-key wall.*

As the pre-recorded voices of the PERFORMER *(pitched high and low) continue, they are layered with synth loops as well as a few of the samples from the Speak & Spell.*

Each of the video call duet roles is projected as a fish-eye video sphere; on screen this looks like binocular vision, with two spheres while the rest of the screen remains black. The sphere on the left (pictured above) is a live feed from the onstage camera where the PERFORMER *is aware of the viewer. The sphere on the right is pre-recorded and features a security camera view, from above, where the subject is unaware of being observed. The camera framing allows both subjects to be anonymous on camera, mostly by showing their body and not their face. Their images are distorted through the use of the fish-eye effect that stretches the centre of the video frame. The chart below describes the split screen videos. This takes roughly three and a half minutes.*

Stage Left Video

Performed Live On Stage / Webcam View

The PERFORMER *walks into frame, upstage of the computer desk and stool. Their head is out of the frame.*

Their hands run across their body. As they extend their arms into and away from the camera frame, their body swerves and sways in response to the image they see on camera.

They place their hands on their body, one on their chest, the other on their belly.

The pre-recorded voices stop but the loops continue.

Their hands come inside their black clothing. The cloth is stretchy, allowing them to distort how their body shape is seen. They stretch the shape of their clothing from the side. They bump out the chest and later the crotch area, creating exaggerated body shapes.

The loops cease.

Stage Right Video

Recorded Action / Security-Camera View

The PERFORMER *is sitting on a stool; the camera angle from above allows for the tip of the seat to be seen between the figure's legs, below the edge of their laptop keyboard. They mimic typing actions with their fingers.*

They fidget between pretending they have a mouse on their thigh, their pointer finger clicking the imaginary mouse and touching their chest and mimicking typing gestures. Their hands eventually settle and run down their body to their thighs; they start to shake. Their hands draw up their thighs to grab the phallic bike seat seen between their legs. They hold on to the seat while shaking the stool.

They stand up while holding the bike seat between their legs and back out of the camera view until only their feet are visible.

They bring one arm out of their clothing and then the other. Their torso can now be seen. They drop their pants and hide their crotch by crossing their hands.

As they work their pants off their legs, they bring their hands onto their belly and move the flesh into various shapes.

They walk forward into the camera frame, ending with their finger in their belly button. They quickly straddle the stool and roll backward while seated, carefully avoiding their pants on the floor.

The Speak & Spell sounds return. These include LOL, OMG, and arbitrary letters.

They face the camera sideways, arms hugging around themselves. They stand up from the stool and quickly grab it, facing the legs of the stool toward the camera as though in self-defence. The legs of the stool resemble antlers.

They drop what appears to be a piece of their black clothing.

They start walking forward with their pants at their ankles, their feet initially wide apart and then coming together. Only their legs and feet are seen. They stop and pull down their black underwear.

They step forward out of the pile of clothes and a bit of their pelvis becomes visible.

Their hand covers their crotch and a single finger, outstretched for a brief moment, mimics a phallus while their other hand, also with an outstretched finger, hovers over the laptop keyboard.

They stand up tall, holding the stool upside down on their head, and walk toward the camera, which currently only sees their hips and lower torso. As they come closer, their belly button becomes the centre of the image on screen. They lower the stool, placing the bike-seat point/phallus into their belly button. This action makes them "deflate" and they lower out of view of the camera.

The figure encroaches on the laptop and they are seen in full frame. They seem to be panicking at the sight of the chair antlers visible on the other screen. They grab their head with their hands, and then their legs . . . and then they back away from the screen until they are out of view.

On stage, as the PERFORMER *slowly lowers to hide behind the stool and laptop table, their face is revealed on the large projection screen, passing the camera lens, and then the screen fades to black.*

SCENE 7: BEDROOM

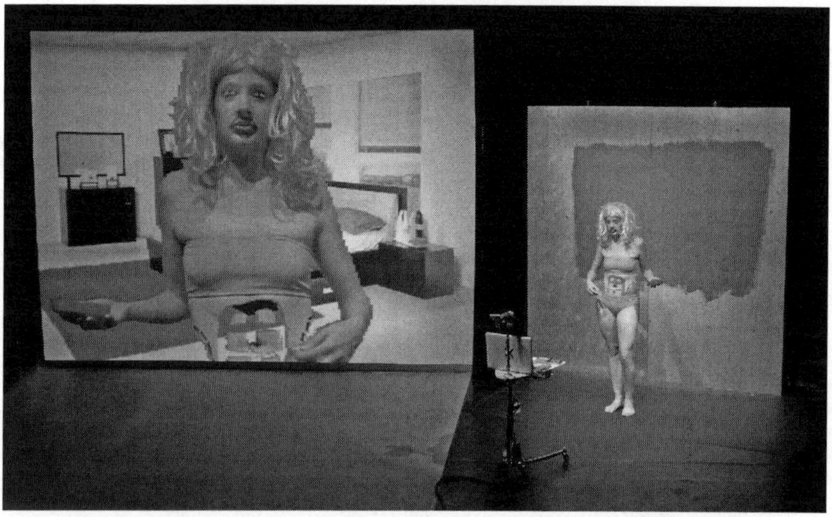

In this scene, the PERFORMER *lip-synchs intentionally in and out of sync with the pre-recorded text while customizing their onscreen/virtual body using the chroma-key paint on stage.**

The sound score heard throughout this scene layers an extremely slowed down version of the Marilyn Monroe song "I Wanna Be Loved By You" with other looped sounds.

The PERFORMER *stands up from behind the laptop and turns on the camera, which faces the blue screen. On the projection screen, the* PERFORMER *appears to be in a bedroom.*

The PERFORMER *lip-synchs along to the pre-recorded text of an* INTERNET USER, *who is heard through the sound system.*

INTERNET USER:† Hi, YouTube, okay, okay, I need to, like, look normal in this.

---

* Photoshop and augmented-reality video filters are used widely online to modify and craft representations of bodies. This phenomenon has only grown with the increase in user-friendly tools available to modify digital images or videos. Consider the additional exploration of AR filters within a remix of *AVATAR*.

† As the original source for this vlog is unavailable, consider finding new text to support a remixed transformation of the Performer's body through reframing the vlog, enacting deliberate actions on stage, and digitally transforming the image on screen.

After adjusting the camera, the PERFORMER *stands back and looks at themself on the laptop while fiddling with their underwear.*

Basically, my thighs are huge.

The sound of skin being slapped.

And um, my belly . . .

The sound of skin being slapped.

Mmmmmm . . . belly gonna eat some more.

This phrase is repeated quietly three times: "belly gonna eat some more."

The PERFORMER *brings their hands onto their stomach and deliberately moves their flesh as though it were soft clay.*

And um, my love handles . . .

The PERFORMER *gently gathers some flesh of their love handles in their hands. The* PERFORMER *leans in to speak directly to the camera.*

WHATEVER, I can't stop eating.

At the end of this line the PERFORMER *pauses their movement as if the video stream froze. One arm leans forward into the camera frame while the other is outstretched toward the background. The* PERFORMER*'s mouth is agape, frozen mid-speech. This awkward pose is held for four beats or so to create tension.*

Then they start to move into a normal standing position while they continue the lip-synch.

I can't stop eating too much, so I am trying to now, like, pretend to cut down on carbs and sugar and stuff like that.

The PERFORMER *points directly into the camera which, when viewed through the projection screen, points right at the viewers.*

I need your support and your advice . . .

The PERFORMER *starts to lower their pointing finger while lip-synching.*

And you're going to watch me shrink so that this will look normal on me, in the summertime. So here is your front view . . .

The PERFORMER *stands with their front facing the camera.*

And here's your side . . .

The sound of skin being slapped.

The PERFORMER *stands with their side facing the camera. Their hand slaps their belly, then rebounds and their outstretched fingertips touch their belly button.*

NOT sucking in.

The PERFORMER *releases their stomach into its natural distended relaxed shape. In response, their fingers trace toward their pubic bone and the hand collapses. A horn sound from the slowed-down, muffled Marilyn Monroe song is heard.*

Back . . .

The PERFORMER *stands with their back facing the camera.*

And your side again.

The PERFORMER *stands with their other side now facing the camera.*

Muffled Marilyn Monroe music is heard. Some indiscernible mumbling about body shape continues.

The PERFORMER *gets a black eyeliner pencil and draws a dotted line on their love handles. They proceed to paint their love handles with blue* paint so that they disappear on camera, thanks to the chroma key. The*

* Blue paint was used for chroma-keying on stage—green paint also works well.

PERFORMER then draws a six-pack on their stomach with the blue paint. They begin with an arched window shape, then create a line down the middle followed by two horizontal crossbars to create the illusion of abdominals. They draw three little lines to indicate ribs on the lower ribcage. The PERFORMER stops lip-synching when the following text plays through the sound system:

SPEAKER:* Do you dress to impress? The best approach is to dress not to impress. What you wear can and will have an impact. Most often, any lasting impression left by your clothes can be a negative one. Your goal is to be remembered, not for what you are wearing, but for who you are as a person.

The PERFORMER uses the blue paint to draw a heart shape on their chest. Next, they use the paint to erase their shoulders and expand to paint their entire chest. The PERFORMER gets a microphone from off stage and sits at the stool in front of the laptop to begin the closing scene. Due to the chroma-key effect and the placement of the PERFORMER's torso in the camera frame, the PERFORMER now appears to be a floating head on screen. The AVATAR is born; this digitally augmented iteration of the PERFORMER enacts the closing scene.

* Original source for Speaker: https://www.youtube.com/watch?v=F-uxoXdqwkU.

SCENE 8: CLOSING MONOLOGUE / Q & A

The AVATAR *sits on their stool, still located in front of the chroma-key wall. They hold a microphone in their hand and the laptop lays open, glowing on the small table in front of them. The image from the laptop webcam is projected onto the big screen up stage. The live web camera footage of the* AVATAR *is chroma-keyed to create the illusion that they are a floating head in the sky (see image above). This composited image is overlaid on a screen capture video of the YouTube interface,* which shows related videos, the comment section, and search bar. Scene 2's pre-recorded footage of the* PERFORMER *filmed from above is composited overtop. The* PERFORMER*'s voice is amplified, and the pitch has shifted to support the transformation into the* AVATAR. *They stare into the camera with their fake eyes as they deliver the following monologue:*

AVATAR: Hi, everyone! I have been gone because of personal things . . . Um. I got a new room; this is it.

---

* Consider other platforms that broadcast live streams: Twitch, Instagram, Zoom, TikTok, etc.

The AVATAR *gestures to the painted wall behind them.*

As you can see, I had to paint it. It's awesome now. Oh yeah, I got a new computer, it's awesome.

The AVATAR *touches their laptop and then twirls their hair.*

I was sick, then I got over it. By the way, this is the new computer I am recording with. Oops. Sorry, I wasn't sure if it was still recording. Can you see me?? Hope you can see me?

The AVATAR *adjusts the camera to see if it is working; their fingers cover the video frame, causing the camera focus to react.*

I was looking at one of my old vlogs—holy crap, there is a reason I put it on private. Um, I was talking like this and I wasn't looking at the camera. But, GEEZ, I sounded so boring. It was like two and a half minutes long I could barely sit through thirty seconds of it. I was like, "Uh . . . ugly." But other than that, the video quality was horrible and, yeah, so everyone, tell me if, like, tell me what you think.

And to all those who have stuck with me from vlog day number one—thank you—I wanna say thank you so much to all my subscribers. I have got such wonderful "subbies." I love you all so much. I love talking to you. I have gotten to know so many people, I feel I am making such awesome friends, from everywhere. I don't have very many close friends here. One of them I am happy to announce just gave birth to twin girls.

The AVATAR *leans in close to the camera.*

Linda, if you are watching this, I am so happy for you and your new babies—happy and healthy, congratulations so much. Congratulations to your family. Again, thank you to all my subscribers. I am happy to announce I am at 998, almost at a thousand. When I hit that mark, we're gonna do a contest. Oh yeah, there was one message, I don't want to describe, I just wanna say thank you . . . I was very flattered . . .

Ahhh. Stupid screen, it went off again.

The AVATAR *adjusts the camera again to see if it is working.*

Can you see me??
I hope you can see me.
Be a shame if this recording wasn't working; we got some good stuff here.

Anyway, moving on, I have little notes here . . .

The AVATAR *picks up a little piece of paper from the table.*

About the Marilyn video, I am not obsessed; I often google her. My grandmother would always talk about her. They had the blond hair with the curl, you know, the Marilyn look. Anyways, I am not obsessed.

Um, in the next two to three weeks, if I look any different whatsoever—I am not ashamed to say it—I am going for some Botox. I used to do this, so if I look any different, don't give me any lectures about it.

I am getting tired of trying to arch my brows . . .

The AVATAR *leans in close to the camera to inspect their brows. Their hand holds the wig out of the way. Their fingers trace the side of their face as they turn their head slightly to one side.*

And, ahhh . . . I hate these wrinkles that my dad gave me. Well, if it makes me feel better, then I say go for it.

Uh, wait . . .
Can you see me??

The AVATAR *adjusts the camera view again to see if it is working.*

Can you see me??

The background sound score shifts to something upbeat and simple, signifying a change to a Q & A *with the in-person viewers.**

* Consider the possibility of broadcasting the web camera view of this performance. Perhaps in this closing scene viewers both online and in-person could engage in the Q & A.

Now is the time where I'd like to ask all of you to ask me questions. 'Cause I love answering questions, especially from you. Popular questions I get asked are things like: How do you get your lips so red?

Actually, I steal a little trick from Marilyn and use a lip plumper to enhance the natural pigment of the lips, and then I slather on L'Oréal 26, Rouge, till it goes into your eyes . . .

The AVATAR *pretends to cover their lips with makeup and then twinkles their fingers toward the web camera.*

Anyways, enough about the popular questions. I want to know what you want to know!

Now don't be shy. I am an open book, an unlocked vault; I am transparent for you, tonight.

What do you want to know about me?

The AVATAR *invites audience members to ask questions.*

There is no such thing as a stupid question. Remember, what you ask says nothing about you, and everything about me.

The AVATAR *improvises answers to questions that arise from the audience. See Appendix for an archive of viewer questions. The following is a sample of questions and responses from various performances.*

VIEWER: How old are you?

AVATAR: Ageless . . . I live in the sky . . . All right, thank you for that question. What else do you want to know about me?

VIEWER: Why are all of your teeth different shapes?

AVATAR: Because I am unique, and special, not just because my mom says so . . . Anybody else?

The AVATAR *raises a hand to their ear to signify they are ready and listening.*

VIEWER: Are you having any rivalries with other vloggers?

AVATAR: Ohhhhhhh, yeah, let me tell you. It is a tough dog-eat-dog, vlog-eat-vlog world out there and we just have to pick up our bootstraps or bare feet and try and, you know, impress with quick skills and improvising, and you really just have to pop those digital pixels . . . Does anyone else have something they want to know about me? Anything, anything at all.

A VIEWER makes an indiscernible sound.

Oh, we have someone hiding in the dark, anonymous on the web, lurking in the shadows. What does this person want to know? . . . Anything? . . . Anything at all?

The AVATAR lowers their mic to signify they are making space for the viewers to speak.

VIEWER: What time is your next episode?

AVATAR: Actually, I am making one right now. Thank you for that question.

The AVATAR guides the audience Q & A periodically with the text noted below. These markers lead toward the end of the piece and serve as cues for the person running sound and lights.

(cue 1) I am starting to feel a little underdressed for the occasion. I am going to slip on something a little more appropriate? *[or]* I have something to put on that might make us all more comfortable. How do I pause this thing . . . As you saw earlier, I'm having issues with this . . . thing here *(points into the camera).**

The AVATAR places their mic gently on the stool and goes to put on a black silk robe that is placed behind the wall. Now wearing the silk robe, the AVATAR picks up the mic and sits back down. The pitch of the AVATAR's voice starts to change very subtly throughout the rest of the Q & A, changing back to their natural voice by the end.

I wanna know . . . still . . . what you wanna know. Okay, Okay . . .

---

* Depending on the setting, sometimes the Avatar would play with being cold as the reason to get the housecoat, other times because they were conscious of being the only person in their underwear.

The AVATAR *fidgets with the mic, their wig, and the camera view.*

All right . . . now I'm ready for you. Um, what else do you want to know?

VIEWER: How long have you been using the net?

AVATAR: Or . . . how long has the net been using me? That's more like it, ha ha ha. Hold on a second . . .

The AVATAR *slowly takes off their wig. As they speak the following line their voice is becoming less distorted.*

Holy, I'm getting tired. So many questions.

The AVATAR *gets a makeup wipe that is stored within the table holding the laptop.*

(cue 2) Just trying to keep you guys entertained. Usually my vlogs are around ten minutes. You are a special group; it's been more like fifteen minutes already. Anybody else out there? What do you want to know?

The AVATAR *begins to remove their makeup, starting with the mouth, gently erasing their fake smile. Their voice is becoming less distorted and you can start to hear their original voice alongside the effected voice.*

VIEWER: How do you escape?

AVATAR: Ummmm, ahhh . . . I don't know. I'm not sure I have an answer for that question.

During the final few question(s) encompassing cues 3 and 4, the AVATAR *continues to remove their makeup, now from their eyes, one at a time. As they erase their fake eyes, they can look into the camera with their real eyes.*

VIEWER: You could always delete your accounts.

AVATAR: That's really wise. I'll definitely take that advice. Thank you.

(cue 3) We have time for one more question. What else do you want to know?

VIEWER: What is your greatest fear?

The AVATAR takes their time answering the last question(s). Gently they complete the ritual of erasing their eyes, simultaneous to their voice becoming less and less affected.

AVATAR: Greatest fear . . . I think I'm feeling it right now actually . . .

Without makeup, the wig, and vocal effects, the PERFORMER that was buried beneath the layers of affects/effects to create the AVATAR is present again.

(cue 4) I think that is it. We are about at the end of the tape.* I just wanna say, thank you all for coming. *[or]* Thank you all for watching.

The stage goes black.

---

* This worked when the piece was performed with an external SD camera, but not when it became the web camera. In later iterations of the performance the Avatar would improvise, sometimes saying the computer hard drive was almost full and needed to stop recording or worked toward the Avatar being tired of questions. The ending always depended on the energy and response from audiences.

APPENDIX: ARCHIVE OF Q & A QUESTIONS FROM VIEWERS

What is your phone number? Are you still going to school? Are you having any rivalries with other vloggers? Are you a natural blond? Was that your bedroom? What is your favourite aspect ratio? Who is one person that you would really, really like to see your vlog? Are you seeing anybody? Do you think Canada should get out of Afghanistan? What is your workout routine? Do you dye your hair? Who do you call when you are looking for a little something interesting? How do you make the blue? Can you tell me about shoes? Are you wearing coloured contacts? How is your relationship with your mother? What is your exercise routine? I would like to know what colour your eyes are. Is that your hair? How do you get the nerve to stand there in front of everybody in your bra and blue skin? This is probably personal, but what is your age? Why are all of your teeth different shapes? Who is winning the Yankees game? Why do you feel the need to blog about yourself? Have you met someone online who you have developed a human relationship offline with? Do you feel more connected online or offline? Is that a wig or is that your real hair? This is fairly personal, but what is your age? Why are all of your teeth different shapes? How was Austria? What sign are you? Where are you from? Why do you love Marilyn so much? What is your favourite website? How do you do your hair so beautifully? How much do you pay your technical support? Where do you go to work out? Have you ever been on Chatroulette? Do you play online poker? How do you escape? How much money do you make from your subscribers? What is in it for you? How does Marilyn influence you in other ways? Do you want to be famous? How old are you? What does a normal day look like for you? Do you have a boyfriend? Are you ever sad? Do you go on Chatroulette? If you could choose to be murdered or a suicide, what would you pick? How long have you been using the net? You could always delete your accounts? Greatest fear? What if we don't ask any questions? Why are you alive? Have you ever been in love? With who? What is the most embarrassing question you have ever been asked? What is your age? How much do you weigh? What is your favourite food? Where do you see yourself in five years? What is your favourite song? Are you enjoying this? Why? What do you do when you are alone? Why is your sky a royal blue? How much can you see? Do you believe in God? Do personal questions scare you? Can you take your wig off, please? What are you most afraid of? Can you please dance for us? How old are you? Do you ever get nervous? What is your name? Do you have a significant other? Why are you still online? How many Facebook friends do you have? How many friends do you have in real life? Why are your teeth so white? What is your name? What is your shoe size? How are you so grounded? Do you love yourself? Do you have a lover? How many people subscribe to you? How many people use your site? How often do you use hair dye? What do you call your hairstyle? Who do you want? Do you feel alone? What do you do when you feel alone? Do you like being avatar? When did you start dancing? How old are you? What do you do when you are not in front of the camera? Is your hair naturally that blond? What is your favourite colour? Are you single? What shoe size do you wear? Do you have any diplomas? Will you stay at home while in college? What is your favourite beverage? How old are you? Do you believe in God? Would you say you are happy? And why? Have you had Botox before? Where do you live? What are your favourite YouTube channels? Do you have any friends? Do you have a boyfriend? How many boyfriends do you have? Where do your boyfriends live? What do you look for in a man? What kind of music do you love? Is your hair naturally blond? What age are you? What zodiac sign are you? What is the subject of your thesis? What do you dream about? What is your idea of a great night out? Your age? What is the colour of your eyes? Do you do drugs? Who are your friends? What is your natural hair colour? What is your name? How often do you film yourself? Are you a cougar? How many hours do you spend on the internet? Do you consider yourself a big deal on the internet? What age are you? What time is your next episode? Do you like Ecuador? Do you like your body? Can I come visit you? At what speed do you travel? What do you want?

Compiled by Jillian Groening

HELEN LAWRENCE

STORY BY CHRIS HADDOCK AND STAN DOUGLAS, SCREENPLAY BY CHRIS HADDOCK

Helen Lawrence was first produced by Canadian Stage, Arts Club Theatre Company, Banff Centre, Stan Douglas Inc, Festival TransAmériques, and the National Arts Centre, with contributions from Arts Partners in Creative Development, Presentation House Gallery, the BC Arts Council, and the Canada Council for the Arts. Special thanks to Kim Collier for her participation in the development of *Helen Lawrence* and to Kelly Robinson for his dedicated support. The production featured the follow cast and creative team:

Mary Jackson: Crystal Balint
Henry Williams: Sterling Jarvis
Percy Walker: Nicholas Lea
Buddy Black: Allan Louis
Eva Banks: Ava Markus
Harry Mitchell: Hrothgar Mathews
Inspector Leonard Perkins: Tom McBeath
Julie Winters: Haley McGee
Rose George: Mayko Nguyen
Police Chief James Muldoon: Gerard Plunkett
Helen Lawrence: Lisa Ryder
Edward Banks: Adam Kenneth Wilson
Emile: Brett Dahl

Bass: Andrew Downing
Drums: Davide Dorenzo
Piano: Dave Restivo
Baritone sax: Perry White
Tenor sax: Peter Lutek and Mike Murley
Alto sax: Andy Balantine and Tara Davidson
Trumpet: Kevin Turcotte, Lina Allemano, and Jake Wilkinson
Trombone: William Karn and Tom Richards
Guitar: John Gzowski

Conception: Stan Douglas
Story: Chris Haddock and Stan Douglas
Writer: Chris Haddock
Director: Stan Douglas
Associate Director: Sarah Garton Stanley
Dramaturg: Rachel Ditor and Matthew Jocelyn
Set Design: Kevin McAllister

Costume Design: Nancy Bryant
Lighting Design: Robert Sondergaard
Composer and Sound Design: John Gzowski
Director of Photography: Brian Johnson
Video Programmer: Peter Courtemanche
3D Production Design: Stan Douglas
Lead 3D Artist: Jonny Ostrem
3D Artists: Trent Noble, Prajay Mehta, and Martin Gilbert
Video Operator: Joel Adria
Stage Manager: Jan Hodgson
Assistant Stage Manager: Peter Jotkus
Apprentice Stage Manager: Molly Pearson (only for Banff and Arts Club)
Fight Director: Paul Gelineau and Jonathan Purvis

CHARACTERS

Nurse
Aide
Helen Lawrence
Julie Winters
Eva Banks
Percy Walker
Police Chief James Muldoon
Henry Williams
Rose George
Edward Banks
Buddy Black
Mary Jackson
Harry Mitchell
Inspector Leonard Perkins
Cashier
Emile

NOTE

Helen Lawrence is set in 1947 Vancouver and uses language that reflects the play's era and setting, including racial slurs.

1.

Int. ECT *Ward. Los Angeles—1947—Day.*

A downstage scrim is in place and will remain so throughout the play.

Title over: Los Angeles 1947.

Stage lights up as an AIDE *stands in a sparse electroconvulsive therapy ward beside a gurney with a woman,* HELEN*, lying on it. A* NURSE *enters carrying a clipboard: the* AIDE *is affable, the* NURSE *irritable,* HELEN *unconscious.*

NURSE: Where's the doctor?

AIDE: He said for you to go ahead and do it.

NURSE: Fine, make sure she's restrained properly.

AIDE: You know who this is.

NURSE: I should hope so.

AIDE: You think she did it?

The AIDE *restrains* HELEN *with straps on each limb.*

NURSE: No. Not that she didn't have a good reason. Takes two to tango.

AIDE: I think she did it. Maybe even faked having a mental problem. Working up sympathy. Setting herself up for an insanity plea.

NURSE: Doesn't look much like she's faking it to me.

AIDE: You think it was the boyfriend.

NURSE: Odds are pretty good. Vaseline.

The AIDE finds and hands her a jar of gel. She applies it to HELEN's temples.

AIDE: She coulda made it all up.

NURSE: She was married. In the society pages. He was her lover. They were sneaking around. They aren't going to stroll down Sunset Boulevard together.

AIDE: I don't think there ever was a boyfriend. I think she made that up.

NURSE: You think everybody makes everything up.

AIDE: We can't help it. Here's a for instance. For instance—I ask you how you're doing today, and you say?

NURSE: Same as always. Fine.

AIDE: Which you just made up, when in fact you're in a pretty foul temper. Same as always. You lie just to grease the wheels. People start telling the truth and it just jams up the system, the world grinds to a halt. You ever notice how when someone starts telling the truth things get real quiet—

The NURSE hands him the mouth bit.

NURSE: Now put that bit in so she doesn't bite her tongue. I don't care to see that again.

The AIDE attempts to insert the mouthpiece bit.

AIDE: Your pictures in the papers don't do you justice—say ahhh honey—let's see you wag a tonsil—

NURSE: She can't hear you. She's out cold.

AIDE: She hears me. She may look unconscious but it all seeps in. Every little thing. Don't it honey? All bubbling and simmering down in the bottom, every little thing that ever happened to ya—

She hands him the padded electrodes—

NURSE: This ought to take a few troubles off her mind. Ready, steady—

The AIDE *applies the electrode pads to both of her temples.*

AIDE: Let her have it.

The NURSE *applies the electrical current and* HELEN *arches off the table in a stiffened spasm as she's hit with the current—the stage is bathed in white light as a close-up of* HELEN *appears on the scrim.*

As the scream of a train whistle comes up from under, a surly score and titles begin.

Cut to:

2.

Ext. Washington State—1948—Night.

Projected on the scrim: a night train rockets along the tracks.

Main title: Helen Lawrence

The train's POV *from the cowcatcher reveals parallel tracks stretching into the night, lit by the headlight of the train. We pass a sign that reads: You Are Now Crossing 49th Parallel.*

From a high angle, the camera swoops over the train as it slows, then fixes on a passenger car window and approaches it.

Cut to:

3.

Int. Train Compartment—Night.

For the remainder of the play, except at exceptional moments, actors on stage will be composited live into virtual environments projected on the downstage scrim.

As the train comes to rest the compartment's sole occupant, HELEN *Lawrence, checks her watch. Footfalls approach and the cabin door suddenly slides open:*

A BC *provincial police officer.*

Tips his fingers to his hat, and says something. She produces ID*; he glances perfunctorily at it. He tips his hat and exits.*

Fade to black.

Ext. Vancouver—aerial view.

Title over: Vancouver 1948

The camera zooms into an overhead shot of a grand Edwardian building. Push into a view of the ballroom.

Title over: The Old Hotel Vancouver

4.

Int. Old Hotel—Lobby—Day.

A girl of sixteen, JULIE *Winters, attired in shirt, vest, and slacks, with a short haircut, works the front desk. The first look suggests she is indeed a young man. She bristles with energy and reads a newspaper with interest.*

EVA, twenty-four, a recent German immigrant and war bride, approaches.

EVA: Juliana—have you a moment for me?

JULIE: Call me Joe, I told you that a million times already.

EVA: Yes, Joe. May I ask why you have a new name?

JULIE: Just sending it up the flagpole.

(off her puzzlement) Trying it on for size. Seeing if it suits me. Kicking the tires.

EVA: I think I like Julianna up the flagpole.

JULIE: I don't care what anybody thinks, I like the sound of it better.

EVA: I was going to ask you Joe when Mary comes you will come tell me please?

JULIE: Black Mary.

EVA: If I am working please send her to the cafeteria.

JULIE: I guess you slept on it.

EVA: Yes. But not much sleeping.

JULIE: No regrets.

EVA: I have too many already. But maybe you won't make my mistake and you will have no regrets.

JULIE: Ha. Don't worry about that sister. I ain't goin' down that road. Not in this lifetime.

EVA: But please don't speak about it.

JULIE: Keepin' it zipped—I know the drill. Hey how do you say asshole in German?

EVA: Arschloch.

JULIE: Arslock. Thanks.

EVA moves off—JULIE watches her thoughtfully, then returns to her reading.

5.

Int. Old Hotel—Telegraph Office—Continuing.

Off the cafeteria, in a converted telegraph office. Percy WALKER, in his forties, a bookmaker, is on the phone, impatient with his explanation—he's got phones to answer and betting slips to keep straight.

WALKER: *(into telephone)* Take the hay outta your ears Phil—it's my last coupla weeks in this shithole here then we're moving over to the Dodson Hotel. This is it, I hit this one outta the park or I'm fucking doomed. Yeah we got a liquor licence, wasn't fucking cheap—

EVA enters with a cup of coffee. Another phone rings. He grabs it.

Keep the joe coming would ya honey?

(into phone 2) Taxi service hold the line—hold your horses, Hollywood Park doesn't go off for another hour—

(into phone 1) Okay, Phil, gimme your bets. Shoot. Got it . . . Got it . . . Wait. That horse has been scratched. How the fuck would I know, maybe he's hungover. Not the horse. The Jockey. Jesus. No wonder you owe me two grand. It's two grand Phil—I write this shit down pal—

6.

Int. Old Hotel—Lobby—Day.

Police Chief Jim MULDOON, in his forties, enters like he owns the place. He wears a civilian suit and a fedora. He is a flatfoot, a lurching narcissistic bully, the alpha dog who must put his scent down wherever he goes. The Right Man who is never wrong.

JULIE gives Chief MULDOON a lazy, sarcastic salute as he strides past.

JULIE: Morning Chief. Catch any crooks lately? There's one in Percy's office if you're looking for an easy collar. Looks just like Percy.

MULDOON stops abruptly.

MULDOON: What's your name?

Beat.

JULIE: It's Joe.

MULDOON: Joe, if I asked you to do a little something for me, could you do it, no questions asked, on the q.t.?

JULIE: Sure.

She leans in conspiratorially.

MULDOON: Mind your own fucking business. Can you manage that?

JULIE: Got it. Yeah. Okay. I'll give it a go. I can do that.

He strides on.

Easy-peasy. All you had to do was ask—I know how to keep my yap shut—goes with the job. Mum's the word. Making like a clam. Arslock.

She casually grabs the house phone and dials three digits, then:

7.

Int. Old Hotel—Cafeteria—Continuing—Day.

Harry MITCHELL, *in his forties, appears on the mezzanine balcony to view the chief as he enters—feeding off the crumbs of corruption, his means of existence. He is sycophantic and malevolent by turns and simultaneously. A confident but unsuccessful ladies' man.*

EVA *is tying her apron as* MULDOON *enters.*

MULDOON: Eva! There's my little Fräulein—

He approaches EVA. *She tolerates his crudeness, used to being harassed by the male veterans of the hostel, the cruelty of the war and refugee camps, and so rebuffs him coolly—*

I was hoping I'd catch you here.

EVA: You always forget, it is Frau, not Fräulein—I am married.

MULDOON: I wanted to make sure I had a chance to say goodbye before you disappear into the wild blue yonder. Where are you headed anyway?

EVA: Edward and I found a new apartment in the veteran's housing—

MULDOON *hands over his card.*

MULDOON: Give me your address and call me when you get a telephone. This is my number—go on, I just had them printed up—never hurts to have a friend on the force—particularly if he happens to be the chief. Go on. Keep it handy.

EVA *takes it—rude not to.*

—I can always come over and put a scare into the neighbours if they're making too much noise—call the paddy wagon if need be—

EVA: I'm sure that won't be necessary—

She keeps on the move, sliding just out of his impending reach.

MULDOON: —or if that husband of yours ever gets out of hand—what's his name again?

EVA: Edward. He's not that kind. If you met him you would know—

MULDOON: I don't need to meet the man. Quit dodging around a minute. I got a little something for you—

He produces a twenty-dollar bill and extends it to her.

Go on, take it; it's just a housewarming present—

EVA: Thank you, but my husband wouldn't like it.

He manages to stick the twenty in her pocket—and press himself closer, his hand in the small of her back.

MULDOON: What he don't know can't hurt us. Make sure you give me a jingle once you've settled in—I'll come round and let the neighbours know you've got the right friends—

EVA: You cannot be visiting. Edward wouldn't like it.

MULDOON: But you'd like it. And I'd like it. Majority rules.

EVA: No, I would dislike it.

WALKER hovers at the doorway—

WALKER: Chief—we got business to take care of—

MULDOON just waves him off and keeps on at EVA.

MULDOON: I seen you giving me the once over, same as I give you—

EVA: I'm warning you—stop—you're embarrassing me—

She fights off one hand, only to feel the other grasping—

MULDOON: *(sotto voce)* I want you to know if you ever get the itch—you know who to call. You know what the itch is—sure you do—it's what you scratch—

She finally slaps his cheek, hard.

WALKER: All right, break it up you two.

MULDOON rubs his cheek and laughs as EVA retreats.

MULDOON: Okay, Schmelling, I get the message.

8.

Int. Old Hotel—Telegraph Office—Continuing.

MULDOON: What's her problem? I was just giving her a hard time—

WALKER: You shouldn't have been going on about her old man. He's got shell shock.

MULDOON starts to read his newspaper.

MULDOON: Hell, who doesn't. You got shot up, you got over it. Don't hear you whining about it.

WALKER: Yeah, you never know when it's gonna rise back up and bite you. Give the kid a break.

MULDOON: He's probably just faking a twitch or two for the pension. Half of 'em do. She'll come around when she gets fed up with that.

(off newspaper) Fucking Liverpool—three nil over Tottenham.

WALKER: What do we know about the Dodson? That licence come through?

MULDOON: Jumping the gun a little bit aren't we? We haven't completed our deal yet.

WALKER: What's the holdup? You said we were done.

MULDOON: It's this Buddy Black business.

WALKER: —it's all arranged. He's buying the last guy out today.

MULDOON: I'd like to be able to tell the mayor I've cleaned up nigger alley like I promised. What's the name of that other shine joint down there?

WALKER: The Scatt Inn. At the top of the alley—Henry Williams.

MULDOON: Henry. That's the place. He's the man we're going with.

WALKER: Henry's a hophead, he'll run it into the ground in a week—

MULDOON: Then we'll be rid of the alley for good, precisely as city council wants it.

This reversal bewilders WALKER.

WALKER: We already closed the deal with Buddy. He's taken care of it. He's buying Henry out.

MULDOON: I was unaware we'd closed any deal.

WALKER: That's what you wanted. That's the only reason I partnered with Buddy in the Dodson, so he wouldn't kick up a ruckus over you closing three of his joints down. That was his compensation—we went all over this a dozen times.

MULDOON: Sometimes you just have to shoot the big crow and hang him in the yard as a warning to the others. Knock off the number one and everybody else falls in line. We're going with the other shine, Henry.

WALKER: You can't change the deal at the last minute—I gave Buddy my word . . .

WALKER trails off as MULDOON deadeyes him—

MULDOON: I'll tell you what I can do—I can shut down whoever the hell I like.

WALKER: I'm only pointing out that Buddy's bought out all the other joints for us—the Italian and the Jew, Mae Lu's hook shop—on the condition he'd be allowed to stay. There's a lot of action down there—that ain't scraps, it's good income.

MULDOON: Which will drift over to the Dodson. Command, control, and contain.

WALKER: And where's the hoi polloi gonna go when they want to go wild and tie one on? You know they drag a naked blue blood outta there every night of the week—that city councillor two nights ago, you know the one. Folks like to go down the alley there and get a little raw, it makes them feel good. Where they gonna let off some steam if you shut them all down?

MULDOON: There's no shortage of skin joints on the west side. And you don't need Buddy to run the Dodson neither—you can do that yourself. More dough for you.

WALKER: Have you talked to the mayor about this?

MULDOON: I already have a mandate.

WALKER: The reason he's sitting on the throne right now is Buddy brought him the Chinatown vote, and that's what put the mayor over the top.

MULDOON: Exactly, so we don't need him anymore. I like this Henry kid, he's cooperative.

Phones begin to ring.

WALKER: You know Buddy's a fighter. He's going to cause a riot.

MULDOON: That's a coincidence, I just bought all the boys new billy clubs. When you get Eva's new address, let me know.

He exits—WALKER lets his phones ring.

Ext. Vancouver—aerial view.

The camera zooms into an overhead shot of a city block on the city's east side. Push into a view of Buddy Black's Beer Garden.

Title over: Hogan's Alley.

9.

Ext. Hogan's Alley—Scatt Inn—Day.

It's early enough that we hear songbirds. At the head of the alley is the Scatt Inn, a ramshackle gambling house, where HENRY *Williams, in his thirties, African American, veteran of the* US *Marine Corps, long a resident of Vancouver and Hogan's Alley, peels himself an apple with his jackknife in one patient peel.*

With HENRY *is* ROSE*, a seventeen-year-old Japanese Canadian, in a robe and silk pyjamas, watching as* HENRY *finishes his artful peel of the apple.*

ROSE: Hey Henry, you ever been to California?

HENRY: Sure, all the time. I used to work the Frisco to Seattle route on the train. Why?

ROSE: Emile wants to take me there.

HENRY: Who's this?

ROSE: Emile. We got a lunch date today. He's a cook in a lumber camp.

HENRY: Probably makes good money.

ROSE: I sure hope so. I can't keep this up much longer.

HENRY *hands her the apple.*

HENRY: Here you go—hang on, it's got a worm in it. Let me cut that out.

ROSE: I don't mind. Even a worm's gotta eat.

EDWARD*, twenty-five, veteran* RCAF*, and unshaven husband of* EVA*, in a rumpled suit, hurries down the alley toward* HENRY*.* EDWARD *starts talking long before he lands beside him.*

EDWARD: Henry! I've got a payout coming, an advance on a job. I'll be designing the new bridge, a fine piece of engineering work—

HENRY: When's payday?

EDWARD: Next Friday. I'm good for a fifty if you can spare it. I only need grocery money for a week.

POV of EDWARD, HENRY, and ROSE from above.

HENRY: Edward, you don't look like you ever met a grocery in your life.

HENRY peels a few bills off a wad.

EDWARD: Well, I've got a home in the veterans' housing to cook in now, don't I? A hundred would keep the wheels on, if you've got it.

A reverse angle reveals—Buddy Black, scowling down from his second-storey window across Park Lane.

HENRY: Fifty. That makes it seven hundred even.

EDWARD accepts HENRY's cash.

EDWARD: I don't suppose I could wet my whistle.

10.

Int. Hogan's Alley—BUDDY's Bedroom—Day.

BUDDY Black, African American, forties, turns away from his window at the tail end of the conversation above, and returns to sit at the desk, wearing a robe (an old boxing robe with the name BUDDY Black on the back) and pyjamas and a homburg. He takes the shoebox from under his arm and places it on his lap, removes the lid, and begins to sort the bundles of cash within. MARY, in her early thirties, in the bedroom, pulls on her stockings. As from the top:

BUDDY: I didn't sleep a wink last night—that goddamn rooster at three o'clock, just as I'm settling into a dream. Who owns that bird?

MARY: I think he wandered over from Chinatown.

BUDDY: I'm gonna shoot that thing tonight. Gonna wait up for him if I have to. Pick him off from the window with my deer rifle.

MARY: Buddy, you know how superstitious they are. You don't want to shoot that bird.

BUDDY: There's other ways to do it. He's out there tonight and there's gonna be a showdown. I got a big day today: I got to be sharp—that rooster cost me sleep—

MARY: I had a dream last night—

BUDDY goes back to his bills making sure they all face the same direction.

BUDDY: Don't want to hear about it. I got enough running around in my head already. Tell me later.

MARY in the door of the bedroom now—

MARY: I have to tell it while I remember it. You were in it, and so was Henry. You were fighting over a dog.

BUDDY: I'd like to get a dog. What kind was it? Not one of those little ones—

MARY: Well, it started out as a little dog but it seemed to get bigger. Then you got bit.

BUDDY: What he do that for? Dogs like me, I like dogs.

MARY: Dog didn't bite you. Henry did.

BUDDY: What for?

MARY: I don't know—he didn't bite me.

BUDDY: You look good. Where you off to?

MARY: Down to the beer garden to put on some coffee. Same as every day.

She stands into her shoes now and comes to him.

BUDDY: Then where you going?

MARY: Over to the butcher to pick up the steaks you say the chief likes. Zip me up.

BUDDY rises to zip her up.

BUDDY: After that?

MARY: Nowhere. Maybe a cup of coffee someplace.

BUDDY: Up to the old hotel.

MARY: If you know why you ask.

BUDDY: There ain't gonna be no letter from him up there today, or tomorrow. And he ain't gonna come whistlin' round the corner neither.

MARY: Who's that now?

BUDDY: Your husband. You up at the hotel every other day to see if Charlie sent you a letter up there.

MARY: What do you know anyway. I have some other business up there.

BUDDY: Been four years sweetheart. If he was coming back don't you think you woulda heard something by now?

MARY: If he's dead I would have received the official letter from the air force, wouldn't I?

BUDDY: They're supposed to send one.

MARY: Why we got to go through this?

BUDDY: It's just been a while—

MARY: You think I don't know how long it's been?

A silence as he watches MARY *put on lipstick.*

BUDDY: As long as you're going up to the hotel, you might as well drop in on Percy, see if he's going to have his cash tonight. I don't want to be worrying about that on top of it all. I want it all wrapped up tonight. This bullshit been going on too long already.

MARY: You better concentrate your worrying on your brother.

BUDDY: Why you going on about Henry.

MARY: I told you—he was in my dream.

BUDDY: Thought you said it was about me and Henry. Now you say it was about Henry—

MARY: Don't forget the dog. You going to grill me about him too?

BUDDY: Dog didn't bite me. Henry did.

MARY: I just know he's going to make you pay for doing him wrong.

BUDDY: I never did him wrong. I did right, still am. He made it wrong.

MARY: If you say so. But just because you admit you were wrong, doesn't mean you have to believe it. That's what he wants to hear. He doesn't care about anything else. Your little brother is a proud man.

She kisses him.

I'm putting on a pot so don't sit around up here all morning—and put some clothes on. I don't like it when you wear that old rag around all day.

Where's my bible?

BUDDY: Under the bed.

MARY *retrieves her Bible—*

MARY: What you looking all funny for?

BUDDY: I don't appreciate you trying to create a peace pact between me and Henry.

MARY: You catch more flies with honey than vinegar sweetheart.

She exits. BUDDY cinches his robe.

Int. Old Hotel—Main Entrance—Day.

Travelling shot moving toward the revolving doors at the hotel's entrance.

11.

Int. Old Hotel—Lobby—Day.

HELEN enters and lingers a moment to look around the deserted lobby before approaching the front desk.

JULIE: *(off-screen)* You look like you musta made a wrong turn somewhere.

HELEN—henceforth called BETTY—approaches.

BETTY: I was just hoping the same thing.

JULIE: You probably want the new hotel. It's a block over. This is for veterans only. No exceptions.

BETTY: Ah. Then I'm afraid I'm in the right place after all. I'm looking for a gentleman by the name of Harry Mitchell.

JULIE: We got a Harry here, I just never heard him described as a gentleman before.

BETTY: That would, no doubt, be him.

JULIE: Make yourself comfortable. I'll try and find him.

BETTY: I'll be in the bar—

JULIE: Let me know if you find one and I'll join you. We're a dry house.

BETTY: That's not very civilized.

JULIE: Welcome to Vancouver. You want a drink in this town, you got to do it out of brown bag. Can I say who's calling?

JULIE dials.

BETTY: It won't mean anything to him. We have a mutual friend.

JULIE: What's it about?

BETTY: It's of a personal nature.

JULIE: *(into phone, while checking BETTY out)* You got a young lady here asking for you. Not your usual type—

Beat.

Of a personal nature she says. A mutual friend—

Angle on MITCHELL—on the mezzanine—as he appears, with phone in his ear. He looks down upon the main lobby and JULIE and BETTY.

She ain't coughin' up a name. Okey-doke.

Sets phone aside.

Mezzanine level, straight ahead. You want me to watch your bags—

BETTY: I can manage—

JULIE watches her walk to the elevators.

JULIE: I'd keep an eye on my valuables, if you know what I mean.

BETTY: *(over her shoulder)* I believe I do.

EDWARD now enters the lobby and scoots past JULIE as her back is momentarily turned—but she senses him.

JULIE: Hold up there Hopalong. Back your truck up.

EDWARD: Oh, I didn't see you there.

JULIE: You and the little lady are moving out today.

EDWARD: That's right, we're hoping.

JULIE: And I was hoping to collect the five dollars you still owe.

EDWARD: Ah, thank you for reminding me.

He searches his pockets.

I must have left my cash in another pocket—

JULIE: I wouldn't put it past ya. What was her name?

JULIE sniffs as if she's smelling perfume—

EDWARD: As if it's any of your business, I'll have you know I was out on a job interview this morning—

JULIE: Horse manure. The only thing you've been interviewing is the nags in the Hastings barns. If you don't have the five spot I'm going to need some collateral.

EDWARD reaches for the medal pinned to his lapel. A moment.

EDWARD: I have a keepsake. It's not worth much to anyone but me I guess—

JULIE: Ixnay. No medals. Got a shoebox full of those. No watches neither, I got enough of those to keep Switzerland tickin' for a year. Don't make me get it from your blushing bride.

Beat.

(calls out) Eva!

EDWARD: Quiet! Here. Take it and shut up.

EDWARD hands over a fiver and exits quickly.

12.

Int. Old Hotel—MITCHELL's Office—Day.

A makeshift office in the loges overlooking the ballroom, filled with shelves of liquor, cigarettes, and other black-market goods. MITCHELL adjusts his rug. BETTY raps on the door.

MITCHELL: It's open.

BETTY: Mr. Mitchell?

MITCHELL: At your service. And you would be . . .

BETTY: Elizabeth Mansfield. Betty.

MITCHELL: Harry. I understand we have a mutual friend.

She spies the store of black-market smokes and booze.

BETTY: That's why I'm here.

MITCHELL: So I understand.

BETTY: Are those American cigarettes?

MITCHELL: Uh-huh.

BETTY: You look like you could spare one.

MITCHELL: Sure. Have one of these.

She accepts his offered cigarette.

You were saying?

Lighting it.

Our mutual friend—

BETTY: Raymond McLeish. You served together overseas. He said we'd get along.

MITCHELL: Yeah. Why's that?

BETTY: Ray has the impression you're a man who doesn't mind breaking the rules.

MITCHELL: That sorta depends on what rules we're talking about.

BETTY: Let's start with the one that says you can't rent me a room and go from there.

MITCHELL: Is it just for yourself.

BETTY: I'm alone. For a night or two. See how it goes.

MITCHELL: Playing it by ear then.

BETTY: Uh-huh. Raymond implied you'd be willing to hum along. How about it? I'll be on my very best behaviour.

MITCHELL: That's not necessary.

MITCHELL fishes up his key ring.

Okay. Okay. The old girl's kissing the wrecking ball in a couple of weeks, and most of the rooms have been stripped out, but I got one that's at least got a lock on the door and cold running water.

BETTY: Wonderful. Sounds just like home.

She starts out. He grabs her bags and follows.

MITCHELL: Right this way. I'll take these.

OMITTED.

14.

Ext. Hogan's Alley—Brothel Doorway—Day.

ROSE lounges on a chair, wearing her robe and silk pyjamas and reading a magazine. A man, PERKINS, approaches and tilts his hat back on his head. ROSE advertises a leg. The radio drifts down the alley.

ROSE: Spare a cigarette, hon?

PERKINS: I believe I can.

ROSE: Hallelujah. I've been having a fit.

PERKINS: You're a fresh face. I don't think I've met you before—

ROSE: I just came into town a week ago.

PERKINS indicates the brothel and hands her a smoke.

PERKINS: And you've landed on your feet already.

ROSE: That's only temporary in this business.

She grins. PERKINS laughs.

PERKINS: I suppose it is. Well, you're quite an exotic specimen. I'm curious about your background.

ROSE: You want to see my background you gotta pay five dollars like everybody else.

PERKINS laughs.

PERKINS: I meant your home. How'd you end up here?

ROSE: Just followed my nose.

PERKINS: What's your name sweetheart?

PERKINS takes out a notepad as—

ROSE: Rose, like the flower. Why are you writing that down?

PERKINS: Oh, excuse me. Let me introduce myself properly. Inspector Perkins, vice squad.

He flops out his badge for her perusal. ROSE takes the badge to examine it closely.

ROSE: Are you kidding me?

PERKINS: I'm afraid not, no—

ROSE: Please—you can't arrest me, not today—I'm supposed to meet a friend—

PERKINS: Well, isn't that inconvenient now—

ROSE: We were just talking anyway, there's no law against that is there—

PERKINS: Not yet

ROSE: *(beginning to tear up)* Buddy told me it was all right out here, that you were paid off already—

PERKINS: *(laughs, delighted)* Look at that face. Aw, isn't she the cutest thing. You can turn off the taps now love of course it's all right. I was just having some fun with you—

ROSE: That ain't very nice, trying to fool me like that. You really going to let me off the hook?

PERKINS: I suppose I might.

ROSE: You want to come inside?

PERKINS: What a lovely invitation. After you—

ROSE heads inside tentatively, returning his badge.

ROSE: I guess this comes in pretty handy.

PERKINS: Now and again.

ROSE: Impresses the ladies I bet.

PERKINS: You tell me.

ROSE: Well, you ain't much without it, that's for sure.

PERKINS laughs and follows her inside.

15.

Int. Old Hotel—BETTY's Room—Day.

A bed, table, coat rack, sink in the corner. A window, which has no curtains. A cityscape rises beyond. BETTY watches MITCHELL set down her bag on the table.

MITCHELL: There's a cafeteria off the lobby if you feel like a meal. It ain't great but we haven't lost anybody yet—well, maybe one or two old timers, but they were on their last legs anyway.

BETTY: I've not got much of an appetite I'm afraid.

MITCHELL: If you want something better, or where to get a drink, whatever you need, I can help you out, no questions asked—

BETTY: I like the sound of that.

MITCHELL: What part?

BETTY: The no-questions-asked part. You mean it?

He chuckles.

MITCHELL: Sure.

BETTY examines him a moment. She opens her suitcase on the table, retrieves a bottle of whisky, and pours two drinks.

BETTY: All right. Ray said you might be able to help with a problem I'm having. I'm sorry, I poured doubles—can you forgive me?

MITCHELL: Everyone's entitled to a little mistake now and then.

BETTY: Where was I?

MITCHELL: You were having a problem.

BETTY: Yes. I'm looking for a friend of my late husband. There's some niggling matters with his estate that need tidying up.

MITCHELL: Sorry about the husband.

BETTY: Don't be. I'm not.

MITCHELL: I wasn't really.

She lifts her glass in toast.

BETTY: I only have a name.

MITCHELL: Let's see if it rings a bell—

BETTY: Percy Wallace.

MITCHELL hides in his drink a moment.

MITCHELL: *(re: whisky)* This is nice. We don't see it much up here. Percy. That's an unusual handle. What was the last name again?

BETTY: Wallace. I understand he may be working as a bookmaker.

MITCHELL: Taking bets.

BETTY: He was at one time anyway. A card player when I knew him. Among other interests.

MITCHELL: How'd he meet your husband, this Percy—

BETTY wags her finger at him.

BETTY: There you go, breaking a promise before you even finish your drink. Percy Wallace. Bells or no bells?

MITCHELL: No, no bells. I suppose you've looked in the phone book—

BETTY: I suppose I have.

MITCHELL: I can ask around—I know a couple of bookies in town—

BETTY: It's a fair sum of money Mr. Wallace is in line to receive, the sort of dough that attracts flies.

MITCHELL: Oh. I see—

BETTY: I need to find Mr. Wallace, quickly, discreetly, without the flies.

MITCHELL: In this scenario, I might get a fee of some sort if I was to locate this Percy fella?

BETTY: Even more so if you manage it quickly.

MITCHELL: Well, I better get started then.

BETTY: Good. Let me know when you have any news.

BETTY abruptly indicates the door.

Bottoms up.

MITCHELL: Sure.

He downs his drink; she takes his glass.

BETTY: You know where I am.

MITCHELL: *(exiting)* I'll send somebody up with a couple of towels.

BETTY: Lovely. Wrap them around a couple bottles of whisky, will you?

16.

Int. Old Hotel—Corridor—Continuing—Day.

MITCHELL runs immediately into JULIE—

JULIE: What's her story—

MITCHELL: It's all about some missing towels. She needs some.

JULIE: Aw, come on. A broad like that don't come into a joint like this asking for you unless something fishy's going on. C'mon give me something to work with.

He walks on.

MITCHELL: Towels. Clean ones. Those'll get you in the door—

JULIE: Towels.

MITCHELL: Yes.

JULIE: Really?

MITCHELL: Yes.

JULIE: That's what you're giving me?

MITCHELL: Let me know what you find out.

JULIE: Yes, boss.

She watches MITCHELL *exit.*

17.

Ext. Hogan's Alley—Scatt Inn—Day.

HENRY *sits out front, rolling a cigarette.* BUDDY *appears, still in his robe.*

BUDDY: Henry, come on down and have some breakfast and we can talk—

HENRY: Ate already.

BUDDY: Coffee then. Mary's making a pot.

HENRY: Got my own going.

BUDDY: All right then, let's get this business sorted out.

HENRY: We don't have any business.

BUDDY: Here I stand, offering you cash money, more than you make in a year.

HENRY: It ain't about money. You remember back in '42—

BUDDY: Here we go. If you're gonna start reminiscing how about if I meet you halfway back in '45 and save ourselves some time—

HENRY: '42's the year you stole my plan.

BUDDY: Which plan was this.

HENRY: The beer garden. We stood right here, having a conversation about my plan for a beer garden out back, right here. You remember.

BUDDY: Get to it.

HENRY: Beer garden was my idea, you said so loud and clear. You said, "that's a good idea, Hank." Then as soon as I went to the army—you stole it.

BUDDY: The army was your idea too. Don't hear you making a claim for that one. When they blew the trumpet down south and said, "All fools line up over here," nobody made you go. You went on your own ticket—

HENRY: To fight for my country while you called in sick.

BUDDY: Your country. You been here in Canada as long as I have. Some place you can't even remember blows a trumpet and you get a lump in your throat. That's a fool's game.

HENRY: You were plain scared is all.

BUDDY: Scared of being a fool.

HENRY: You a coward.

BUDDY: At least I ain't pretending I ain't. I don't need to go to war to learn that. I prefer sticking to my own affairs and leaving others to theirs. If you done the same you wouldn't be cryin' about a beer garden now.

HENRY: I'm not crying about it. I'm telling you how it is. Let's get right back to the main idea. The idea was my property just as much as this dirt is. You were just laying in the weeds waiting for me to go to the army. You always got a strategy cooking.

BUDDY: That's just being a natural man.

HENRY: You were just laying in the weeds—

BUDDY: Hold up right there. It's all coming back. 1942. The night before you went off to boot camp. Didn't I get you cross-eyed drunk and feed you a Mickey Finn so you'd miss your train?

HENRY: I got drunk all by myself—

BUDDY: I paid for every drink—

HENRY: —and it was that cute redhead Doris who doped me.

BUDDY: I didn't try and stop her did I? I did everything but chain you to the radiator—like a man seeing his brother volunteering for some foolishness should do.

HENRY: Point is, I come back and you had all my business and the whole alley stitched up like a goddamn combine.

BUDDY: Where else they gonna let a nigger get some business but this alley?

HENRY: Now you got a piece of Carlo's, you buying Mae Lou's hook shop, Levi's card game—

BUDDY: You think I was gonna go hide in the woods and live off squirrels till the war was done? You leave the game you lose your spot. And while you're at it, tell me something that ain't stitched up. Go ahead, tell me one thing. Just one. See? You can't.

HENRY: All I ever thought about over there was coming back here, building my beer garden, planting shade trees all around, puttin' up a string of lights and having people dance underneath. That was my heaven on earth, only thing kept me going.

BUDDY: What kinda fool turns his back on heaven and grabs the first train to hell? You shoulda stayed and fought the war right here on the home front. You shoulda planted trees, you shoulda played your music. But you didn't. I swore on our mama's grave to keep your ass alive— You decided you were going to join the herd, and off to the slaughter yards you go. And what'd you get out of it anyway? You get benefits? Pension? Nope. Just a one-horse parade on a rainy afternoon and a duffel bag full of sad-sack stories, complaining about everything being rigged.

HENRY: It ain't the riggin' I mind so much as not being in on it. I just want to be in on it one time—

BUDDY: And here you go—more money than you've ever had in one place.

He takes out the bundles of bills from his pockets.

HENRY: I want reparations.

BUDDY: Call it reparations, payback, fuck-you-jack, whatever you want, I'll give you fifteen thousand dollars' worth right now.

HENRY: I lie awake all night till the rooster crow—

BUDDY: I'm taking care of that rooster too. Fifteen thousand and a dead rooster. We got a deal or not?

HENRY: You ain't even listening. You never ask me, "Henry, how was it over there, what happened?" Never wrote me one goddamn letter. You know, I think you woulda been happy if I never came back.

BUDDY takes this one to heart.

And now you don't even want to hear about it. Ain't I got the right to tell my story?

There's a long beat.

BUDDY: Go ahead. Tell your story. And then we can get down to the goddamn business at hand.

HENRY: You think there's a line we won't cross—things you won't ever do to another human being. I'm telling you, there ain't one.

HENRY is about to elaborate . . . but just goes quiet.

BUDDY: Well, I'm glad you learned something out of it all. But now, now you gotta learn this—because this is right now, not yesteryear. If you don't take my fifteen, Chief Muldoon's gonna send down his black shirts, they're gonna lay the devil's own beating on you, and maybe even burn you out if they feeling a little frisky that evening. Muldoon is going to allow one nigger down here. That's his whole damn consolidation policy. One of us has to go.

HENRY: That part I understand. Why's that nigger gotta be me?

BUDDY: 'Cause I been feathering my goddamn nest. 'Cause I play by the rules, instead of whining about what coulda been.

HENRY: I want a piece of the beer garden.

BUDDY: That ain't never gonna happen.

BUDDY walks off.

Blackout.

18.

Int. Old Hotel—BETTY's Room—Day.

Sound effect only: JULIE raps on BETTY's door. No answer. Another knock, still no answer.

JULIE: It's Joe. Got some towels and a couple pillow cases . . .

JULIE takes a key and slowly opens the door. BETTY is lying on the bed, in her slip. On the floor beside the bed sit an open bottle of whisky and a vial of pills.

If you're sleeping, I can come back another time.

Still no answer, so JULIE approaches the bed.

Miss? Hey, Miss. I got the towels.

She picks up the pill vial and reads the label.

Insert: the vial in her hand.

Then she sees the whisky bottle and puts it together as BETTY suddenly grabs her by the wrist—

BETTY: May I help you?

JULIE: Ahhhh! Jesus!

(gains some air) I thought—it looked like—the pills, the whisky—you was hardly breathing. I thought you pulled the plug.

BETTY: I like to think if I was going to kill myself I'd do it somewhere they change the linen a little more regularly.

(rising) What are you doing here?

BETTY finds her skirt.

JULIE: I got the towels—I knocked—you weren't moving—Jezuz, you made me jump.

BETTY takes the pill vial from her and opens it.

BETTY: None of your business.

JULIE: What?

BETTY: In answer to your question.

BETTY rouses herself enough to pour herself a drink.

JULIE: I wasn't asking . . .

BETTY takes a pill and a drink.

You mix those babies with the booze and you'll feel no pain.

BETTY: I've been given those promises before.

She washes the pills down with the drink. Finally:

Who are you?

JULIE: I'm Julie, some people call me Joe.

BETTY: And what are you doing in this dump?

JULIE: I'm an orphan. Sorta. My dad was killed in Holland, so they let me stay here.

BETTY: You have no other family?

JULIE: My mother, but she ran out on us when I was still nibbling on the furniture. She and my dad were working the carnival, running the shooting galleries and the dart game, then my mom ran off with the lover boy on the roulette wheels. Dad used to say if he'd had a real rifle he'd a used it on him. Put three darts in his chest instead. And we're talking about those big darts, not those bitty ones. One, two, three, bull's eye in his chest. That's about the time he joined the forces.

BETTY: Tell me about that man you run around after.

JULIE: Harry. He's the manager. My dad asked him to keep an eye on me until he came home, which never happened.

BETTY: There's something about him I don't like very much.

JULIE: It's probably that long bit between his eyebrows and his socks.

BETTY: I hope you keep a knife under your pillow.

JULIE: Only when I'm sleeping. I won't be around much longer anyway. I'm probably going out with the carnival when this place closes. They said they might need somebody in the fortune-teller booth to read palms. You want, I can read yours. G'wan, can't hurt, can it?

BETTY flops her hand out for JULIE to read.

BETTY: Make it a good one, will you? I could use the encouragement.

JULIE: I just read 'em as I see 'em. Let's see now. Hmm. You've been married to a guy with a pretty big bankroll.

BETTY: True.

JULIE: But that didn't work out so well.

BETTY: You could say that.

JULIE: You've been sick recently.

BETTY: All right, you little carny sharpster, that's enough. Go now and leave me in peace. You're just a cheap fraud like all the rest—go on, shoo.

JULIE: What do you mean? I'm three for three.

BETTY: The ring—I'm married. The pills—I've been ill—

JULIE: There's more I didn't even tell yet.

BETTY: Save it for the hayseeds on the midway—

JULIE: One last thing—

BETTY rises to steer her out.

BETTY: Out.

JULIE: You're on the run from something—tell me how I know that.

BETTY: Why else would I stay in a dump like this?

JULIE: 'Cause you're looking for somebody and you don't want him to know you're here while you're looking.

BETTY: Well, aren't you clever. I suppose you learned that in the carnival too.

JULIE: Every other clown in the carnival is on the run, so you pick up some tricks. Like, you gotta know who's a flatfoot trying to catch you doing something shady, which is most of the time, or how to pop the button on Friday night's paycheck or clock a plainclothes cop at a quarter mile on a moonless night.

BETTY: All the makings of a very promising career.

JULIE: Keeps me out of juvenile hall. Most of the time anyway. Sometimes I let 'em pinch me so I can visit some of the old gang and get my teeth fixed. Ask me anything, I know lots of stuff.

BETTY: You're familiar with the city?

JULIE: We passed getting familiar a while ago.

BETTY: All right. I've got one for you.

JULIE: I get this one right, and you take me out for drinks.

BETTY: All right.

JULIE: And dinner.

BETTY: And dinner.

JULIE: I choose the spot.

BETTY: Fine.

JULIE: Go ahead, shoot.

BETTY: I'm looking for a gambling house run by a negro by the name of Buddy Black.

JULIE slaps her hands in victory.

JULIE: Drinks and dinner, my choice, on you.

BETTY: That's what we said.

JULIE: Eight o'clock, I'll have a cab waiting, we'll have drinks and the best chicken-fried steak you'll ever eat.

BETTY: Buddy Black. Where do I find him?

JULIE: That's what I'm saying. Buddy Black, Hogan's Alley, chicken-fried steak, we'll have a ball.

BETTY: He'll be there?

JULIE: He's gotta be there. He's Buddy Black.

19.

Ext. Hogan's Alley—Brothel Doorway—Day.

ROSE exits the brothel, dressed conservatively by her standards, followed by PERKINS, who pauses on the stoop to button up his fly. BUDDY emerges from his bar directly across the alley to call after ROSE.

BUDDY: Rose!

You going up to the hotel to meet that fella of yours sometime?

ROSE: I'm heading there right now, but I wouldn't say he's my fella exactly, I only met him last night. But he's a good opportunity; he's a cook in a lumber camp.

BUDDY: Give this letter to the front desk.

He hands over a letter.

Tell them to give it to Mary when she comes in.

ROSE: Why don't you give it to her yourself.

BUDDY: Never you mind any of that.

PERKINS: Buddy! Top of the morning!

BUDDY: Tell the desk to tell Mary it just arrived—don't forget now.

ROSE moves off.

PERKINS: Buddy Black! King of the Alley!

How's my man on this fine day.

BUDDY withdraws a wad of bills and hands it over to PERKINS as—

BUDDY: You talked to the chief, everything's arranged, he'll be here tonight?

PERKINS casually thumbs the bills.

PERKINS: That young Rose is a welcome addition down here. You've got your own little geisha girl, right here in Hogan's Alley.

BUDDY: Uh-huh. Muldoon, you talked to him, we're all set?

PERKINS puts the bills away and takes out a little stub of a pencil to make notes on a pad.

PERKINS: Ah, there's been a little bump in the road I'm sorry to say—the chief's had a change of mind.

BUDDY: How's that now. You said yesterday it was all arranged—

PERKINS: It was, it was all arranged, except for a detail or two that's changed. Isn't that what they always say, the devil dances in the details—

BUDDY: Which devil.

PERKINS: I'm surprised Percy hasn't told you. I had the impression the chief took a meeting with him this morning at the old hotel.

BUDDY: Come on now. Tell me what the chief changed his mind on—

MARY emerges to overhear the rest.

PERKINS: Of course, you have a right to know.

(sees MARY) Top of the morning Mary, you look lovely as usual.

MARY: Mr. Perkins.

BUDDY: Gimme what's on the wire right now. What about the chief—

PERKINS: Yes, the chief. We had a meeting and decided it'd be best for all parties concerned if you were to quietly move along.

BUDDY: Move along. You shutting me out of the Dodson deal too?

PERKINS: I wouldn't know about that.

BUDDY is baffled. PERKINS enjoys the moment. MARY is equally concerned. She moves to stand by BUDDY's side.

BUDDY: With all the money you know comes through here—you just decided to shut me down?

MARY: Why would you do that?

PERKINS: Well, the chief—after some consultation—with Buddy's profile—has decided to let Henry stay open.

BUDDY: Henry. You picking my brother over me? He agreed to that?

PERKINS: You're too loud, too well-known. If we can say we shut down Buddy Black—well, that's news that's all over town. That makes a better impression with the citizens. You're the devil they know and want to see go. If I'd been appointed chief, it might have been an entirely different story, but here we are.

BUDDY: I've been stuffing your pockets for the last ten years, greasing all you gambling squad boyos, buying your houses out in the country for your whores, you and Muldoon—

MARY slips her arm in BUDDY's, holding him by her side.

PERKINS: Careful now son. You know we're both happily married men. It wouldn't do to spread rumours—

BUDDY: That young cooze you got stashed down by the river, that ain't rumour. And that brand new Chevrolet every other year, that ain't no rumour, and all the time gettin' your oil changed here on my dime. You killing the golden goose, man!

PERKINS: That reminds me, I'd like to see Rose again. Make sure she's available this evening, will you? She's a bit of a treat.

PERKINS heads off.

20.

Int. Old Hotel—MITCHELL's Office—Day.

MITCHELL's on the phone—mostly listening.

MITCHELL: *(into phone, whistles to himself)* A big shot, huh. Newspapers, no kidding. When—hang on—back up. When was this exactly? Get me details and call me back.

JULIE enters and helps herself to a cigarette.

What's the lowdown?

JULIE: Nothing much, 'cept when I go in there—I knock, no answer—and there she is, laid out on the bed—with a bottle of whisky in one hand and a bottle of pills from some bug ward in LA.

MITCHELL: She ask you about Percy?

JULIE: Nope. He got something to do with her?

MITCHELL: You keep that to yourself.

JULIE: Why?

MITCHELL: Just you stay away from Percy, I don't want you talking to him.

JULIE: Why not?

MITCHELL: And don't let her know he's downstairs. I gotta keep those two apart for a while—here, take this.

He hands her a bottle of whisky and a carton of cigarettes.

JULIE: That's mighty white of you boss.

MITCHELL: Not for you, for her. Go on, tell her it's with my compliments.

He urges her out the door and follows, locks up.

Int. Old Hotel—Corridor—Day.

JULIE: This ain't gonna do it. You can't hit what she's pitching. This won't even get you close to first base. You won't get outta the dugout.

MITCHELL: Beat it.

They head in opposite directions.

JULIE: Just trying to save you from another humiliating humiliation . . .

21.

Int. Old Hotel—Telegraph Office—Day.

WALKER: *(into phone)* Taxi service. Yeah, I just called you. We need to settle up.

He listens to an excuse a moment, as MITCHELL *enters, unseen by* WALKER.

I'm moving the office over to the Dodson. Yeah, we bought the licence. Big step up, you ain't kidding. Thanks. You bring that money over today, all right. All right.

He hangs up.

(to himself) Jesus fucking Christ.

MITCHELL: Morning Sergeant.

WALKER *whirls around—*MITCHELL *mock salutes him.*

WALKER: What are you always sneaking around for. How long have you been there?

MITCHELL: Don't get your shorts in a twist, I already knew you and Buddy were going for the Dodson. Congrats.

WALKER: Yeah, another fucking headache.

EDWARD: *(peeks into the room)* Percy—

WALKER: Answer is no, Edward. Take a walk.

EDWARD steps out of view.

What do you want?

MITCHELL: It's about the Dodson, now you happened to bring it up.

WALKER: What about it.

He writes down some figures on a pad.

MITCHELL: I'd like to come along on that.

WALKER: Come again?

MITCHELL: Dodson's a legit beer parlor. You gotta start keeping a couple sets of the books, you need a manager, I need the work. I'm a good front man, that's what I do. I'm a decorated officer, I make a good show. That's what I did in the army. Any time anybody needed something pulled off with a little class, they came to me.

WALKER: I heard you were pimping for the officers' corp.

MITCHELL grins ear to ear.

MITCHELL: Sweet work if you can get it.

WALKER: So what's the worry, you won't starve, you can always turn your little chicken Julie out for a buck till something comes along.

MITCHELL: It's not like that.

WALKER: What's it like?

MITCHELL: Not like that.

Mayko Nguyen, Nicholas Lea, and Hrothgar Mathews;
photograph by Stan Douglas.

WALKER: It sure looks like that.

WALKER reaches to answer a ringing phone, giving MITCHELL his back. MITCHELL begins to darken and pace as—

Taxi service. Shoot. Got it. Got it. Okay. We need to settle up today. Because I need the cash. Before six.

He hangs up. Makes some more notes.

MITCHELL: I've done a good job for you around here. No complaints.

WALKER: I'm not the complaining type. That's how I get along. It seems to be a successful philosophy. You might try it.

MITCHELL: My point is—you've done well here—I gave you this spot when you needed someplace outta the limelight. I thought we had a pretty good partnership. Thought that might continue, help you make a smooth transition over to the Dodson—

WALKER: I'm not much of a partner type either.

MITCHELL: You go partners with Chief Muldoon, partners with Buddy Black.

WALKER: They're essential to the operation.

A phone rings again.

(cupping the phone to his chest) I'll keep you in mind if a position opens up, that's the best I can do.

He reaches for the phone.

MITCHELL: Maybe you forgot how I helped you out of that trouble down in Los Angeles. I was pretty essential then.

WALKER stares at him a moment, then takes the ringing phone off the hook.

WALKER: We weren't going to talk about that. And here you are, bringing it up.

MITCHELL: You know a woman by the name of Elizabeth Mansfield?

WALKER: What are you on about?

Another phone rings and he takes that off the hook too.

MITCHELL: Blond, real good-looker. About your age. From Los Angeles.

WALKER: They grow 'em by the dozen down there.

MITCHELL: This one spent some time in a sanitorium. Had some sort of mental breakdown.

Beat.

WALKER: I know who you mean now. Where'd you run into her?

MITCHELL: Didn't say I did. Just said she was looking for you.

WALKER: She called you here, at the hotel?

MITCHELL: I just spoke to her, but she had your name wrong. Called you Percy Wallace, not Walker. Then I figured out that Wallace was the name you were using down south. I said I'd never heard of you but I'd ask around. She's pretty eager to track you down.

WALKER: A good-looking blond.

MITCHELL: Uh-huh.

WALKER: You can tell the difference between a redhead and a blond just by talking on the telephone? That's quite a talent.

MITCHELL: She described herself, in case I ran into you, so you'd know who I'm talking about.

Beat.

WALKER: Brother, she's as nutty as they come. Made up all kinds of stories, how I seduced her to get after her old man's money, all kinds of lunatic stuff. So I'd appreciate it if you didn't point her in my direction.

MITCHELL: A woman scorned, is that it?

WALKER: Ain't no fucking joke.

MITCHELL spreads his arms in a friendly gesture.

MITCHELL: Sure. I didn't want to put the squeeze on you. I'm not the squeezing type.

WALKER: But you're a pretty good bullshitter, Harry. Pretty good.

Beat.

I could use a man like you. Be good to have somebody watching my back instead of looking at it like a good spot to plant a butcher knife.

MITCHELL: That's my line of work: seeing what you can't see. Taking care of it before it becomes a problem.

A phone rings.

WALKER: How about I come up and see you a little later on. We'll have a drink, chew the fat, and work something out we can both live with.

MITCHELL: You know where I am.

WALKER: Thanks for the heads-up. We'll work something out.

MITCHELL: Sure. No complaints.

MITCHELL exits. WALKER is clearly rattled. EDWARD slips in.

EDWARD: What do you say, Percy. Gimme a chance to get even.

WALKER: Listen Edward, you're walking around under a black cloud of bad luck, and I don't want any more of it. The only reason I let you bet with me is because I like your wife.

EDWARD: What's that supposed to mean?

WALKER: How hard is that to understand? I like your fucking wife.

EDWARD: You got something going on with my wife?

WALKER: Just handicapping the contest. She's a good-looking woman, hard worker, with her eye on the finish line. You on the other hand—you can't get out of the barn let alone the gate, and if you don't put some money in her pocket, she's got a few opportunities just waiting in the shade for you to fade.

22.

Int. Hogan's Alley—Scatt Inn—Day.

HENRY: —I said it was on the condition, if I went along on this, that Buddy would be well taken care of—

PERKINS: Am I backing the right horse here? I'd expect a little more spine from the man about to inherit the alley.

HENRY: You said he'd be taken care of and go along quietly—

PERKINS: And he will.

HENRY: Well, we're down to the wire and he ain't showing any signs of it.

PERKINS: I admit the chief hasn't handled it well. Myself, I would have taken a more reasonable approach, but here we are.

HENRY: Buddy ain't just gonna roll over and scratch his balls—he's gonna raise hell—

PERKINS: I have a solution for that, tell me what you think. You recall there was a sailor killed in the alley six months back—

HENRY: What about it.

PERKINS: If somebody was to come forward—

HENRY: Uh-huh

PERKINS: —and finger Buddy for it—

HENRY: I'm not going down this road with you. If that's what it's gonna take, I'm out. That wasn't Buddy.

PERKINS: You sure about that?

HENRY: Sure, I'm sure. He was up here buying a couple of kegs off me when that happened. I gave a statement about that.

PERKINS: Maybe you were mistaken.

HENRY: No chance. Buddy never killed a man. He don't have that in him. I've seen men who do, and them who don't. He may take out his blackjack when he have to, but Buddy don't have murder in him.

PERKINS: How can we know what a man's really capable of when he's been betrayed?

Slaps him on the back.

Anyway, my point is, if you want to take over the beer garden—you've got to pay the piper.

23.

Ext. Hogan's Alley—BUDDY's Beer Garden—Day.

BUDDY makes his way in a deep funk into the garden; he sees someone's back, at the bar.

BUDDY: We ain't open yet. Come back 'round supper time.

BETTY: How's business? Still reeling in the suckers?

BUDDY stops in his tracks. She turns to him.

I figured you wouldn't deny a thirsty girl a drink, so I helped myself. After all we've been through together.

BUDDY: Does Percy know you're here?

BETTY: I'm trying to keep it a surprise. Please don't spoil my fun. I haven't had much lately.

BUDDY gets himself a drink.

BUDDY: I think I'll join you.

BETTY: You'll probably need a double.

BUDDY: I heard they picked you up for it.

BETTY: Nine months in the sanitorium.

BUDDY: You all right?

BETTY: The professional opinion is split fifty-fifty. Some say I'm fit to stand trial, the others think I'm unstable. It's a dead heat. Hold all tickets. I hopped the fence while they were checking the photo finish.

BUDDY: Must be people after you.

BETTY: That's a safe bet. Tell me. Does he miss me?

BETTY lays out her heartbroken ploy.

BUDDY: I wouldn't know. We don't talk about you.

BETTY: Ouch. Does he have a new lady friend?

BUDDY: He leaves you holding the bag for murder, and you come back for more.

BETTY: The professionals can't figure me out either. I told them it's obvious they've never been in love that way. I'd just like to see him. Won't you tell me where he is?

BUDDY: Depends on what you plan on doing when you do see him.

BETTY: Depends how I feel when I do.

She shrugs.

Love's a funny little thing, isn't it?

BUDDY: I laugh till I cry.

BETTY: He ruined me you know. You remember how I was?

BUDDY: You were a breath of fresh air.

BETTY: I was. With hardly a care.

BUDDY: And always up for a party if I recall.

BETTY: Likewise and vice versa.

BUDDY: You know I'd like to help you out, but Percy and I, we're in some good business together right now—

She lashes out with a slap—he stops her and holds on as:

BETTY: He ruined me. You understand? He reached inside me and squeezed the evil in me. And you did nothing! Nothing! You're as guilty as he is!

She draws her arm back and fumbles in her purse and finds a pen to write a note.

I could put you in it you know. I can say how you and Percy came down and roped my husband into that poker game.

BUDDY: That's all I did.

BETTY: I could tell the whole story, beginning to end, and you'd be right in there along with Percy.

BUDDY: I got no blood on my hands.

BETTY hands him a slip of paper on her way out.

BETTY: Call me at this number, in case you want to change sides before the bombs start dropping. It's the gas chamber, if you're wondering. That's how they do it in California these days. But I imagine you knew that already.

24.

Int. Old Hotel—Lobby—Continuing—Day.

MARY enters to find no one at the desk. She rings the bell. No one appears.

Int. Old hotel cafeteria, continuing.

Where ROSE occupies a table, near the door in a sulk, worrying a handkerchief.

MARY: You see the desk clerk anywhere?

ROSE: No. Can you believe it? I think the son of a bitch is standing me up.

MARY: Which one is this?

ROSE: The Frenchie, Emile, throwing his money around at Buddy's last night. I thought he was different, you know, I don't think he even knows I'm a working girl. On top of everything, it's my birthday.

MARY: You should have told me. I'll make you a cake.

ROSE: Screw him anyway. Why I believe a word anybody says I don't know. Just like that Inspector Perkins tried to sucker me this morning—

MARY: I saw him giving you a hard time.

ROSE: That's all right, I got even.

She shows the badge.

MARY: That's Inspector Perkins's badge.

ROSE: And the beauty of it is he don't know I got it.

MARY: And he better not find out. That man's dangerous.

ROSE: I know it. I plan on putting some miles between us the next day or so anyway.

MARY: That's a very good idea. You don't belong in the alley.

ROSE sees her date—EMILE—arrive in the lobby, with flowers. ROSE's POV: EMILE talking to a man in uniform.

ROSE: Hold on—there he is. Looks a little different in daylight doesn't he.

MARY: They all do honey.

ROSE: What do you think?

She brings out her compact.

MARY: Not bad at all. Flowers are a good sign.

ROSE: They are, aren't they.

MARY: You still better take your time. You're too young to get hooked up.

ROSE: My mother used to say watch out, 'cause while you're looking for something better to come along, something better just walked by. This might be my something better and he's taking the train back to the woods tonight, so I better give it a chance. How do I look? Not too cheap? A little is okay. Gives 'em something to think about.

MARY: Here, take my bible. Let him know you want to see a church before he sees your bedroom.

She hands ROSE the Bible. ROSE giggles.

ROSE: Thank you. Oh, I was supposed to give this to the front desk, but it's for you anyway.

ROSE waves to EMILE and hands over the letter. MARY stares at it. Frozen.

MARY: Where'd you get this?

ROSE: Buddy gave it to me. He said it just arrived. Wish me luck.

She hurries off—MARY pulls the letter from its envelope and immediately knows what it is.

EVA appears, and hurries to MARY.

EVA: Thank you for coming. Is it arranged?

MARY looks up—takes a moment to register. Her eyes brim with tears.

MARY: What?

EVA: You will be ready for tonight?

MARY: *(finally)* Yes. Yes, I'll be ready.

EVA: I have the money now.

MARY refuses the money.

MARY: You can pay me later.

EVA: I just have to go ahead with it. I can't keep it. I can't wait another week.

MARY: It's halfway down the alley between Gore Street and Park Lane. There'll be a light on in the upstairs window.

EVA: Thank you.

She sees that MARY *is distraught.*

Is something wrong?

MARY *can't speak and so hands her the letter by explanation.*

From the air force . . .

MARY: My husband—

EVA: Oh

Blackout.

25.

Int. Old Hotel—Corridor—Day.

JULIE *raps at* BETTY*'s door. She has a carton of cigarettes and a bottle of whisky.*

JULIE: *(off-screen)* Room service.

No answer. She raps again. Keys herself in.

Anybody home? Room service.

No answer, so she steps in.

Int. Old hotel, BETTY*'s room, continuing—day.*

JULIE sets the carton of smokes on the bedside table. She takes the moment to poke around, keeping an eye on the door. Sees the suitcase on the bed, flips it open, and ruffles through it. Finds a silk slip. Runs it through her fingers. Smells it. Lays it against her body, modelling it, mimics BETTY's sultry long-legged walk. Puts it back, closes the suitcase.

Notices the hat box beside the bed. Examines it, takes the lid off. Removes the hat, tries it on, realizes there's something else beneath the hat, and delicately removes the pistol.

Now she hears the distant bing of the elevator and leaps to her feet, putting the gun back, closing the lid, and scampering for the door—then realizes she's still got the hat on. Back to the bed, the hat box, and swiftly to the door again to casually meet BETTY as she arrives.

Room service. I brought a carton of smokes and a bottle of whisky.

BETTY steps past her, glancing around at the room.

BETTY: I didn't order any.

JULIE: On the house. From Harry. He's got a crush on you.

BETTY: Aren't I the lucky one.

JULIE nervously follows BETTY's glance around to check the room. They both come to rest on the hatbox.

JULIE: I didn't want to leave the smokes in the hall in a joint like this—

You don't look so good. You feeling okay?

BETTY: Aren't you the little Nazi.

JULIE: Huh?

BETTY looks at the hat box—JULIE tenses.

BETTY: Always poking your nose where it isn't wanted.

JULIE: I wasn't snoopin' if that's what you're thinking—

BETTY: No?

BETTY studies her a long moment and approaches.

You act like you know something you might want to tell me.

JULIE: No—

BETTY: Get it off your chest.

JULIE: Nothing, nothing.

BETTY: Then why are you still here?

JULIE: Well, I was just gonna ask you if we were still on for going down to Buddy's tonight.

BETTY: I'll be taking a rain check.

JULIE: Rain check, okay.

JULIE exits. Cracks the door open again.

The rain check, when do you think—

BETTY: Later.

JULIE: Later tonight or—

BETTY: Out.

BETTY closes the door on her. JULIE as blue as can be.

26.

Int. MULDOON*'s Staff Car—Intercut—Day.*

Parked on Main Street, PERKINS *sits in the rear of* MULDOON*'s car, passing over envelopes he's collected from the bookies and checking his notepad.*

PERKINS: This is from Red the barber, this is Little Tony at the loggers' club, this is from Fat Slim's poolroom—hang on—no, this is Slim's and this is Tony's—

MULDOON: Good Christ, you see what I mean, you see my point? I can't be always fussing with all this cash. It's ridiculous. From here on it's one stop for collections, at the Dodson, once a week, instead my having to chase everyone around all week. I can hardly get any work done anymore.

Tucks money in his coat.

Did you go 'round the alley and talk to Henry—

PERKINS: He's getting cold feet, and Buddy's putting up a fuss.

MULDOON*'s car phone rings.*

MULDOON: Well, go back and hammer those fucking nig-nogs' heads together.

He answers the car phone.

Muldoon.

*Int. Hogan's Alley—*BUDDY*'s Apartment—Intercut—Day.*

BUDDY: Chief, what's this hitch in the deal Perkins told me about?

MULDOON *looks at* PERKINS*—*PERKINS *shrugs.*

MULDOON: A hitch? I've heard of no hitch.

BUDDY: Your Inspector Perkins came by here telling me I'm out of the deal and Henry's in—

MULDOON holds the phone so PERKINS can hear—

MULDOON: Well, my Inspector Perkins is a fucking moron isn't he? I'll see you this evening and straighten it out.

He hangs up and turns to PERKINS—

PERKINS: Henry must have said something to him. I'll take care of it—

MULDOON: No you won't. You'll finish your route, and stay out of trouble for five fucking minutes.

PERKINS: I can deposit the cash if you want—

MULDOON: You fucking well will not.

Int. Old Hotel—Telegraph Office—Intercut—Day.

WALKER: *(answers phone)* Taxi service.

Int. Hogan's Alley—BUDDY's Gaming Room—Intercut—Day.

BUDDY: How's it look over there?

WALKER: I'm pulling in the cash. How you sitting—Henry coming around?

BUDDY listens closely, ear tuned to any hint of betrayal.

BUDDY: Sure, he's coming around.

WALKER: Let's not fuck this up now.

BUDDY: I'm good on this end. Any problems come up with the chief?

WALKER: No problems. Smooth sailing. See you tonight—

BUDDY: The chief's on board?

WALKER: On board, just waiting on the money.

BUDDY: See you tonight.

He hangs up, realizing that he's probably being screwed.

27.

Int. Old Hotel—EVA and EDWARD's room—Day.

EDWARD sleeps in a chair, fully clothed as EVA enters. The room is dingy and grim.

EVA: Where have you been all night.

EDWARD: What?

EVA: Where were you?

EDWARD: Uh, Christ. I had an interview for a job. They're putting up a new bridge, they need engineers.

EVA: In the middle of the night?

EDWARD: Come sit with me.

EVA: Please, Edward, I only want to get out of here and settle in. To get on with things.

She busies herself with packing a suitcase. EDWARD finds a smoke and lights it.

EDWARD: Maybe now we're here you don't like me so much. Maybe you like Percy a little better.

EVA: That's ridiculous. For god's sake, stop before you start.

EDWARD: Well, go ahead, you're here now, all legal, go ahead and leave me. I'm sure you'll be better off.

EVA: These are foolish ideas.

EDWARD: Are they?

EVA: Why don't you ask the doctor.

EDWARD: I've seen all the doctors I need.

EVA: You go out all night, you lie about looking for jobs, who looks for job in the middle of the night—

EDWARD: People don't stop working when the sun goes down. I met that man about the bridge, didn't I?

EVA: Why must you always lie. You've been at the racetrack.

EDWARD: That's where the rich people are. Who you think owns all those horses?

She's not buying.

At least it's not here.

EDWARD heads for the door.

EVA: Why do you want to get away from me?

EDWARD: I'll go up to the apartment and meet the moving van.

EVA: Edward! Why do you want to get away from me.

EDWARD: Because I can't stand to see the goddamn disappointment in your eyes every time you look at me. There's no escape from it.

EVA: I don't look at you like that. That is in your head only. You are creating these things.

EDWARD: No. I see it. Plain as day. You've lost faith in me.

EVA: Only in you? Not in everything? Who hasn't lost faith? Tell me, what faith have you? In what? In nothing. I'm tired of it.

EDWARD: Tired of me.

EVA: Yes, all right, tired of you. Ich bin müde.

EDWARD: I wouldn't blame you if you're looking at other men. You've got to look after yourself—

EVA: Stop it! You are saying things that make me anxious.

EDWARD: I know. Sometimes I'm afraid to fall asleep, that I might do something—that I might hurt somebody.

EVA: These are the things you should talk about with the doctor—

EDWARD: What's he gonna do? Declare me a lunatic. That's a life sentence. You think anybody will give me a job with that on my record? I've seen what happens. Here's your disability paper, bugsy—now take a hike. See you on the soup line.

EVA: He's a nice young doctor. He will listen and you will talk. These new doctors are different—it is new approach—

EDWARD: A nice young doctor with a new approach. Why are you at the doctor?

EVA: I was there—trying to tell him you weren't a lost cause. He said you could come by. You could talk about what you saw in the war.

EDWARD has no response.

EDWARD: But things can't be unseen. Things can't be undone.

EVA: He can help you put it out of your mind.

EDWARD: As if there never was a war.

EVA: As if there is a future.

EDWARD: Is there?

EVA: You used to think so.

EDWARD: Had an army paycheque then.

EVA: You were full of hope.

EDWARD: I guess I sprung a leak. I'm sorry Eva.

She exits. EDWARD sits in a chair, dejected then reaches into his coat pocket to retrieve his service revolver.

Fade to:

OMITTED.

OMITTED.

OMITTED.

Ext. Old Hotel—Day/Night.

In apparent time lapse, sun moves across the facade of the hotel, then gives way to night.

Cut to:

31.

Int. BETTY's Room—BUDDY's Bedroom—Telegraph Office—Split Screen—Night.

WALKER, BETTY, and BUDDY are arranged in a semicircle at stage left, with WALKER upstage centre, BETTY upstage left, and BUDDY centre-stage left. Only BETTY and BUDDY appear on screen.

Each character simultaneously prepares for the evening to come. WALKER slips a fifteen-thousand-dollar wad into his coat jacket, slides a hat pin into his lapel, grabs a bottle of fancy whisky, and then exits stage right while—

On the left-hand side of the split screen BETTY, *now in just the slip, straightens her stockings one leg at a time. What appears to be a garter on her right leg turns out to be a holster: she conceals her pistol then takes a turn at the mirror to see if it's effectively concealed. She puts on her jacket and then exits upstage while—*

On the right-hand side of the split screen BUDDY *puts on his jacket then retrieves some items he will need tonight: a fifteen-thousand-dollar wad for* MULDOON *and the sap he always has on his person. He takes a glance in the mirror to make sure he looks sharp, and then exits downstage.*

32.

Int. Old Hotel—Lobby—Night.

WALKER *crosses to the elevators, and presses the button.* EDWARD *meets him—*

EDWARD: Percy. Can you give me a little something for my service revolver?

WALKER: You're on your own pal.

The elevator doors open and WALKER *enters.* EDWARD *is left alone in the lobby, revolver in hand.*

33.

*Int. Old Hotel—*MITCHELL*'s Office—Night.*

MITCHELL *finishes knotting his tie. He has dolled himself up as best as can be, and splashes some cologne on. A rap on the door turns him. It's* WALKER. *He has a bottle.*

WALKER: Peace offering. I was wound up a little earlier. Moving headquarters is more of a pain in the ass than I expected. I always underestimate the trouble.

MITCHELL *accepts the bottle.*

MITCHELL: You should let me take some of that weight off your shoulders.

WALKER: I guess that's what we're gonna talk about.

MITCHELL: Just gimme the say so. On the rocks?

WALKER: Straight up.

WALKER finds a seat, checks MITCHELL out.

You're all dolled up. Going out somewhere?

MITCHELL: Over to the Penthouse, I got a date with the hat-check girl.

WALKER: So—the blond. Let's drop the bullshit—what do you know.

MITCHELL: What do I know? Nothing, just guessing you had something to do with her old man's kicking the bucket. Something about a big poker game. Am I right?

He tosses a glance over his shoulder for the reaction. WALKER cracks a grim smile.

WALKER: She said that? See, that's why they put her in the puzzle palace. But proceed, Mr. Prosecutor. Members of the jury, suspend your disbelief.

MITCHELL: Maybe it had nothing to do with poker at all. Maybe you and the blond had a little romance going and made a deal to snuff the geezer.

WALKER just raises an eyebrow.

WALKER: I'm not the type. I faint at the sight of blood.

MITCHELL: But you melt at the scent of pussy.

WALKER laughs. MITCHELL turns to give him his drink.

She came all the way up here for some pretty good reason. What'd you do—leave her holding the bag? Or maybe you left her a little Percy Junior. She sure didn't bust out of the nuthouse and come up here for the climate.

WALKER: You've got a vivid imagination. Who feeds you this stuff?

He loosens his tie.

MITCHELL: I just talked to Ray McLeish. He said it was all the gossip in the LA papers for a month. The husband was killed with a ladies' hat pin to the heart.

WALKER: *(laughs)* You don't say.

MITCHELL: They say if you do it right it looks just like a heart attack. It fills the chest cavity with blood or something like that. Apparently the scheme was all going down good until some junior medical examiner found a piece of the hat pin in his heart. Turns out it was her hat pin. But—maybe your idea.

WALKER: That would make me a pretty clever fellow.

MITCHELL: That's what you are. No doubt about that.

WALKER: Aw shucks. I better not get a swelled head about it.

MITCHELL: I think you talked her into taking the temporary insanity bit, then you vanished.

WALKER: You testing this theory out on anybody else?

MITCHELL: Not so far.

WALKER: And the blond, she's here?

MITCHELL: She's floating around somewhere.

WALKER: She might come to the hotel here.

MITCHELL: Good chance.

WALKER: Probably be a good idea if I avoided her.

WALKER tastes his whisky.

MITCHELL: I'll put the stall on her.

WALKER extends his glass.

WALKER: You mind putting some ice in this?

MITCHELL takes the glass and turns to get ice—WALKER now pulls a hat pin from his lapel.

MITCHELL: By the way, I don't mind if you helped her kill the old man.

WALKER: That's a big relief.

MITCHELL: Woman like that, millionaire husband,

WALKER turns up the radio.

I'd be tempted to knock off the old man myself. And with her in the deal? You bet.

I just point all this out to demonstrate this is the kind of thing I can help you with—give you an alibi when you need one—

He turns with the drink—as WALKER lunges to drive the hat pin deep into MITCHELL's heart—

MITCHELL drops the whisky glass and looks at his chest—bewildered. He staggers.

What'd you do that for?

WALKER now seizes MITCHELL around the throat to suppress his moans as they stagger around the room in a violent dance. Finally, he succumbs. The music continues under—same radio station—as we cut to:

34.

Ext. Hogan's Alley—BUDDY's Beer Garden—Night.

ROSE attaches a boutonniere onto BUDDY's lapel, illuminated by strings of light bulbs strung in the air. The radio on the same tune as the previous scene. She is giddy from her date and helps herself to a drink as:

ROSE: He's a riot! He's really funny, and boy does he love to eat. I had two desserts and could have had three but I got too drunk from the champagne. Real champagne, not the usual vinegar, and we're going out again tonight for dinner and dancing—he loves to dance, that's why I need a favour—

BUDDY: Who's this?

ROSE: Emile!

BUDDY: You see my Mary?

ROSE: Up at the hotel, uh-huh—she lent me her bible, and it turns out Emile is kinda churchy, so he thinks I'm a fine young lady. He kept saying that—you're a fine young woman—I said that makes me feel good, and he said that's all he wanted to do was make me feel good. He's coming back in a month and gonna take me on a trip to California—

BUDDY: The letter—you leave the letter at the desk for Mary?

ROSE: The letter, uh-huh, she got it.

BUDDY sighs as if the air has gone out of his life.

BUDDY: I guess that's that.

ROSE: I won't be working tonight if that's all right with you—Emile's taking me dancing at the Commodore Ballroom.

BUDDY: Go ahead.

She slips off happily. BUDDY *listens to the distant sounds of the city for a few moments.* HENRY *approaches.* BUDDY *sees him. Finally:*

I never thought you'd turn on me like that.

HENRY: They came to me. The chief and Perkins. I didn't have much choice.

BUDDY: Percy in on this too?

HENRY: I'd bet he is.

BUDDY: As long as we're in the confessing mood, I got a confession myself. I did take your plan for the beer garden. Never woulda thought of it if you hadn't brought it up. I didn't think about stealing, I just took it without even thinking about it, like it wasn't stealing, it was just an idea. I thought it was mine, just come to me in a daydream, you know.

HENRY: That's how I come up with it.

BUDDY: I realized when you came back what I done, and I said to myself, well, fuck him until I believed it.

HENRY: You may have said it to yourself, but I heard it loud and clear.

BUDDY: Everybody was grabbing up everybody's land, the Japs, the Germans, and I thought they were gonna come for us. People were scared, they needed a place to cut loose. So I built the beer garden.

HENRY: Somebody has to run the card games and the whores. That don't stop just cause there's a war on.

BUDDY: Now it's gonna all be cleaned up, divvied up and made scarce again. That's the plan.

HENRY: Muldoon and Perkins got another plan too. Gonna try and lay that murder of the sailor down here on you—

BUDDY: Everybody and the police knows that wasn't me—

HENRY: They asked me to say I saw you do it, but I drew the line. I won't set up a frame on no man.

BUDDY: It don't matter. Mary's gonna have a piece of my hide when she gets back home. Maybe the whole thing.

HENRY: Why's that?

BUDDY: Charlie's dead.

HENRY: Charlie. Oh man.

BUDDY: Now the cat's outta the bag, she knows it, and I don't feel any better about it at all. Ain't no man alive I'm jealous of, but I'm jealous of a dead man. I got the letter from the air force up at the hotel. And I kept it. Gave it to her this morning.

HENRY: That's gonna be hard on Mary.

BUDDY: I been hanging on to that letter for almost four years.

HENRY: Ooo. I wouldna done that.

BUDDY: Couldn't stand the idea of seeing her in pain I guess. You know how that is. She tear a fingernail and I'm about to cry.

HENRY: She told me to come down and smoke the peace pipe with you. Now what say we smoke the pipe and talk some business. You still got that fifteen thousand you was offering?

BUDDY: Right here.

HENRY: Say you gave that to me for my place and I give it back to you for a piece of the beer garden and we'd call that reparations.

BUDDY: Say what now.

HENRY: I was thinking maybe I'd serve drinks, toss the riff raff out, and maybe, if you was all right with it, play a little guitar now and then in the beer garden. What you think about that.

Allan Louis, Crystal Balint, and Sterling Jarvis; photograph by Stan Douglas.

BUDDY: I—I think I'd like that—

MARY enters, the letter dangling from her hand.

HENRY: Hello Mary.

She waves the letter at HENRY.

MARY: You part of the conspiracy?

HENRY: What now?

MARY: Do you know about this letter?

HENRY: What's it say?

BUDDY: He don't know about it—

MARY: Wasn't speaking to you.

A beat.

It's from the air force. Official notice. Charlie's dead.

HENRY: I'm sorry to hear that.

MARY: See that stamp?

She shows the letter to HENRY, jerks her thumb at BUDDY.

Four years he's had it. Didn't even have the courage to own up to it. Had to have somebody else do his dirty work, as usual.

BUDDY: Sweetheart, I apologize—

MARY: I'm talking to your brother.

HENRY: It was good intentions Mary. Buddy just trying to keep you from the bad news—

BUDDY: I didn't want to see you grieve.

MARY: *(to BUDDY)* I was grieving every day, four years of grief. You think I didn't want the thing over with? And today, now I know Charlie's dead and I'm suddenly seeing things—the trees and the birds and all the things that I didn't even notice yesterday. I'm suddenly . . .

Waking up, like I've been in a trance.

I'm waking up.

(to HENRY, re: BUDDY) Tell him he owes me four years. Ask him how he's gonna pay that back?

She exits. BUDDY takes it in for a moment.

BUDDY: I'm a fool, ain't I?

HENRY: Can't argue with you there.

BUDDY: You know she's not ever gonna talk to me now. That's what her people do. Her mama didn't talk to her daddy one time for three years in a row. You just invisible, snap, just like that. That goddamn letter be the death of me.

He walks off—

HENRY: We got business to talk about. How we gonna deal with Muldoon tonight?

BUDDY has gone. HENRY has a thought that he considers.

35.

Int. Old Hotel—Telegraph Office—Night.

WALKER's hands tremble as he uncaps a bottle. He takes a drink straight from the bottle, settles a bit. He picks up a small suitcase and heads for the exit.

36.

Int. Old Hotel—Lobby—Night.

JULIE is at the desk. BETTY approaches—

JULIE: Message from Buddy for you—

BETTY pauses to accept JULIE's note, reads it, crumples it—and exits without a word. JULIE sulks, then dials the phone.

WALKER appears and crosses into the lobby.

Hey Percy—you seen Harry around?

WALKER: I've been in my office all day. If I'd seen him you'da seen him.

JULIE: Harry! Hey, Harry!

37.

Ext. Hogan's Alley—BUDDY's Beer Garden—Night.

EDWARD finds BUDDY behind the bar.

EDWARD: Buddy—

BUDDY: Not tonight Eddie.

EDWARD: I was hoping to get in a game—give me a chance to settle up—I feel lucky.

BUDDY: Your luck is all used up. You gone dry.

EDWARD: It's back, I know it. You know how sometimes you can just feel it, and tonight, I feel the tide turning—

BUDDY: Yeah, it's going out and you going with it—come on now.

He takes EDWARD by the arm and leads him out.

EDWARD: I can't go home without any money. My wife's going to leave me.

BUDDY: Can't you see what everybody else can? You used up your luck overseas man; all your chances, just staying alive. You ain't gonna see another lucky day in your life.

EDWARD throws off BUDDY's arm angrily.

38.

Ext. Hogan's Alley—Shed Beside the Brothel—Night.

EDWARD exits the beer garden and crosses BETTY as she enters. He lingers then finds a hiding spot beside the brothel facing the entrance to the building where BUDDY keeps his gaming room.

39.

Ext. Hogan's Alley—Night.

We find HENRY comforting MARY.

HENRY: Charlie was a good man, and I'm going to miss him too.

MARY pulls away.

MARY: Thank you Henry. I'll be all right. I knew the day was coming. It's time to move on.

HENRY: I'll sure be missing you if you go. Won't be the same at all around here.

MARY: The way he treats you—the way he treats me—he can be so mean sometimes.

HENRY: He'll fall apart without you. Go off the rails again.

MARY: I can't do anything about that. I need to get away from him, at least for a while.

HENRY takes her hands.

HENRY: You know he cried when I left for the army, and he cried when I came back. He was mad at me because I caused him grief. And I understand now he had every right to be mad, because I was a fool, because I could have ended up the same way as Charlie. Same way he thought he was doing the right thing by keeping your letter, he was just trying to save you from all the grief you were gonna suffer, and he was gonna suffer along with you. Grief piles up on a man, and it makes him hard. And it makes a woman hard too. Makes us mean and evil. Don't it sometimes?

MARY: Yes.

HENRY: I have to ask you something, to help us all out. You, me, and Buddy. We need the names of some of the society folks Chief Muldoon might have steered your way.

MARY: Henry! You can't ask me that!

HENRY: I know what I'm asking.

MARY: You're asking me to break a confidence that's important to me.

HENRY: I know what I'm asking.

MARY: Did Buddy send you here?

HENRY: No. This is me asking you.

MARY remains quiet. Finally—

MARY: If I gave you names, those women could go to jail.

40.

Ext. Hogan's Alley—BUDDY's Beer Garden—Night.

BUDDY steers BETTY toward a table out of the way.

BUDDY: I'm expecting some police a little later, so you and Percy just work out your problems without spilling any blood. You hear me?

BETTY raises her right hand as if to pledge.

BETTY: We'll be sweet as kittens.

41.

Ext. Hogan's Alley—Shed Beside the Brothel—Night.

BUDDY and HENRY chat. The chief appears walking down the alley.

BUDDY: Evening, Chief—you know my little brother, Henry Williams.

HENRY: Chief.

MULDOON: Brothers now are we?

BUDDY: My brother and I have a proposition we'd like to share with you—

MULDOON: I'm not in any mood for a lot of hagglin', boys. I just want the good news—

BUDDY: And maybe one of Mary's chicken-fried steaks.

MULDOON: Wouldn't say no. But no bullshit on the side—I'm not in the mood.

BUDDY: Why don't we go on upstairs and Mary can get started cooking that steak the way you like it.

42.

Int. Hogan's Alley—BUDDY's Gaming Room—Night.

As EDWARD watches the trio enter the building and ascend the staircase.

MULDOON: I don't want to hear any argument from you. If you want the liquor licence for the Dodson, you've got to give up your spot in the alley. That's just the way it has to be.

BUDDY: I can't see how that makes any sense. Henry can't run this place anywhere but into the ground and that's why you giving it to him.

HENRY: That's right. Straight into the dirt.

BUDDY: But he's my brother, and about as honest as you'll find, and he'd make me a good partner.

MULDOON: Well, that's all fucking lovely, but it's not the way it's going to be. Now let's get this done. Have you got my money or are you wasting more of my time?

BUDDY: I got your money. I got something else besides. I don't like to play it this way, but you don't leave me much of a choice—Henry, would you mind giving me and the Chief of Police some time alone?

HENRY bows out.

MULDOON: Bringing out the blackjack are we now. Be careful son. I won't be trifled with.

BUDDY: That gives us something in common I guess.

43.

Int. Old Hotel—MITCHELL's Office—Night.

JULIE walks down the hall and enters MITCHELL's office to find him—sprawled out on the floor—

JULIE: Jeez, it's a little early for the blackout ain't it, Harry? It ain't even midnight—

She realizes MITCHELL is dead.

Blackout.

44.

Int. Taxi—Travelling—Night.

JULIE shouts directions from the back seat—

JULIE: Hang a right on Main—and boot it, a right at the library—run the light, run it!

She slumps in the seat, brain running uptempo, frantic. She takes a handkerchief out of her jacket as—

Close on her lap, as she opens the handkerchief to reveal the hat pin, blood on the hankie—her mind racing. A moment for thought, then—

C'mon, you got squirrels under the hood of this thing? Take this next right—head south to Union—war's over, Jack, give it some gas!

OMITTED.

46.

Int. Hogan's Alley—BUDDY's Gaming Room—Night.

BUDDY: You've come to see my Mary a few times, to help out a few of your friends. To save them some embarrassment.

MULDOON laughs.

MULDOON: You think you can blackmail me because I've knocked up a cross-eyed lass or two?

BUDDY: It's not your whores I'm referring to. It's the mayor's wife I'm thinking of. I don't think she'd appreciate seeing her name in the gossip columns.

MULDOON: I don't suppose the mayor would take to it either when he hears about it.

BUDDY: I didn't drag half of Chinatown to the voting booth to elect a mayor, who in turn appointed you, on my recommend, who is now tryin' to throw me off the goddamn gravy train. So if the mayor and his wife don't make you think, I got a list as long as my arm of abortions facilitated on your recommend.

MULDOON contains his rising temper. Finally—

MULDOON: What's your proposal?

BUDDY: It works for everybody. Henry and I run the beer garden here; Henry closes down the Scatt Inn. That's one more place you can say you shut down, but it still keeps the money coming.

BUDDY hands him a fat wad of bills.

That's just my half of the liquor licence for the Dodson. Percy's coming along shortly with the rest.

MULDOON looks at him a long moment, then grins, laughs.

MULDOON: You've been at this game a long time my friend.

BUDDY: A little while.

OMITTED.

48.

Ext. Hogan's Alley—BUDDY's Beer Garden—Night.

JULIE beelines it to BETTY.

BETTY: I said I'd see you later. It's not later. Go on, shoo.

JULIE: Listen to me a goddamn minute.

She fixes BETTY with a look—she needs to see her reaction.

Someone just killed Harry.

A beat. She then produces the hat pin in the hankie.

They stabbed him with this hat pin—the same way your husband bought it.

BETTY realizes who's done this.

BETTY: Percy— He knows I'm here—

JULIE: Yeah, he's setting you up for this one too. You gotta get outta here—

She tugs at BETTY's elbow—BETTY throws her off.

BETTY: You told him—

JULIE: Whaddya mean? You think I don't care about Harry? You think I don't care about you?

49.

Ext. Hogan's Alley—Beer Garden Gate—Night.

PERKINS strolls down the alley, fully pissed, sloppy drunk.

PERKINS: Buddy Black!

He bulls his way past HENRY.

HENRY: You sure you need another drink Mr. Perkins?

PERKINS: Stand aside.

Ext. BUDDY's Beer Garden—Night.

PERKINS swaggers in.

Buddy Black, King of the Alley! Where's my little geisha girl?

MARY moves swiftly to corral PERKINS at the bar.

MARY: Mr. Perkins—

PERKINS: Where is she? Get her over here. That light-fingered whore has something that belongs to me.

MARY: Rose has the night off—come have a drink on me—

PERKINS: BUDDY BLACK!

(to MARY) What kind of whorehouse lets the whores have a Friday night off?

MARY: She's probably gone up to Henry's, you could find her up there.

PERKINS: I was just up at Henry's, not a soul around—and Henry's down here. Something's going on here that's not quite right.

MARY: Don't know what you mean—

PERKINS: Why is the chief upstairs? Hmmm?

MARY: You're mistaken—

PERKINS: I just saw his car parked over on Union Street—driver told me he was over here. You think I'm a fool?

MARY: You just a little drunk is all. Sit tight now, I'll see if I can find Rose for you.

OMITTED.

OMITTED.

52.

Ext. Hogan's Alley—Shed Beside the Brothel—Night.

WALKER approaches.

WALKER: *(finally)* Chief show up?

BUDDY: Upstairs—hold up. Before we go deal with the chief, we got to get something straight.

WALKER: Buddy, I got a train to catch. I gotta be in Seattle, let's get this deal over and done—

BUDDY prevents him from passing.

BUDDY: You planning on backstabbing me?

WALKER: Where'd you hear that?

BUDDY: Didn't have to hear it. I'm feeling it. You making for the high road to Seattle, chief upstairs saying it's Henry gonna take over the alley. That leaves me with just about nothing, don't it?

Allan Louis and Nicholas Lea; photograph by Stan Douglas.

WALKER: Jesus Christ—what the fuck's got into you? This deal is my last best shot in this town—I'm getting outta town because I got somebody on my tail. Now, here's my end like I promised.

BUDDY: Somebody on your tail. Who's making you run like that?

WALKER: It's all that LA business come back to bite me. You better keep your head down too, 'cause she's around, asking about you—

BUDDY: That right? Asking about me.

WALKER: I think she's trying to put you in it, trying to put both of us in it. Keep your eye out.

BUDDY: All right, thanks for the heads-up.

WALKER: Sure. You'd do it for me.

WALKER checks his watch.

I'll call you from Seattle soon as I get there. Close the deal man. Close the deal.

He dips away into the night.

53.

Ext. Hogan's Alley—BUDDY's Beer Garden—Night.

BETTY listens distractedly to JULIE.

JULIE: —gimme fifteen minutes, I could boost a nice car, we'd be halfway to Saskatchewan by tomorrow night. Gimme twenty and I'll find a convertible. We can head south to Florida, for the carny circuit, lay low till it blows over—

BUDDY interrupts, shoving JULIE aside.

BUDDY: Bug off kid—

(in BETTY's ear) Your Mr. Percy just left to catch the night train to Seattle.

BUDDY exits. BETTY quickly rises, heads for the exit—JULIE is just as quick to follow.

JULIE: Wait. He ain't worth the trouble—

BETTY: Get lost. Go on, it's past your bedtime.

OMITTED.

55.

Ext. Hogan's Alley—BUDDY's Beer Garden—Night.

PERKINS: Where is he?

PERKINS looks about the beer garden—HENRY tries to steer him aside.

HENRY: Nobody you know out here Inspector.

PERKINS: Careful now Sunny Jim—

He elbows past HENRY and plants his feet to yell up at BUDDY.

Buddy! Come on down here!

MARY drifts past—PERKINS focuses on her.

Mary!

PERKINS lurches after MARY and grabs her. HENRY moves to intervene, but PERKINS clings tight—HENRY grabs PERKINS by the collar and hurls him across the yard as BUDDY appears in the entrance to the garden.

HENRY: That's enough now!

PERKINS, drunk, confused, wild with anger, fires off three wild shots into the air.

HENRY, BUDDY, and MARY stand frozen as PERKINS waves his gun around.

PERKINS: *(chuckling)* Well, that got your attention. Let's have that drink now.

BUDDY: You're a little out of hand Mr. Perkins—

MARY lets out a bloodcurdling scream. HENRY staggers suddenly. Blood seeps from his chest.

MARY: Henry!

MARY rushes to grab HENRY as he collapses in her arms. PERKINS seems befuddled by the events.

PERKINS: What happened?

MARY is holding HENRY; BUDDY moves toward PERKINS.

BUDDY: You killed my brother

PERKINS: No. I— Don't worry, we'll work something out. Well, nobody here saw anything, did we?

PERKINS wipes his gun with his handkerchief, drops it, and kicks it across the ground. BUDDY approaches him, blackjack in hand, and whips PERKINS in the head. He crumples.

56.

Ext. Hogan's Alley—Shed Beside the Brothel—Night.

Crowds flee up and down the alley.

Chief MULDOON cuts across the alley and alongside the brothel porch and down the side of the cathouse. In the distance a siren is heard rising.

He fumbles along in the dark.

EDWARD: Hold it right there!

MULDOON: Good Christ!

EDWARD, army issue pistol in hand, scarf over face—

EDWARD: Give me everything you got.

MULDOON: Do you know who I am? I'm the goddamn chief of police.

EDWARD peers at him.

EDWARD: By god, you're right. Hands where I can see 'em, Chief.

MULDOON is spun around—raises his hands. EDWARD frisks his coat—MULDOON begins to chuckle—as EDWARD finds the two packets of cash, he whistles low.

Jesus H. Murphy! You're loaded!

EDWARD finds a couple more envelopes.

MULDOON: It's your lucky day today son. But not tomorrow. No. Tomorrow every copper in the country will be after you. You won't get five miles—

EDWARD: How's that going to look Chief? You gonna say somebody stuck you up while you were getting paid off at Buddy Black's?

MULDOON: More likely I'll tell them it was the funds raised by the constables for the crippled children's hospital. They'll find you hanging from a tree—

EDWARD boots MULDOON in the ass.

EDWARD: Off you go. Hustle up!

MULDOON moves off. EDWARD quickly scoots into the alley, the thrill rushing over him in waves, and trembles as he flips through the packets of cash.

A moment later, a grave and nervous EVA appears, searching for an address—she spots the upstairs lights of the house at the end of the alley and heads for it.

Blackout.

OMITTED.

Ext. Great Northern Railway Station—Night.

WALKER enters, hat pulled down, collar up.

58.

Int. Great Northern Railway Station—Ticket Wicket—Night.

WALKER finds his way to the ticket wicket.

WALKER: One for Seattle. First class, alone if you have it.

CASHIER: I believe there's an empty compartment. Name?

WALKER: Percy Walker.

CASHIER: Nine dollars. Track seven.

WALKER pays and disappears into the depths of the station.

59.

Int. Great Northern Railway Station—Night.

BETTY approaches the wicket, JULIE behind. BETTY produces her ID at the wicket.

BETTY: One for Seattle—first class.

CASHIER: *(off-screen)* Name?

BETTY: Lawrence. Helen Lawrence.

CASHIER: Nine dollars. You better hurry—track seven.

JULIE, aching to be cool, but distraught—sticks a cigarette—wrong way—in her mouth.

JULIE: Let's not make a big fuss. If you want to write—it's in care of Nobody, General Delivery, Nowhere.

BETTY takes the cigarette from her, kisses her, sticks the smoke back in her mouth the right way, and walks off into the station. JULIE watches her go, and the tears start to come, and she fights them. She sees the cashier is staring at her.

What are you lookin' at?

She sulks a minute, then sees ROSE.

You seeing somebody off?

ROSE: Yeah. I think I just got sorta dumped.

JULIE: Yeah. What you doing now?

ROSE: I was gonna go back up to the alley. Buddy's is open.

JULIE: Probably be pretty hot up there now.

ROSE: We could go someplace else.

They head off.

JULIE: We could go anywhere. Who's gonna stop us?

ROSE: Nobody. Not when we got one of these.

ROSE reveals the badge and JULIE snatches it with delight.

JULIE: Where'd you get this?

ROSE: Inspector Perkins. I bet he's missing it right about now.

JULIE: We're gonna have some fun with this.

60.

Int. Train Compartment—Night.

The slowly gathering rhythm of the train as WALKER settles in the window seat and takes out his handkerchief, and dabs at the sweat on his brow. He relaxes, takes a sip of the whisky he's been served. As he does so—there's the sound of the door sliding open. He turns—suddenly alarmed. He manages a charming smile.

WALKER: Hello darling—

Title: End

TOWN CHOIR

THEATRE REPLACEMENT

NOTE

Town Choir was a performance by Theatre Replacement that took place in the atrium of the Vancouver Public Library's Central Branch during the 2017 PuSh International Performing Arts Festival. The work featured four writers, located in different cities across Canada, who wrote the texts for the performance in real time, from their respective homes. On site at the library in downtown Vancouver, a choir received these texts and sang a selection of them out to the awaiting public in four-part harmony. A multimedia interface, also on site, included four screens—one for each writer—which projected their complete texts.

The writers were responding to a series of prompts, sent to them just before the performance began. The prompts made up ten sections, which moved through everyday observations from the writers' lives, including descriptions of the physical space around them, their wants and desires, their fears, as well as questions they had for each other.

After they wrote each line, the texts were immediately uploaded and sent to the choir.

The choir and the conductor utilized "choral frameworks" in order to sing each section. These frameworks were known and rehearsed by the choir beforehand, however, the texts were new every time, which added to the overall liveness of the show.

This script contains the complete texts sent in by the writers for the performance on February 5, 2017.

Some of the choral frameworks for the sections, as well as photos, are also included. The text in bold are the lines sung by the choir for this particular performance.

Town Choir was first produced by Theatre Replacement at the 2017 PuSh International Performing Arts Festival. Over the three Sundays of the festival, the performances took place at the Woodward's Atrium, Roundhouse Community Arts and Recreation Centre, and the Vancouver Public Library Central Branch Atrium in Vancouver, Canada. It featured the following creative team:

Director: Maiko Yamamoto and James Long
Writers: Kim Barlow, Christine Fellows, Raghu Lokanathan, and Radwan Ghazi Moumneh
Performers: Vancouver Youth Choir (VYC)
Conductor: Robbie Blake
VYC Artistic Director: Carrie Tennant
Composer: Robbie Blake
Multimedia Designer/Operator: Remy Siu
Technical Director: Carey Dodge
Producer: Corbin Murdoch
Associate Producer Interns: Chelsea MacDonald and June Fukumura

Would you say you're having a pretty good time right now?
SORENTO
Canada Trust

In the atrium of the Vancouver Public Library Central Branch, the conductor rings a large, brass bell. The choir begins to sing:

Live from Prince George
This is Raghu Lokanathan!

Live from Winnipeg
This is Christine Fellows!

Live from Montreal
This is Radwan Ghazi Moumneh!

Live from Canning, Nova Scotia
This is Kim Barlow!

SECTION 1: OBSERVATIONS ABOUT PLACE

SECTION 1

observations about place

Full Choir

music by
Robbie Blake

RAGHU: I am in my top-secret laboratory.
It's just coming on to noon.
There's a small glass of red wine beside me.
Someone's doing dishes.
I've got cold feet.
The neighbours across the street just got back with their groceries.
The house next door is still not rented out.
There is a large calendar lying near the closet.
There is a washtub on a chair full of the piano keys my friend Peter gave me.
There are many pieces of rolled up paper on the floor.
The piano keys, a bunch of papers, and some cut up letters are arranged on the floor for a poster I'm designing.
The person doing dishes sang a line.
The heater is on.
There's a tin on top of a cable on top of an envelope I got by courier.
I am typing the sixteenth of seventeen lines about where I am.
There's bumpy ice on the roads.

CHRISTINE: I am in my studio.
It is cloudy and minus twenty degrees.

It is early afternoon.
There is a big window in this room that looks out onto the backyard.
The backyard is covered in three feet of snow.
There are a lot of rabbit tracks in the snow underneath the bird feeders.
There is one long icicle hanging from the corner of the shed.
There is a squirrel hunched into a tight ball at the very top of the maple tree.
This room is full of road cases that have yet to be unpacked.
There is a dog sitting in the doorway looking at me meaningfully.
There are three mechanical pencils on the desk in front of me.
There is a small, green bird asleep on my shoulder.
I am still in my pyjamas.
I am wearing a blue baseball hat and the new scarf I bought in LA.
My pal Smithy is texting me. She's going skiing and wants me to come.
The little green bird is nibbling on my hair and it feels funny.
I am pretty sure the bird just pooped on my shoulder.

RADWAN: **I am in my house.**
It is yet another cold and wet winter day.
It is in the middle of the afternoon. I am home with my wife.
We are patiently awaiting the grand arrival of our baby!
The house is quiet and very calm.
My wife is reading a book.
The mood here is very positive, although anxious.
I can hear the distant sound of kids playing outside.
The weather is a bit more damp than normal.
It makes me feel like it's a good day for a child to be born.
Music playing on the sound system is relaxing us quite a bit.
I look at my dinner ingredients that I prepped and I wonder if I will actually get to making dinner.
There is a big, black suitcase by the door full of baby stuff.
Next to the suitcase is a very intimidating stroller.
I am surrounded by new baby stuff in my house, and it does feel a bit odd.
I envision a new member in this house and it makes me very happy.

KIM: I am in my room.
It's almost time to make supper.
The kids are downstairs demanding books be read to them by their father.
They are finishing up a book about Olivia the pig.
The Fairy Princess, in which she has an identity crisis
The house is cold today—the fire doesn't ever fully address the draftiness of this old wooden frame.
The bed is littered with laundry and stuffies.
There is another pile on the chair, and the dresser.
The walls are mostly bare and uncluttered, at least.
There are two needlepoints in frames, made by the mother-in-law.

One has her son's initials in large calligraphic swoops.
The other has our initials intertwined, with swans.
There is a small painting by my grandmother.
Outside, the sky is gray and dimming.

It smells a bit stale in here—will be nice when it warms up and we can open windows!
There are several partially read and overdue library books on my nightstand.
There is a sippy cup on my nightstand, not mine.

SECTION 2: WANTS AND DESIRES

SECTION 2

wants and desires

Full Choir

RAGHU: **I want to eat some chicken curry.**

I want the rehearsal to go well tonight.

I want my dog to get to chase her ball every day.

I want to be tough.

I want to be patient.

I want to be kind.

I want to tell stupid drivers why they're being so stupid.

I want to forgive stupid drivers.

I want to walk through the woods along a stream.

I want to make a fiddle out of a cardboard box and a hockey stick.

I want to put on a show where I recount the Hindu epics.

I want the last line to be the best line.

CHRISTINE: I want to catch up on my sleep.

I want another cup of coffee, but I know it's a bad idea.

I want a day off.

I want the sun to come out.

I want to make a pot of hot and sour soup.

I want to go skiing in the forest with the dog tomorrow.
I want to have long, hot bath today.
I want to phone my mom and dad.
I want someone to do the grocery shopping for me.
I want to spend a whole day without talking to anyone.
I want to go to bed early tonight.
I wish I had the energy to go skiing right now.

RADWAN: I want to be a better writer.
I want to be a better singer.
I want wars to end.
I want to learn how to make all types of pickles.
I want to buy a house in Lebanon.
I want to live by the sea.
I want to swim in the sea every day.
I want to adopt a child.
I want to open an orphanage.
I want to feed people who cannot afford food.
I want to make a history film.
I want to learn how to make complicated meals like my mother.

KIM: I want to find that perfect life balance.
I would like to enjoy my kids and also get all the work done.
I desire peace.
I want no one to suffer.
I would like more empathy all around, please!
I would like these noisy, brash men on the news to shut up and let someone else decide.
I want them to learn to be kind, and generous, and to read a good book.
I would like the husband to cook supper tonight!
I desire pizza, or a roasted chicken, but we are vegetarians.
I want us, the people, to rise up!
I would like to finish a good song tomorrow.
I would like to take a nap.

SECTION 3: ABOUT VANCOUVER/QUESTIONS FOR THE CHOIR

SECTION 3

questions for the VYC

Full Choir

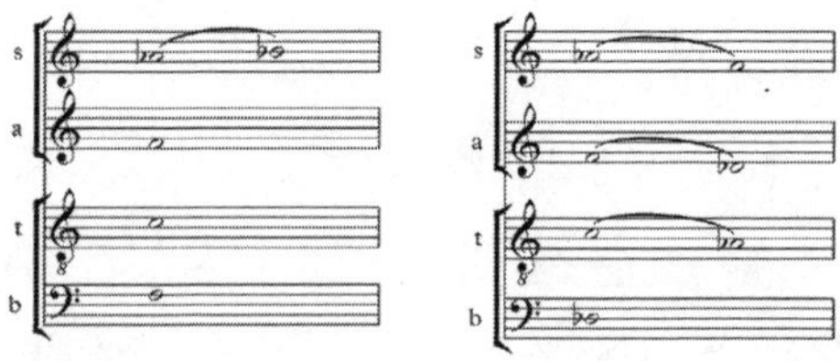

Criers

thoughts on Vancouver

RAGHU: **Vancouver's big. There are lots of pretty, green areas.**
You see logs on the water when you fly into it.
There's lots of art in the airport.
There are accordion buses.
Sometimes you have to cross several bridges to get where you're going.
There was a boatload of Indians that got turned away in the early twentieth century.
I often feel cold there.
There are quite a lot of Persians in North Vancouver.
There's a big main public library with many smaller branches.
You can get Djarums at a tobacco shop near the library. It's beside a sushi place.

CHRISTINE: **Would you say you're having a pretty good time right now?**
Are you going to be sad when this show is over?
Are you going to go out and celebrate today after the show?
Do you ever get distracted and start thinking about grocery lists while you're performing?

Do you wish you were playing electric guitar right now?
Have you ever been to Nunavut?
Do you ever dream you're flying and wake up disappointed?
Can you do the splits?

RADWAN: Did you all do your vocal warm-ups?
Do you feel my words make musical sense to you?
Are you able to not laugh at some of the silly things we are saying while singing?
Have you looked up any of our music?
Did you like any of it?
Do you have any questions for us?
What will you wear for the actual performance?
Are you as curious about us as we are about you?

KIM: What is the highest note you can sing?
What is the weirdest gig you've ever done?
What do you SOUND like? I'm so curious!
Where will you go after you're done today?
Will you go out with some friends from the choir?
Are you pleased with the results of this performance so far?
What's your favourite section of the library?
Do you ever lose track of time when you're reading and forget where you are?

SECTION 4: A MOMENT THAT GAVE YOU PAUSE

SECTION 4

a story that gave you pause

RAGHU: I woke up at about midnight to the sound of a bang. I thought Jody must have closed a door harder than she intended. I heard another bang and the door opened and she said, "Get up! The truck next door is on fire!" She got Leah up from downstairs. I went down there and caught the cat. We looked out the kitchen window and saw Joe's truck in flames. We called 9-1-1 and so did several neighbours. Jody had gone next door and banged on their door, but no one answered. When the truck caught the fence on fire, we were worried our fence, and then our house, would catch fire, but the fire trucks were there pretty quick and put it out.

CHRISTINE: At the library, there is a long, polished cement staircase. As I walked down those stairs yesterday, I noticed there was a dime-sized pool of fresh blood on every other stair, all the way down. I followed the trail of blood down the stairs, past the elevator, past Reader Services, past New and Noted, through the turnstiles and stolen-library-book detectors, and out the revolving doors. That's where the trail of blood ended.

Or is it possible that's where the trail of blood began, and the end of the trail was at the top of the stairs?

RADWAN: I performed a show in Belgrade last week. It was a show in a massive warehouse.

The soiree was packed and everyone was smoking. I got up on stage and started the performance, and immediately I noticed a man roughly my age behaving in a very scary manner. He was rolling his eyes back and moving in random ways that were causing a little bit of concern in me. I decided to ignore him and continue on with the performance. All of a sudden, he started praying at me. It confused me so much to the point where not only did I mess up my words, but I then forgot them. In the moment, all I could do was silently stare at him until the words came back to my mind.

KIM: My three-year-old son wanted a yellow-barrette ponytail in his hair, so I put one in. He ran around with that cute ponytail all morning, sticking straight up on the top of his head because he has very short hair. We got in the car to do some errands, and when we got out to go into the store, he pulled the barrette out. I asked him why, and he said, "Because the men won't like it." He didn't seem upset or worried. He did it very matter-of-factly and continued on into the store. I don't know where he heard this idea. It's strange and sometimes heartbreaking observing cultural norms becoming entrenched in the minds of small children.

SECTION 5: ABOUT THE PLACE YOU LIVE/QUESTIONS FOR EACH OTHER

SECTION 5

questions for writers & where I live

Full Choir

CHRISTINE: **I live in a prairie city with two big rivers running through it.**
The closest major city is almost seven hours away.
This city is in Treaty One Territory.
Even when it is really, really cold the little old ladies wait at bus stops to go downtown for lunch.
In summer, there are mosquitos like you wouldn't believe.
This city is home to the oldest contemporary dance company in Canada.
The film *Capote*, starring the late Philip Seymour Hoffman, was shot here.
Two winters ago, it was colder here than on the planet Mars.
A lot of Icelandic settlers fled to Manitoba after the volcano Askja erupted in 1875.
In May, the snake dens at Narcisse are filled with writhing masses of tiny garter snakes.

RADWAN: Dear Christine, do you ever wish you could join those motorcyclists and ride across your town?
Dear Christine, are the owls that you see in your town active?
Dear Christine, if so, are you scared of them?
Dear Christine, why are the rivers muddy where you live?
Dear Christine, when these rivers freeze, do they turn brown from the mud?
Dear Christine, how far of a ride is it from the forest to downtown?
Dear Christine, can you remember the first time you performed in your town?

Dear Christine, did you feel love from the audience, seeing as you were a local?
Dear Christine, have you written any songs about your town?
Dear Christine, if so, which song(s)?

KIM: Canning, Nova Scotia, is a small town, population four-hundred-ish.
We have a post office, a Lion's Hall, a gluten-free restaurant.
We also have an ice-cream parlour!
Everyone owns a snow blower and likes using them.
When we got the big snow two years ago, Maritimers invented "storm chips."
Our road was not ploughed for three days. Others were snowed in even longer.
Many people sat home and ate chips, I guess. Hence the storm chips.
Now when there's a storm coming, everyone stocks up.
Canning is in the Annapolis Valley, where the Honeycrisp apple variety was developed.
The valley is known for its apples and wine, and the world's highest tides.

RAGHU: Dear Kim, what do you like to drink before a show?
Dear Kim, have you ever punched someone in the face?
Dear Kim, what do get up in arms about?
Dear Kim, who's a teacher you loved?
Dear Kim, what was the name of your elementary school?
Dear Kim, what is your mother's maiden name?
Dear Kim, are you now, or have you ever been a member of the Communist Party?
Dear Kim, are there moose where you live?
Dear Kim, do you know what I mean by the sucking-in "yep, yep, yep"?
Dear Kim, are you wearing a toque?

SECTION 6: A SONG BY CHRISTINE FELLOWS

The choir sings all together:

Oooh . . .
Every morning on the way to school
They torment us and call us names
they're mean and rude

But me and Carmen, we will show them
All night we are as free as owls
Flying high above the trees and houses
Hunting mice and squirrels, together
Oooh . . .

CHRISTINE: I wrote this song, along with a whole bunch of others, during a really cold winter.

RADWAN: This song is by Christine Fellows. We haven't met yet, but I have heard so much about her for so long!

RAGHU: This song is by Christine Fellows. The letters in her name can be rearranged to make "rich wolf's ten lies."

KIM: This song is by Christine Fellows. She is funny, and a very good Scrabble player.

SECTION 7: PLACES YOU WANT TO GO AND WHY/PLACES YOU'VE BEEN

SECTION 7

places you want to go and why

Full Choir

Criers

Proclaiming out

CHRISTINE: **I want to go to Naples, to wander in the caves.**

I want to go to Hofsós, to swim in the pool overlooking the Isle of Drangey.

San Francisco, to see a baseball game.

Düsseldorf, to shop for mustard.

Florida, to see alligators (from far away).

Fredericton, to see my pal Sandy.

Morden, for the Corn and Apple Festival.

Iqaluit, to visit the Nunatta Sunakkutaangit Museum.

Bugat Soum, for the Golden Eagle Festival.

Perth, to swim at City Beach.

RADWAN: I want to go to Xinjiang, China, because it has been a place I've really wanted to go for a long time.

I want to go to Iran, because my grandparents had Iranian passports.

Russia, because all of my friends have been there.

Saudi Arabia, because Saudi music has been some of my favourite music.

Kurdistan, because Kurdish Iraqi music is so beautiful to my ears.

Syria, because I really long to go back there after a long absence.

Oman, because I spent my childhood there and have not been since.

Yemen, because of how close to Omani culture it is.

Brasilia, because I want to see the Oscar Niemeyer buildings that I find absolutely stunning.
Azores islands, because I have so many friends who have been there.

Cried out by members of the choir throughout this section:

KIM: **New Minas!**
New Ross!
New Canada!
New Germany!
Lunenburg!
Halifax!
Rivière du Loup!
Edmundston!
Montreal!
Yarker!

RAGHU: **College of New Caledonia!**
The Nechako Branch!
George and Anne's house!
Naomi and Sean's house!
Moore's Meadow!
Wilson Park!
Vanderhoof!
Fort St. James!
The Hart!
Timbuktu!

SECTION 8: FEARS

SECTION 8

fears

RAGHU: I am afraid of becoming a drug addict.
I am afraid of singing a really bad harmony.
I am afraid of pissing off my boss.
I am afraid of sounding stupid.
I am afraid of the Christian Right.
I am afraid Canada will become more like America.
I am afraid of certain places in town at certain times of night.
I am afraid of joining a bunch of strangers at a table.
I am afraid that I will be found to be a fraud.
I am afraid of pain.
I am afraid the kind of person I am has no place in the world.
I am afraid I'm all talk, no action.

CHRISTINE: I am afraid of making people angry.
I am afraid of getting lost in the subway.
I am afraid of falling asleep in airplanes.
I am afraid of jumping off cliffs.
I am afraid of strawberries.
I am afraid of stepping on rusty nails.
I am afraid of getting really sick.

I am afraid of breaking other people's things.
I am afraid of cannibals.
I am afraid of the President of the United States of America.
I am afraid of the power of hatred.
I am afraid of confrontation.

RADWAN: I'm afraid of running out of steam.
I am afraid of skidding on wet roads on my bicycle.
I am afraid of dying in a plane crash.
I am afraid of drowning.
I am afraid of the day when I wake up and find out that it's too late to save our planet.
I am afraid of mould (even though I love mouldy cheese).
I am afraid of cockroaches.
I am afraid of forgetting my music on stage in front of an audience.
I am afraid of losing my teeth one day due to my fear of dentists.
I am afraid of dentists.
I am afraid of making bad records.
I am afraid of crashing on my motorcycle.

KIM: **I am afraid of cold fingers.**
I am afraid of grizzly bears.
I am afraid of swallowing eight spiders in my sleep, although I hear that's an urban myth.
I am afraid of rising sea levels.
I am afraid of black ice.
I am afraid of bullies.
I am afraid of what the world will look like when my kids are adults.
I am afraid of suffering.
I am afraid of nothing!
I am afraid you'll have to leave now.
I am afraid of not getting my good work done.
I am afraid of mean men.

SECTION 9: EVERYDAY EXPERTISE

SECTION 9
everyday expertise

Full Choir

Criers

soprano soloist,
tenor soloist,
alto soloist,
bass soloist

RAGHU: The Large Hadron Collider is a ring some seventeen kilometres in circumference that straddles the Swiss and some other border.

It was designed to smash particles at very high energies, simulating the conditions of the universe just after the big bang.

Two streams of protons are accelerated in opposite directions by magnets supercooled by liquid helium. Then the two streams are made to smash into each other, and some kind of record is obtained of the particles that are produced from the collision.

The first series of experiments from a few years ago provided strong experimental evidence for the Higgs boson, a fundamental physical particle predicted by the standard model of particle physics.

Now they're gearing up to run the collider at twice the energy they ran it at before.

CHRISTINE: When I was in Churchill, I learned a little bit about polar bears and sea ice. In winter, the ice on Hudson Bay freezes.

In late fall, the polar bears wait on the shores of the bay for the ice to set in. The bay has to freeze up so they can get out on the sea ice to hunt seals. By the time fall rolls around, the bears haven't eaten anything at all for about four months, and they are very, very hungry.

This year has been unseasonably warm, and there is no ice to speak of. The bears are very skinny, and they sleep in the kelp by the shores of the ocean, waiting.

RADWAN: It had never dawned on me how concrete structures were built until I was at a construction site in Lebanon (where all houses are made from concrete).

I always was amazed how towering buildings were made and how they got all that concrete up so high. And then it dawned on me that the entire structure is a series of many small moulds that get built in sections.

The moulds are all made of two-by-four planks of wood, and then filled with liquid concrete, which then dries up.

The supporting pillars are giant, cardboard tubes that simply get set up and filled with the same concrete.

I was really impressed by the idea and how simple it was once I figured out that that was how these massive hundred-storey buildings are made.

KIM: I thought I would learn to play tenor banjo because it would work with the Celtic music people play around here. So, I borrowed one last

year and watched some YouTube instructional videos. It is a lot harder than I expected—it's played with a plectrum, or type of pick, and because a lot of Celtic music is in 3/4, 6/8 or 12/8 time, there are triplets all over it. On the tenor banjo, you would play them as a rapid down-up-down motion with the pick—die-da-la, die-da-la, die-da-la, die-da-la—with a very fast wrist motion.

The tenor banjo is tuned in fifths, like a fiddle or mandolin, which means the interval between strings is five notes like A to E: A b c d E—five steps. Old time and bluegrass banjo is tuned to an open G chord. Tenor banjo, because it's tuned in fifths, has a more open sound, with more potential, but harder to access because there is not a full chord on open strings. It's better for playing melodic parts rather than chordal accompaniment. It's a lot of work! I decided to hold off on that kind of time investment.

SECTION 10: ONE DAY

RAGHU: One day the sun will burn up its fuel.
One day everything will be so far apart from everything else there'll be no way for anywhere to tell if anywhere else exists.
One day the snow will melt.
One day the ground will thaw.
One day Prince George City Council will authorize backyard chickens.
One day the internet will seem quaint.
One day we'll make salsa.
One day we'll make coleslaw.
One day someone will figure out an equation for everything.
One day the tulips will bloom.

CHRISTINE: One day I will kick this cold.
One day I will remember that it's supposed to be fun.
One day I will unpack those road cases.
One day I will get a really good idea and run with it.

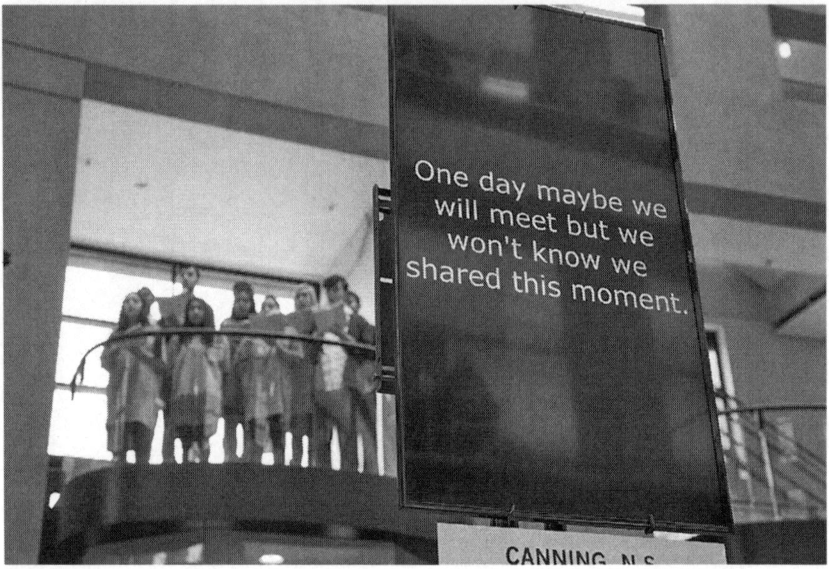

One day I will learn how to sleep on airplanes.
One day I will remember that I can't please everyone.
One day I won't be in such a hurry all the time.
One day I would like to see the Vancouver Youth Choir sing live.
One day the Vancouver Youth Choir should come to Winnipeg.
One day I hope I'll get to see you all and thank you in person.

RADWAN: One day, I'll put an end to my vinyl-buying addiction.
One day I will be vegan again.
One day I will quit sugar.
One day I hope we will live in peace with each other.
One day I will become a good buzuk player.

One day I will become a good singer, good enough to sing to some of my heroes.
One day I will produce a record and feel like it couldn't sound any better!
One day I will be able to learn how to relax and not insanely freak out before performing.
One day I will feel like I have reached my goals with my art.
One day my art will feel like it is making a difference in the world.

KIM: **One day maybe we will meet but we won't know we shared this moment.**
One day your prince will come!
One day is much like the next.
One day my kids will not laugh at my fart jokes anymore and that will be sad.
One day they will roll their eyes at me and say "Mo-m!"

One day maybe I will check everything off the list! But probably not.
One day you and I will have tea.
One day I will fix the weird break in my voice that happens at the middle E.
One day I will learn a fast bluegrass roll.
One day you will swim in the ocean in the warm sun.

Live from Prince George!
Live from Winnipeg!
Live from Montreal!
Live from Canning!

This is Raghu Lokanathan!
This is Christine Fellows!
This is Radwan Ghazi Moumneh!
This is Kim Barlow!

Signing off!

The conductor rings the brass bell once again.

Fin.

MUSE

BARBRA FRENCH

NOTES

Actors and Music: The actor who plays Grace must play a musical instrument well enough to play the song "I Found Peace." In this version, Grace plays the cello, but any musical instrument that is portable and works as a solo instrument can be used (guitar, violin, oboe, flute, portable keyboard, recorder, etc.) A few minor script changes may be made to allow for a different instrument, (references to the cello, descriptions such as curvy, drawing on the floor, etc.) The actor who plays Vicky must be able to accompany Grace's instrument on the keyboard in the most elementary way for the scene up on the roof. She does not need a strong singing voice.

Audience: The house and the audience are the inside of Grace's brain. When she creates "I Found Peace" with the audience, she is creating the song in her head with her creative impulses and insights. When she talks to the audience, she is talking to herself. She only talks directly to Vicky on pages 257 and 258, with the lines "Interrupting cow," "Moo," and "That's good enough for me." Otherwise, she is always speaking to herself/the audience throughout the play.

Digital Media: Video mapping (using the program Isadora or similar software) and sound and light cues are noted throughout. When specific cues are not indicated, the images on the flats could serve as the walls of Grace's room or be left blank. These panels can be painted off-white to represent the institutional setting.

Vicky and the Doctor Vignettes: These are videotaped in advance and projected on the main panel. Sound from these should be somewhat distorted, enough to show how painfully intrusive it is to Grace, but not so much as to make them inaccessible to the audience. We found it best to make the first five or six seconds loud and heavily distorted, and then bring the distortion volume down and the vocals up after that. Care must be taken when videotaping the vignettes to ensure that they may be layered on top of the actual actor playing Vicky when she stands upstage.

Music: Kotarah Rivére generously wrote a version of her song "I Found Peace" specifically for this play. You can find the original version of this song in her upcoming album, *Illuminate* (due to be released in 2021). The lullaby, "When the Night Settles Warm," is an original song written by Barbra French.

Grace uses her own system of numbers that correspond to notes. The numbers can be spoken or sung, as the scene requires. Please see the score for both songs for translations, but here are Grace's note numbers:

"I Found Peace"

4 4 3 2
It's here today

4 4 4 4 3 5
There's nothing I can say

4 4 3 2
It flows through me

5 5 7 6
Can't stop no way

5 5 6 6
In simple ways

5 5 4 3
We learn to play

4 4 3 2
It fills us up

2 2 3 1
It's such a rush

5 6 6 6 5 5
'Cause I can prove to you

6 7 6 5
I'm just me

6 6 7 8 7
They try to tell you

6 6 6 5 6 5
That I'm crazy

6 6 6 6 5 5
This is the world I've built

6 7 6 5
Inside me

6 6 6 6 5 5 5
I'm sad that you think this way
4 5 4 3
But I found peace

Song-building Sessions: Grace composes a song with the audience throughout the play. The audience is in her head; she uses them as part of her creative process. The actor can use the audience to create rhythm (clapping, clicking, stomping, and so on), background vocals, singalongs, or harmonies as appropriate. During production, we found that simple is best, and audiences will happily work with the actor. Each time, she and the audience get a little further along until the song is complete at the end of the play.

Ladybug Drawings: The ladybugs help to illustrate the idea of numbers—whether matching or creating patterns—but they can be very simplistic in design. They can be pre-drawn in permanent white paint, and the lines between them drawn in chalk live on the stage. For the matching game, Grace draws single lines between the matching number of ladybug spots. For the relationships game, Vicky asks "Which one comes after," but Grace creates musical patterns instead of a simple series. Each spot represents the note number that Grace uses. When Vicky questions her, she erases the lines, and then Grace would again draw lines to make the same recognizable pattern. Example (4 4 3 2):

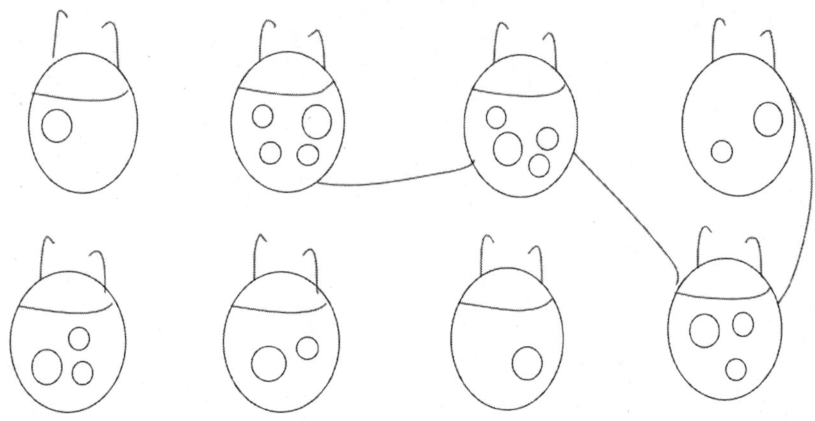

Stage directions represent the media, blocking, and notes taken for the premiere production. As the play relies heavily on imagery, some of these notes have been included for clarity.

Lullaby ("When the Night Settles Warm")

```
   E     E     E    C# C#   C#
When the night settles warm
  D   D      D     B   B   B
And the moon's on the rise
    D   D   D   B    B    B
There's a blanket of love
  B   C#    B    A   A      A
Glowing stars in your eyes.

 E   E     E     C# C#  C#
Mama rock you to sleep
  C#     E     E  D  D    D
Keep you safe in her arms
  E    E     E        B       B     B
And the moon lights your way
  B    C#    B    A    A    A
Floating free from all harm.
```

Muse was first produced by In Other Words Theatre on October 10, 2013, at the Nanaimo Centre Stage in Nanaimo, BC, with the following cast and creative team:

Grace: Natalia Hautala
Vicky: Maureen Molyneaux
Doctor: Brian March

Director: Barbra French
Media Design: Kevin Jesuino
Composer: Kotarah Rivére

CHARACTERS

Grace: A woman in her late twenties. She has been institutionalized for many years.

Vicky: A woman is her late thirties. She is a nurse.

Doctor McDougall: A man in his fifties.

SETTING

Artistically, the world of the play is inside Grace's head. The video projections, sound, and lights represent her memories, thought processes, dreams, and how she perceives the outside world (such as the "invasion" of the doctor scenes into her awareness). The theatre and the audience are included in this world and serve as her inner creative sounding board as she builds her new song.

Practically, and out in the "real world," the setting is a stark, clean room in the Ocean Parks Care Home. A bed, chair, and small table are upstage. There is a window stage right. Behind the bed are flats that frame Grace's room and serve as projection screens for video mapping. The centre or main projection panel consists of five four-by-eight-foot flats joined together to create a wall twenty feet wide and eight feet high. There are two four-foot-wide and ten-foot-high panels (one stage left and one stage right) that help to further define the space (such as the bathroom on stage left) and are also projection screens.

Scenes between Vicky and the doctor are pre-recorded video scenes projected onto the main media panel.

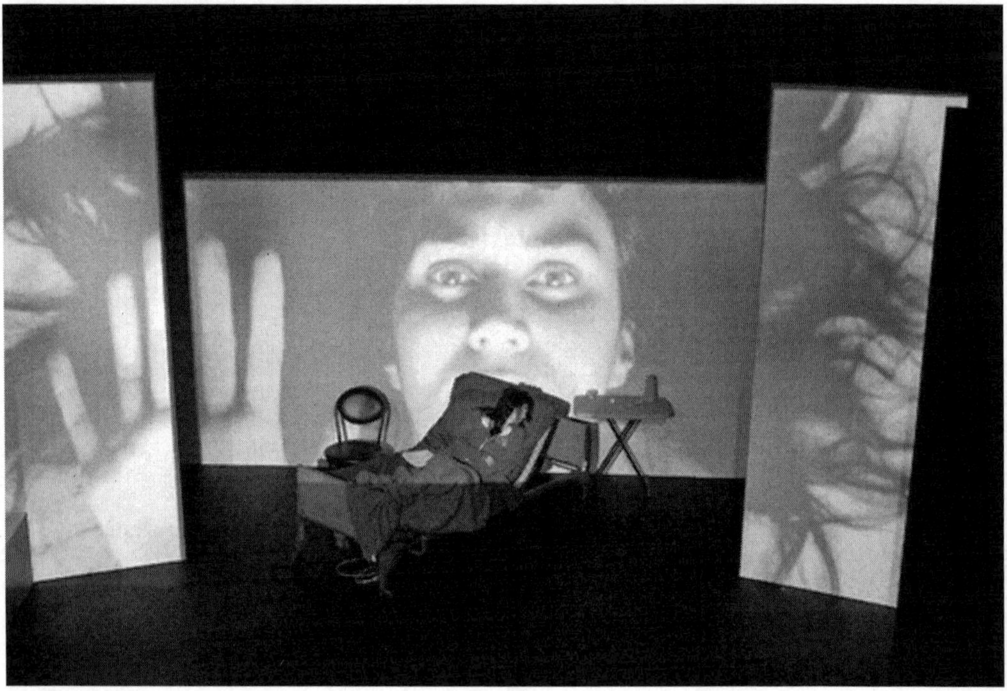

Natalia Hautala; photograph of by Greg Morison.

PRE-SHOW

GRACE is on a chair downstage centre, humming and writing in her notebook.

Video projects on the main and side panels of being underwater. The lights are cool and dim. The feeling should be of a lovely, peaceful, blue dance of water layered on top of GRACE.

SCENE 1: MONDAY MORNING

As lights change and video fades out, GRACE is working on her new song. Sometimes she hums, sings the numbers as notes, or plays with the lyrics. She speaks to herself and/or directly to the audience at all times, except for three lines on pages 257 and 258.

GRACE: It doesn't fit.
(sings) "4 4 3 2. Here it is today—"

No.
(sings) "Today's the day. 4 4 3 2."

Hmm.

(sings) "4 4 5 4? Today's the day. 4 4 5 4."

No. No, that doesn't ring right.

Hums it several ways.

There's a crack. It's still got a crack.

Crack, crack. The ice goes crack when you give it a smack with a big freakin' . . .

Do you remember that time when we went camping that one summer? Remember? And there was a skunk—a big black and white skunk with beady little eyes and a twitchy little nose, and we scared him with our axe and he turned around and lifted his tail and then Dad grabbed us and threw us on the air mattress and he got sprayed, so Mom made us open up all those tomato juice cans, one after another after another after another, and we cut our finger on a lid and the blood came pouring out all over Dad's crossword puzzle, and he ran over to get us a Band-Aid and tripped on one of the cans and fell in the fire?

(sings) "Here it is today. 5 6 5 4 5."

That was so funny.

(sings) "5 6 5 4 5

No, that's too crowded. Too fussy.

(sings) "It's here today. 4 4 3 2. 4 4 3 2."

Heather should be here soon. It's ten minutes to eight. Ten minutes. She should be here in ten minutes. We have our shoes on and our toque and our wallet with eleven dollars and twenty-eight cents exactly. That's how much it costs. Eleven dollars and twenty-eight cents and our shoes and our toque. Ten minutes. Ten—nine minutes. Nine minutes.

(hums 6654 notes) Maybe.

(sings) "6 6 5 4."

Too airy up there, right? Do you think it's too airy?

> *Video of* VICKY *and the* DOCTOR, *vignette 1, is projected on the main panel. They are walking down the hall toward* GRACE*'s room, stopping just inside her open door to talk for most of the scene. As the scene ends, they begin walking away, to the next patient's room. The video resolution should be slightly distorted or have a filter of some kind. Flickering images of brain scans are on the left and right panels. Audio from the video begins as a distorted roar, underscoring the dialogue. This clears up to a more normal*

volume but still somewhat distorted speech after five seconds or so. The overall sound levels should fade in as VICKY *and the* DOCTOR *approach* GRACE*'s room and start to fade out again as they leave. Lights are harsh, bright on stage. The scenes in these vignettes are painful assaults on* GRACE*'s brain, like walking into bright sunlight and motorcycle engines after being in a dark, silent room. She cowers from the onslaught.*

DOCTOR: Welcome to Ocean Parks Care Home. We're delighted to have you join our staff, Ms. Shelbourne.

Despite what you may have heard, sixty percent of the patients have stayed with us through this management and staff changeover. Our new policies and procedures are in effect immediately, with an emphasis on structure. It is your job to see that they adjust with the least disruption possible. You will report directly to me regarding all patients and treatment options, is that clear?

Good! Now, we are a small facility with sixteen non-violent patients, with varying degrees of mental illness. This first patient is Grace, one of our newer residents. She came over from Oaklands and has a history of disruptive behaviour. Her last review did not go as well as expected. Now that I have taken charge, however, I anticipate great improvement. She is noncommunicative, prone to fits of anger and anti-social behaviour, and exhibits compulsive tendencies. She is a bit of a troublemaker, but not dangerous. Her symptoms seem to suggest a psychiatric, rather than neurological condition, but tests have proven inconclusive. Now, over here in room twelve we have Kelly . . .

The video fades out and the lights restore to normal.

GRACE: Psychiatric? Noncommunicative?

We're not crazy. Just because we don't feel like talking, just because we like to have fun. Talking is overrated.

Adjusts position of chair.

Who is this guy, anyway? He just showed up! Talking and talking and talking and talking, like knives. He just showed up. All shiny and smelling like old tree bark rotting leaves burnt paper.

Adjusts position of chair.

He's not supposed to come in our room, that's not the way. That's not the way. Heather is supposed to come in our room. Heather. Heather is supposed to come in our room. And the art therapy teacher. And maybe Kelly. But this guy this guy this guy he's not supposed to be here. He's not supposed to be here.

Adjusts position of chair.

Compulsive. Pfft.

She sits down in the chair, calming herself by rocking and singing.

(sings) "When the night settles warm
And the moon's on the rise
There's a blanket of love
Glowing stars in your eyes"

And now it's 8:03. 8:03, 8:03! Where is Heather? It's Monday. Monday.

(sings) "Mama rock you to sleep . . . "

She can't remember the rest of the song.

"Mama rock you to sleep . . . "

VICKY enters with a breakfast tray. She stands for a moment, not moving, watching GRACE. She speaks her first two lines upstage and then crosses downstage next to GRACE.

The lights are harsh, bright as VICKY says her first two lines, and then return to normal. A loud, distorted roar builds, similar to the one from the VICKY and DOCTOR vignette, almost drowning out her first line. Sound cross-fades to the subtle sound of ice cracking, and then fades out completely.

VICKY: Good morning. How are you today?

VICKY comes downstage next to GRACE.

Good morning, Grace. My name is Vicky. I'll be your new nurse.

GRACE rocks.

I've brought you some breakfast.

VICKY puts down tray. GRACE rocks.

I'm sure you're wondering where Heather is. I know she looked after you for a long time, but Heather . . . had to leave. She wanted you to know that she's sorry she couldn't say goodbye. I'll be taking care of you, of things, from now on.

You can count on me, Grace.

GRACE hums "Hit the Road Jack."

Dr. McDougall mentioned how much you love music. Is that your favourite song? I like to hum when I'm nervous, too. It helps calm me down.

Would you like to go for a walk after breakfast? The sun is shining, and it's not too cold today.

GRACE keeps humming.

All right. Maybe we can do that later. I'll let you eat your breakfast and I'll be back at eight-thirty for the dishes, okay?

VICKY exits.

GRACE: She's wrong! It's only ten minutes after eight. Heather is just late. She wouldn't leave.

Where would she go? It's Monday. Only ten minutes after eight. Mondays we go to Walmart and the Big Mac counter. We get a Big Mac large fries large coke large Oreo McFlurry. For breakfast.

Eleven dollars and twenty-eight cents. Eleven dollars and twenty-eight cents and just the McDonald's cashier. We're not allowed to go through the Walmart cashiers. We're not allowed since . . .

GRACE starts to giggle.

The feathers were floating over all the cashiers and they were running around trying to stuff them back into the pillow or plastic bags and some of them were sneezing and little kids were running around chasing them and a couple of old people were laughing and the store manager's face went really really bright red and he ran right into the cashier and went head first into the pillow and everyone was laughing and having fun and Heather said that maybe we could use the pillows from here instead.

Heather.

> GRACE *paces around the stage, eventually gets her notebook, and starts working on her new song.*

(sings) "It's here today. We have so much to say."

So much to say? Nothing we can say. No. We have too much to say. Too much to say? Or what is there to say?

Crack, crack. The ice goes crack when you give it a smack . . .

We don't know how to talk to people. People are so loud, so shiny. They hurt our head. *(whispering)* There's a lot of crazy people here.

> *She rearranges the dishes and cutlery on her breakfast tray.*

Maybe Heather will be back for lunch. We'll eat after art therapy. We just aren't hungry in the morning. Unless it's McDonald's. Heather knows that. She's our friend. We don't have many friends.

Jodi died. Bill doesn't count; he's too old and senile. Tabatha is cranky all the time and they give her so many drugs she can't even watch TV. We don't know what's up with Sandra; she just sits there and stares out the window without even blinking for hours and hours and hours even if you put her hair in her milk. Kelly is schizophrenic, and Paul is trying to kiss us all the time. Inside our pyjamas.

> *She giggles.*

So we told Paul we would kiss him, remember? We would kiss him if he brought us a chocolate bar—Coffee Crisp—and he did so we stole a leftover fish, a whole fish from the kitchen, and put it inside our sweater and then made him close his eyes and he puckered up and leaned in and we stuck the cold fish in his face and he kissed it!

Heather says we're easy to love, but difficult to manage.

Song-building 1: GRACE goes into audience to work on her new song. She gets them to sing backup vocals, or provide rhythm and percussion, or offer advice on lyrics. Together they come up with part of the first verse. This will take a few minutes. Whatever the actor does with the audience will form the foundations for the song they will co-create throughout the play. The audience is a key part of the song's performance.

When GRACE is song-building with the audience, video of a play of colour and floating numbers could be displayed on all panels. Colours and patterns should be subtle, as they should not distract the audience from their task. This is GRACE's brain in creative play. Directors must decide when to fade out the video, depending on how the work with the audience progresses.

(sings) "It's here today
Nothing for us to say
It flows on through
Can't stop no way"

Hmmm . . . it flows on through; it flows through us?

She sings, hums, and periodically makes notes in her notebook on what she and the audience have discovered.

(sings) "4 4 3 2. 4 4 4 4 5 4."
No.
"Nothing for us to say. 4 4 4 4 3 4."
Maybe.
(sings) "4 4 3 4. It flows on through."
No. 4 4 3 2. 5 5 7 6. 76?
(sings) "Can't stop no way. 5 5 7 6. 5 5 7 6."
(sings) "It's here today
Nothing for us to say
It flows on through
Can't stop no way."

Not bad. Not bad. But there might be a crack.

She sits on the edge of the stage, hums, and writes more notes in her book.

SCENE 2: THAT AFTERNOON

VICKY enters with a lunch tray, interrupting GRACE writing in her book. GRACE cowers briefly and then quickly puts her notebook aside.

As previously, a distorted roar and bright, harsh lights hit GRACE as VICKY speaks her first line, but the effect is not as intense as the first time. GRACE is slowly getting used to VICKY's presence.

VICKY: Hey, Grace, how's it going? Lunchtime! Where did the morning go, hey?

GRACE rocks and hums part of her new song. VICKY putters, making the bed and tidying while she chats. GRACE does not touch her food.

Sorry I didn't get back at 8:30. But I've been so busy! First day on the job, and there's a lot to learn. But now that I know where everything is and I'm starting to figure out who does what, I should be able to keep on schedule. But honestly, the way they run some things around here! Don't tell anyone I said that, though, okay?

You haven't touched your breakfast! Not so big on oatmeal, huh? I can't really blame you. I brought you a chicken salad sandwich for lunch. You like chicken salad, right?

GRACE turns the tray around but does not touch her food.

It's not that simple, is it? When you're on shaky ground who cares about food? In my family, whenever one of us was upset, we'd totally lose our appetites. It's in our genes, I guess. Sometimes one of us would purposely start a fight if Mom made Brussels sprouts.

During VICKY's monologue, GRACE is drawn to the tray and keeps adjusting the dishes and cutlery.

I used to know this little kid—I was a kid, too, but I was older than her. She was the most beautiful, interesting person I've ever known. And funny. She had this goofy laugh. Her little shoulders would shake and then she'd kind of squeak before she started laughing, and sometimes she'd laugh so hard she'd snort. I was always trying to get her to laugh. We used to eat apples with peanut butter and make up knock-knock jokes for hours. Wasn't easy telling jokes with a mouth full of peanut butter, let me tell you. But we had so much fun.

Knock, knock. Who's there? Stopwatch. Stopwatch who? Stopwatch you're doing and open the door!

GRACE smiles but turns her face away.

Well, some jokes are better than others. What are you doing? Drawing a picture? Can I see?

GRACE covers her book with her hands.

I have an idea. How about we go down to the duck pond and feed the ducks? It's just a little bit frosted over. What do you say?

GRACE turns the sandwich upside down and smooshes it on the plate.

I'll just take this away, shall I? Is there something else I can get for you? Soup, maybe? No. Definitely not soup.

Grace. Can you look at me?

Cracks creep in on the edges of both side panels. The sound of ice cracking fades in and slowly increases in volume.

GRACE starts rocking as the cracking sounds slowly get louder.

All right. I know it's hard. I'm practically a stranger.

You know, I think there might be some cinnamon buns in the kitchen. I'll see if I can find one. I'll take this away. Be back in a few minutes.

VICKY leaves with the lunch and breakfast trays.

The cracks on the side panels and the sound of cracking ice fade with her exit.

GRACE: *(rocks and sings)* “When the night settles warm
And the moon’s on the rise
There’s a blanket of love
Glowing stars in your eyes
Mama rock you to sleep . . .
Mama rock you to sleep . . . ”

Heather gave us cinnamon buns on Thursdays. Today is Monday. No cinnamon buns today.

Blackout.

SCENE 3: TUESDAY

GRACE *is staring out the window, humming and swaying back and forth to some unheard rhythm.*

Video of VICKY *and the* DOCTOR, *vignette 2, is projected on the main panel. Flickering medical charts appear on the side panels. A projection of* VICKY *lies on top of the actual actor on stage. The sound is loud and distorted at first, becoming more understandable in a few seconds.*

GRACE *puts her hand over her ears and cowers as the voices slam into her.*

DOCTOR: I see that Grace has stopped eating and won’t go outside for her walks. This is not good news, Nurse. I want her to make progress. She may be a troublemaker, but at least she was following the program before. Now it seems we have taken two steps backwards.

VICKY: Well, I’d say her reaction is pretty normal to all the changes, Doctor. I think she misses Heather. She just needs some time to adjust. She’ll be all right.

DOCTOR: We have inspectors coming next week, Ms. Shelbourne, and I can’t overstate the importance of passing our first inspection. Let’s see if we can get your patient at least eating and exercising by then, shall we?

VICKY: Of course, Doctor. But—didn't you say that Heather had been working with Grace for six months? It may take a while for her to trust me.

DOCTOR: We don't have the luxury of time to coddle her.

VICKY: I don't want to coddle her; I want to connect with her.

DOCTOR: Please find a way to "connect" with her quickly.

Video fades from all panels. As VICKY's conversation with the DOCTOR melts away, she is left standing on stage underneath where her projection was.

VICKY: Hi, Grace! How are you doing?

GRACE hums the song she is working on.

Would you like to go for a walk with me? Everything is melting and the air smells so wonderful! It's a little late in the afternoon, but that means we can have the park all to ourselves.

GRACE hums.

I saw some deer wandering on the lawn. They are so beautiful! Wouldn't you like to go and see them?

GRACE hums.

Or, we can stay in if you're not feeling up to that. How about a game of checkers? Dominoes?

GRACE goes and sits on the edge of the stage. She stops humming.

I brought you a surprise. Look! Cinnamon buns! I'll even let you have one instead of dinner, if you like. They're serving tuna casserole tonight, so I'll spare you from that. Honestly! Who makes tuna casserole anymore? I'll have to see what I can do about the menus here.

GRACE rocks.

You just have to sit on the floor, don't you? All right then.

VICKY sits down beside her.

Are you sure you don't want to go to the park? You look like you could use some fresh air.

GRACE rocks.

When I was a kid, I used to love going to the park, especially after it rained. Everything was so fresh and clean and cool. Do you remember that girl I told you about? The one with the laugh? I'd go with her. We'd go searching for worms and slugs, turning over rocks and logs, looking for things to feed to the birds.

Sometimes I'd sing while we looked for things. I was never very good at it, but she loved to listen. Kids' songs, you know.

"Ten little angels, all dressed in white,
Trying to get to heaven on the end of a kite.
The kite got broke and down they all fell,
Instead of going to heaven, they all went to
Nine little angels, all dressed in white . . . "

GRACE smiles and hums the song she just heard.

Now and then we'd catch frogs and put them in an old ice-cream container and hide it under our beds so our parents wouldn't find them and make us put them back. I guess we weren't very good at taking care of things; there were a few frog casualties long the way. But it was such fun. Feeding the birds, hunting frogs, sliding down the hills on wet grass. Singing songs.

"Ten little angels all dressed in white . . . "

Did you like that song when you were little?

GRACE hums. VICKY breaks off a piece of cinnamon bun.

Would you take a bite, Grace? It's delicious. Please? I could toast it and slather it with buuuuutteeer . . .

GRACE is not tempted. VICKY eats the piece she tore off.

Video of a mother making cinnamon buns, shot looking up from the floor, is projected on all panels.

Hmmm . . . so good! Lots of icing.

My mom used to make the best cinnamon buns in the world. We'd eat them right out of the oven, practically burning our fingers, but we couldn't wait. By the time we cut them in half and buttered them, they were perfect. Warm and soft and gooey and sweet. And the smell!

VICKY tries to get GRACE to look at her. GRACE turns away and rocks.

The video fades out.

That's okay. But you do have to start eating. You really do. Dr. McDougall is—wants—to see you get better, and so do I. If you could just show us that you want to get better, that would help. A lot.

GRACE rocks.

What did the fish say when he swam into a wall? Damn!

VICKY laughs. GRACE stops rocking and hides a smile.

I never said I was a good joke teller, did I?

We're going to do lots of fun things together, Grace. We'll tell jokes and go for walks and eat ice cream and go to art class. I noticed there's a games room here. Could you show me around a bit? Maybe we could find some games to play together.

GRACE rocks and hums her new song.

There's plenty of time for that another day, though. We can just sit here and talk if you like.

GRACE hums and counts the notes on her fingers. VICKY watches, fascinated.

Is that some kind of game you're playing? You like numbers, huh? I know a game with numbers. One minute.

VICKY exits. She comes back drawing on a small, hand-held chalkboard. She continues drawing as she speaks. Explanation and examples of the drawings can be found in the Notes section at the end of the play.

I saw this chalkboard in the games room. I'm not a very good artist, but stick drawings? I can handle those. I used to draw things like this for my friend, the one I told you about. I'd draw the outlines, and she would colour them in. She loved ladybugs, so I got pretty good at drawing them. Rough ones, anyway. There! That's not too bad. One, two, three, and four. Okay.

She shows the chalkboard to GRACE.

VICKY's drawings—ladybugs with spots (two with one spot, two with two spots, two with three spots, two with four spots) are projected. As GRACE draws lines between them, the video shows the lines being drawn for each puzzle. The video and the actors' movements are roughly synced. Pleasant music could underscore the women playing.

Okay, which ones go together?

GRACE draws a line.

That's right! Now what about the other ladybugs?

GRACE draws three more lines.

Good work!

VICKY erases GRACE's lines.

Okay, let's play a new game. Which ones come after this first one?

GRACE draws four lines, indicating a 4 4 3 2 pattern.

Hmmm. That's not quite right. Let's try again.

She erases GRACE's lines.

Which one comes after this first one?

> GRACE *draws four lines again.*

Maybe that's too hard for today. Oh, wait! I think I get it. It's not a series, it's a pattern! That's very good, Grace. Who says we have to count, right? Let's try another.

> *The lines are erased and a new puzzle is started as the scene fades.*

Show me some more patterns . . .

> *Blackout.*

SCENE 4: WEDNESDAY

> *Lights up as* GRACE *enters from stage left. She is laughing hysterically and can barely catch her breath.*

GRACE: Kelly said, she said—
I need some more—I need some more cobalt blue so the—
And the teacher—she opens the cupboard—
The LOOK ON HER FACE!
And now it's EVERYWHERE!

> *She eventually calms down.*

I'm in so much trouble.

> *Song-building 2:* GRACE *gets her notebook and starts working on the song with the audience.*

> *Video of the song-building colours and floating numbers is projected on all panels.*

(sings) "It's here today
Nothing for us to say
It flows on through
Can't stop no way

In simple ways 5 5 6 6
We came to play 5 5 4 3. 5 5 4 3."

We came to play. Here to play?

(sings) "We're here to play. 5 5 4 3."

Hmmm.

(sings) "We're here to play."

No. That's not the way. We came to play. Yes. Together?

> GRACE *has the audience repeat the parts they learned earlier. They run through it together a time or two.*

> VICKY *enters. There is no sound distortion when she enters now. She watches* GRACE *work the song with the audience from upstage. To* VICKY, GRACE *is in her head, her own imaginary world. After thirty seconds or so, she notices the untouched breakfast.*

VICKY: Hey, Grace.

> *The video cuts out.*

> GRACE *stops her song building and sits on the edge of the stage. The breakfast tray is beside her; she arranges the cup, bowl, and cutlery over and over throughout the scene.*

Still not hungry, huh?

I know things are confusing for you right now, but you can't keep going without food. I'll get you anything you want. Anything. Ice cream. Brownies. Mac and cheese. Pancakes? Peanut butter and jelly, hot dog, chicken nuggets? Whatever you want, Grace. Just tell me what you'd like, and I'll get it for you.

> GRACE *continues arranging the dishes.*

At least have something to drink, okay? I brought you a milkshake from the corner store. Don't tell! I had to sneak it in. It's not bad, actually, considering it comes out of a box. This one is chocolate, your favourite, right? Don't you just love chocolate? I know I do. *(reads label)* "Refrigerate after opening. Best before . . . " Oh dear. Well, you've got till next Christmas.

GRACE doesn't take it. VICKY puts it beside the dishes.

I heard what happened in art therapy; news travels fast around here. Kelly is pretty upset, and so is your teacher. Dr. McDougall is not very happy, either, I can tell you. I don't think you meant to hurt anyone, Grace, and I know you probably were just having fun, but I think we should find another outlet for you.

As it happens, I brought a surprise that might just help. A good surprise this time, I promise, and I think it will let you focus your creative energies. I'll be right back. Don't go anywhere.

VICKY exits.

GRACE: Surprise, surprise, a surprise for us. That's what they say. That's what they say. Ward did that he did that. "I have a surprise for you, Grace." Then he put purple blue surprises on our tongue and left. He would come and do and go and come and do and go and come and do and go. That was the other place, but there's a crack here, too. There's always a crack.

We don't like surprises. We like jokes. We like fun.

VICKY enters with a cello. GRACE examines it thoroughly with wonder.

Video fades in on the main panel of a man playing cello. We only see him from the shoulders down, and quite close up. A child's view. Shots of different parts of the cello on the side panels: close-ups of strings, the frets, the bow, and so on. From the video, we hear the cello playing softly.

VICKY: It was my father's. He was with the city orchestra. He used to let us listen while he practiced at home. Oh, he was good, Grace, really good. We loved his music. He'd play and we'd twirl and dance, like ballerinas. I didn't have the heart to sell it after he died; it's been in storage for years. But I think maybe it's found a new home, a new life. With you.

A hospital page is heard: "Nurse Shelbourne, please report to Dr. McDougall's office." The video fades out on all panels.

Oh! That's me. Gotta go. But I'll be back to check in on you this afternoon. I hope—I hope you like your cello, Grace.

She exits.

GRACE: Oh. Oh oh oh oh.

GRACE plays/experiments on the strings with her fingers, then with the bow, and calls out numbers. It sounds awful at first, but as she counts and plays it gets better.

Madeline. Your name is Madeline. That's a curvy name, just like you.

She plays.

That's right, Madeline. That's right. No cracks. We'll just have to practice, that's all.

She continues to play and sing the notes.

(sings) "5 6 5 4 5"

Oops.
(sings) "5 6 5 4 5. 5 6 5 4 5. 5 6 5 4 5."

Our first lesson in speaking, Madeline!

A time-lapse of VICKY coming and going with trays of food, making the bed, tidying up, and so on plays on the panels. Light levels in the video change (morning to afternoon to night to morning, etc.) as several days go by.

As the video plays, GRACE practises downstage, getting better and better. She sips on her milkshake as she works. The lights slowly fade to black as the video and scene ends.

SCENE 5: THE FOLLOWING MONDAY, LATE AT NIGHT

We hear the two women carrying instruments up the stairs.

VICKY: Shhhh! We have to be very quiet. We're not supposed to be up here. And you're supposed to be asleep in bed, remember?

GRACE *giggles.*

We hear a door opening. Lights come up cool and dim. On the stage left panel, video plays of a door opening onto the roof. Cross-fade to video of stars on all panels as the door opens. A subtle crystal-like tinkle of stars slowly is heard fading in until fully audible with VICKY*'s line "I imagine that I can hear the ice crackle . . . "*

What a perfect night. I love coming up here. It's so quiet, so peaceful.

They unpack their instruments: the cello for GRACE *and a mini keyboard for* VICKY*.*

Okay, we're on the roof. That's my part of the deal. Now you have to drink another milkshake. Okay?

Or should we go back to your room?

GRACE *takes the milkshake and sips now and then during the scene.*

I'm not much of a musician. This kiddie keyboard is about my speed. I did practice a few simple tunes last night, though. I know you've been practicing non-stop. You're way ahead of me, as usual.

GRACE *gets ready to play.*

Oh, Grace, look! Look at the stars! So many!

GRACE *stops to look at the stars.*

There is an old story, an Inuit story, about those stars over there. We call that cluster the Pleiades, but the Inuit call it Nanuk, the Great Bear, and the Dogs. The story goes that one day Nanuk was hunting on the ice when he heard a pack of wild dogs. The dogs began to chase him, so he ran as fast as he could across the ice and snow. Nanuk ran for hours, faster and faster, away from the dogs. But they just kept coming and he couldn't shake them. He and the dogs ran so fast and so far that they all slid right off the end of the world, up into the night sky, and froze into stars. See? There's Nanuk, and there's the dogs chasing after him.

I guess that's what happens when you run too fast and too far without thinking.

Sometimes, if I listen very carefully, I imagine that I can hear the stars, crackling, like music. The music of the stars. Shall we play with them? Let's start with something simple.

VICKY starts to play "Twinkle, Twinkle, Little Star." GRACE happily joins in, and they learn to play together.

A night sky full of stars, rotating slowly, continues on all panels while they play. The sound of crackling ice crystals underwrites their music. After a while, VICKY slips out and the scene and stars dissolve away, fading back to GRACE alone in her room with her cello.

SCENE 6: TUESDAY MORNING

GRACE is holding her cello, humming "Twinkle, Twinkle, Little Star" softly.

GRACE: The music of the stars. Ice cubes firecrackers Rice Krispies. Me and Madeline. Me and Madeline and the music of the stars. And her.

She wasn't too loud; she wasn't too shiny. Most people—most people are so crazy.

Madeline isn't crazy. We talk to her all the time now. We don't know how to talk to people, but we can talk to Madeline and she can talk for us. If she feels like it. We talk to her all night now. Shhhh . . . soft, soft quiet. All night! We don't need sleep. We don't need food. Not when we're talking to Madeline. She doesn't sleep. She doesn't eat. She's our friend. She's perfect.

Song-building 3: GRACE and the audience finish the first verse.

Video of the song-building colours and floating numbers is projected on all panels.

"It fills us up. 4 4 3 2 . . .
It's such a rush. 2 2 3 1
It fills us up.
It's such a rush."

That's right. That's perfect, Madeline. Together, together!

(sings) "It's here today
Nothing for us to say
It flows through us
Can't stop no way
In simple ways
We learn to play
It fills us up
It's such a rush"

We are so good at this! We are so freaking good at this! Okay, okay. Let's do that again. Again again again!

The song-building video is rudely interrupted by VICKY *and the* DOCTOR *from the hallway, starting vignette 3. They have obviously been walking and talking, stopping outside* GRACE*'s room.* VICKY *holds a tray of food. The lights and sound are as previously described in the* DOCTOR *vignettes.*

DOCTOR: This is not good news, Nurse. Patients were woken up by music at 2:00 a.m. And 3:00 a.m. The night staff had quite a time getting her to settle back into bed.

VICKY: Oh dear, I didn't realize she'd—I'm sorry about that, Doctor, it's all my fault, really. Please don't blame Grace. I've introduced music as a way to reach her. It seems to be working! You can't imagine how quickly she's learned to play the cello. She's made astounding progress.

DOCTOR: You gave her a cello? You're new here, so perhaps you didn't understand. All treatment regimes must have my approval before being implemented. You are not to make those decisions on your own.

VICKY: Yes, Doctor McDougall, I'm sorry. It won't happen again. I was just trying to help Grace focus her energies. I'll make sure she doesn't disturb anyone from now on.

DOCTOR: Is this "treatment" of yours getting her to eat and exercise?

VICKY: Not yet, but I think she is coming around. She's happier, which will certainly help; there haven't been any more incidents in art therapy class; and . . . she has had a couple of milkshakes. From the store. I sort of brought them in.

DOCTOR: Nurse, you know better than that.

VICKY: Yes, Doctor, I do, but she refused to eat anything from here, and I just had to—

DOCTOR: Our inspectors will be here in a few days, looking at every piece of paper on every patient. There's no solid food intake on her chart, and that is what they'll be looking for. If you don't get something into her—following standard operating procedures and properly recorded—by the time they get here, I shall be forced to tube feed her. Is that understood?

VICKY: Doctor, I don't think we've reach that point yet—

DOCTOR: Is that understood?

VICKY: Yes, sir.

The video and sound fade out, leaving VICKY standing alone by the door upstage.

Understood.

GRACE is still downstage, making notes in her book and humming.

Grace! Were you playing your cello last night? You can't play after dinner time, unless I'm there, okay? We'll go up to our secret place again soon, I promise. But until then, you can only play music before dinner. Okay? Before dinner.

All right. Now, I want to make another deal with you. If you eat half of this breakfast, I'll play music with you, right here in your room. Right now. Would you like that?

I have lovely poached eggs, with runny yolks, and toast with strawberry jam. That's your favourite, right? You love strawberry jam.

GRACE: Running yolks, gross!

VICKY: Come on.

She offers the toast.

Take a few bites, and we'll play some music together.

GRACE: We do like strawberry jam.

VICKY: Three bites. Just one, two, three bites.

GRACE: She did give us Madeline. But we can play music with just us.

VICKY: Please? Okay. I understand.

How about a nice walk in the park, then? Some sunshine—well, maybe not actual sunshine—but some fresh air. We can go down and feed the ducks. They're hungry. They like breakfast.

GRACE is still.

Or how about we go to McDonald's? Heather used to take you there, right? We could go there! My treat. Whaddya say?

GRACE gets up and gets her cello. She sits on the chair downstage.

GRACE: Heather took us to McDonald's on Mondays. Today is Tuesday.

GRACE plays quietly, gently. VICKY listens for a while.

VICKY: Less than a week. You've had that cello for less than one week. I don't know if you've ever played one before—I have no idea where you've been or what you've done for all those years before you came here—but I'm starting to think that you must be some kind of prodigy. And no one has figured that out. Not when you were little, not when you grew up. You were never given the chance, were you?

GRACE plays.

You can have that chance now, Grace. If you start eating. Why aren't you eating? Is it me? Do I upset you? Am I too strict or too mean or something else? I really do want to help you, Grace, but you have to give me some idea about what you need. I know I'm not Heather, but I would like to be your . . . friend.

She reaches out to touch her. GRACE pulls away.

I'll leave the tray here and come back for it later. My offer still stands. Three bites.

She goes upstage and stops.

It's important, Grace. I'm afraid of what McDougall will do if you don't eat. Please.

She exits.

GRACE: Okay, Madeline. Let's play.

Song-building 4: GRACE and the audience review the verse and then start working on the chorus.

The song-building colours and numbers appear on the side panels, the sun crossing the sky or clocks running on the main panel. As her work with the audience continues, all panels fade to the starry night/milky way video from the rooftop scene. On stage, the lights go from warm to cool as moonlight comes through the window.

It's here today
Nothing for us to say
It flows through us
Can't stop no way
In simple ways
We learn to play,
It fills us up
It's such a rush
'Cause we can prove to you
We are free
They'll try to tell you that

We're crazy
This is the world we've built . . .

She hasn't written the end and can't figure out the next line.

(sings to herself) "This is the world we've built . . . This is the world we've built . . . "

We hear the recorded, distorted voice of the DOCTOR *ordering a pentobarbital injection.*

GRACE *quickly puts her cello away when she hears the voice.*

The night sky cross-fades to a blurry montage of needles and restraints and ice cracking. We hear the distorted sounds of nurses calming GRACE *down, getting her into bed. The voices are garbled and mixed up; it all sounds like a drunken memory.*

GRACE *physically walks herself backward and into bed. The lights and sound slowly fade. Blackout.*

Madeline? Are you still there?

SCENE 7: WEDNESDAY MORNING

GRACE *is playing her cello downstage, figuring out the last bits of her song (not with the audience, just on her own). The* DOCTOR *and* VICKY *scene slams into her brain.*

Video of VICKY *and the* DOCTOR*, vignette 4, plays.*

VICKY: With all due respect, Doctor, she is making progress. Please, just give her a bit more time.

DOCTOR: Our inspection is the day after tomorrow!

VICKY: I understand. But she just needs a chance to adjust to her new environment.

DOCTOR: What she needs is food. What she needs is to get out of her room and start interacting with people. What she needs is to start following the rules. All she seems to care about is playing that damn cello! We had to sedate her last night to get her to stay in bed.

VICKY: Yes, Doctor. She does need to follow the rules, and I will try to impress those upon her, but her cello is helping her, and I really feel that too many changes all at once could drive her further inside herself. If we give her some time to—

DOCTOR: I don't have the luxury of time, Ms. Shelbourne! This patient is not responding to your "treatment." The prank in art therapy class, her refusal to eat or go outside, and these late night jam sessions all indicate to me that what she needs is more structure, more discipline. Sometimes you just have to force them onto the right path. Music is distracting her from that path.

VICKY: With all due respect, I strongly disagree! Her music is opening her up to new possibilities, new challenges, new connections. Within herself and with others. Grace is coming alive! She's discovering who she really is, and that's helping her open up to me. Doctor, please. She's counting on us to help her find her way back to herself.

DOCTOR: She can find herself next week! Right now, she has to eat and follow the rules! If she starts behaving appropriately and eating, we'll see. Maybe she can have her cello back for an hour a week.

VICKY: Back? Do you mean you want me to— But she's just starting to trust me. If I take away her cello it will undermine all the work I've done with her!

DOCTOR: The decision has been made, Ms. Shelbourne. This is my treatment plan, and I want it followed. Now. If you can't do your job, I will find someone else who can.

> *VICKY's conversation with the DOCTOR melts away and she is left standing on stage. GRACE begins playing her cello, energetically, after the sensorial assault. VICKY watches her for a while. She paces and fidgets, goes out of the room and back in, all while GRACE is playing downstage. Finally, she goes to speak with her.*

VICKY: Grace, we need to talk. We need to talk.

> *GRACE plays louder, frenetically with her bow. VICKY shouts over the noise.*

Grace! We need to talk.

GRACE plays louder and faster.

Grace, please! Grace!

VICKY takes her bow away.

Listen to me. You were playing again late last night. We talked about that; you can't play—Dr. McDougall thinks that you—he says that you—he thinks it would be good for you if you didn't spend so much time with your music.

Video appears on side panels of cracking ice, accompanied by the sound of ice cracking very slowly getting louder.

Grace, you know that he wants you to get better, right? We all do. And . . . he thinks it will be best if you focus more on other people right now, on making friends.

Wouldn't it be great to have some real friends, Grace? A new boy moved in down the hall. He's very good-looking. We could go for walks and outings with him, maybe go to the duck pond, or even McDonald's someday. Would you like that?

So . . . to help you to do that, to help you focus on people more, I have to take your cello.

She grabs the cello and runs out.

I'm sorry, Grace!

GRACE: Madeliiiiiiiine!

GRACE runs upstage but VICKY and Madeline are gone.

The main and side panels cross-fade to water rising up, higher and higher, up to GRACE's neck. We hear the roar of a huge wave.

She climbs on her bed as the water rises, clutching her notebook. After the wave hits, she gets off the bed. The media fades out.

The duck pond? The duck pond! That's not the way. That's not the way! You can't trust ducks. You can't you can't trust them! Ducks are too shiny! Too quiet. Quiet water smooth wet shiny until. Until. You can't trust them!

GRACE paces around. VICKY enters and gives her a sedative. VICKY tidies the room and turns down the bed during GRACE's monologue.

We saw ducks on TV. They glide through the water quiet quiet like knives. We saw it on TV. And then they all jump on one duck, feathers all over the water, and that one duck tries to get away but they turn on her, push her down down down and that one duck tries to fly but they keep pushing and pushing down down down and that one duck goes down. She goes down. And she doesn't come up again. Then all those other ducks just turn and float down the river. Quiet. Quiet and shiny.

VICKY leads GRACE to bed and tucks her in.

VICKY: The medicine I gave you should help you get a good, long sleep.

GRACE: Madeline, are you okay?

VICKY: Let me get your shoes off.

GRACE: Will I ever see you again?

VICKY: I'm so sorry, Grace.

GRACE: Ever?

VICKY: I wish things were different.

GRACE: Why did she take you away?

VICKY: I wish you could talk to me.

GRACE: We don't know how to speak now. We don't know how.

VICKY: I wish you understood that I'm here for you.

GRACE: We're all alone again.

VICKY: Here's a nice, warm blanket. How's that?

GRACE: It's cold in here.

VICKY: Tomorrow will be a better day. For both of us.

GRACE: We're all alone. Crack, crack. The ice goes crack. When you give it a smack. With a big. Freakin' . . .

GRACE's speech slows as she falls asleep.

VICKY: Do you remember that little girl I told you about? The one with the adorable laugh? She wouldn't speak, either. Just like you, Grace. She never spoke a word to anybody. Not her mom, not her dad, not her sister . . . nobody. But I understood her. She didn't need to speak to me. I knew when she needed to be alone, or when she needed some company, or when she needed a good cry. Or a good laugh. I knew. And she counted on me for that. She counted on me.

VICKY takes the notebook and pencil from the now sleeping GRACE. She opens it.

Numbers. You aren't drawing, you're writing numbers? I didn't know you could write!

She goes over to the window to look at it through the moonlight.

Video of random numbers and scribbles slowly fade in bit by bit on all panels. The main panel cross-fades to the moon rising.

4 4 3 2; 4 4 4 4 3 5; 4 4 3 2; 4 4 7 5. They definitely aren't random. They're more like, like the ladybug patterns, but they're not consistent. Grouped together, all starting with 4? No. This group starts with 5. 5 5 6 4; 5 5 7 5.

Grace, what does this mean? Patterns. Repetition, changes, more repetition. If this is some kind of language, damned if I can figure it out.

As she studies the notebook, GRACE fusses and rolls over. VICKY gets up to straighten the blankets and absently puts the notebook in her pocket to free her hands. After settling GRACE down, VICKY stretches, yawns.

I'll see you in morning. Tomorrow will be a better day. I promise.

VICKY exits.

SCENE 8: THURSDAY, EARLY MORNING

A dream sequence. Video of blue liquid dropping into water cross-fades to flying through the sky with puffy white clouds, a vortex of shining light in the centre. We hear the soft, subtle sound of a woman singing the lullaby before it fades out, pleasant synthesizer music continuing on, layered on top. Peaceful tranquility. The video cross-fades to a dark, starry night, moving from the zenith down, cross-fading into blue, under the water, sinking peacefully under, cross-fading to GRACE's face under the water. Her palms come up and press against the screen, first right, then left. The synth fades to the sounds of ice cracking and a heartbeat. The heartbeat quickens as GRACE begins to panic. We see GRACE beginning to panic and pound her fists against the screen. She pounds faster and faster, heartbeats matching her pounding, her eyes wide with terror. As the character GRACE begins to stir and wake, we see the quick and subtle suggestion of tiny bubbles scooting away on the main panel. The media snaps out as she sits up abruptly.

GRACE: Mama!

She looks around, then searches the bed for her notebook.

Okay, that's a pretty good trick. Playing a joke on your own brain?

She gets out of bed to pull apart the sheets. She grabs her blanket.

Okay, uncle. We give in. Where'd we put it?

She gets up to search the nightstand, starts to pace.

We need to find it. We need to find it. Where is it where is it where is it!

She goes to sit on the edge of the stage, still clutching her blanket.

"When the night settles warm
And the moon's on the rise
There's a blanket of love
Glowing stars in your eyes

Mama rock you to sleep . . .
Mama rock you to sleep . . ."

Song-building 5: She goes to her nightstand and takes out the chalk from the ladybug scene. She begins to write her notes on the floor as she works with the audience on her song.

Video of the song-building colours and numbers is projected on the panels.

(sings) "'Cause we can prove to you
We are free
They try to tell you
That we're crazy
This is the world we've built . . .
This is the world we've built."

VICKY enters, carrying breakfast. GRACE quickly covers her work with the blanket.

VICKY: Good morning, Grace! How are you feeling today? Did you get some rest?

I brought your favourite breakfast! Hard-boiled eggs.

GRACE rearranges the dishes and cutlery. VICKY joins her on the floor. GRACE draws lines and circles on the floor, beside her at first, then eventually around her.

You do like to draw! You're such an artist. Reminds me of my dad. He was a musician, but he'd call himself an artist because his name was Art. "What has no arms or legs and hangs on the wall? That's me!" I don't know if he could draw, but he sure loved jokes. Puns, word games, riddles. Knock-knock jokes. He was pretty quiet, otherwise, didn't talk a whole lot. His music was his voice. But he was thoughtful, you know? He watched. He listened. He knew what was going on around him, and he knew how to make bad things feel better.

When I was six or seven, he came home with a kitten. I remember how shocked I was, because he grew up on a farm and animals were not allowed in the house. But I'd begged him for a kitten for so long, and there he was. Black and white, with big green eyes and a twitchy tail. Dad sat me down and he said, "Vicky, you can keep him if you feed him and make sure he stays outside. I don't want him running all over the house." So that's what I did. I fed him and kept him outside most of the time. I named him Follow because he'd follow me around all day, every day. To the park, to school, to the store, to baseball practice. He was always there, lurking in the bushes somewhere. Then one day when I wasn't paying attention, he followed me right across a busy street and he was gone.

My dad came and picked him up, laid him in the ground in our backyard, and covered him with dirt. He planted a rose bush right on top of that cat. I'd never seen him plant anything before. He said that Follow would feed the roses, and the roses would feed my heart. You'd have liked him, Grace.

She sees what GRACE *has drawn.*

Oh, my goodness! Is that your cello? I know you must miss it. I'm so sorry.

It's beautiful. You're so darn talented, aren't you? Just like Dad. Making something beautiful out of something sad. Aren't you hungry? Even a little bit? Here, just take a small bite . . .

GRACE *turns away and rocks.*

Okay. We'll try something else later.

VICKY *picks up the chalk and writes on the floor.*

Cello. C-e-l-l-o. Cello, Grace! *(as in "Hello, Grace!")*

She writes some numbers.

Grace, what does this mean? 5 5 6 4?

GRACE *stops rocking.*

How about 4 4 3 2? 4 4 7 5?

GRACE turns away and tries to hide inside herself. The women speak the following simultaneously:

VICKY: How do I get in? I don't know how to get through to you, Grace. You don't understand what I'm saying most of the time. I'm trying to figure out those patterns, and I thought we were getting somewhere, but you're so quiet and withdrawn still. I know I took your cello . . . but I'm sure that's only temporary.	**GRACE:** We wanted to like you. You think we don't listen, we don't understand what you're saying? You don't know. You don't understand. We're getting somewhere but you keep making us stop! You took Madeline away. You won't last long here. You're just temporary.
Is it because you recognize me? Or because you don't? No. You don't know who I am. I've been here almost every day for ten days and you don't know who I am. But I refuse to believe that I'm wasting my time.	You keep telling us what we like as if you know us. That's not the way. "It's your favourite, Grace." You haven't been here very long; you don't know us. You don't know who we are. You're one of them. You're just wasting our time.

VICKY: I am not going to give up, Grace.

GRACE: Please go away.

VICKY: I'm not. I'll be back with your lunch.

VICKY leaves with the dishes.

GRACE: Hard-boiled eggs! Gross! They stink! Heather, when are you coming back?

"Mama rock you to sleep . . .
Mama rock you to sleep . . . "

Crazy. Dr. McDoodoo thinks we're crazy. He took away Madeline because he thinks we're crazy.

(to audience) Do you think we're crazy? Never thought to ask you before.

Everyone thinks we're crazy. They think stupid things. They talk too much, they're too loud too shiny too crazy sad inside, all the time. All the time. Even when they're nice, even when they give good surprises. There's always a crack.

Crack, crack. The ice goes crack when you give it a smack . . .

Then you're alone. All alone. No one else to hear, no one else to talk to. Just you. Just you and the blue. Blue world inside.

Is everybody alone inside? Everybody? Or is it just . . . me. Just me. The world inside. Me.

(sings) "'Cause I can prove to you
I'm just me
They try to tell you
That I'm crazy
This is the world I've built
Inside me
I'm sad that you think this way . . . "

She hums and hurriedly writes the new lyrics on the floor. Fade to black.

SCENE 9: LATER THAT DAY

VICKY enters, bringing food and bubble-blowing supplies. GRACE covers her work with the blanket.

VICKY: I'm ba-ack! I thought we'd have lunch together today. Oh, a picnic! What a good idea! May I join you?

We used to have picnics when I was a little girl. Me and my sister. Did I tell you I had a little sister? She was a gorgeous little thing, with a smile that would light up a room. We'd go down to the lake— Well, it wasn't a real lake, it was one of those man-made lakes that they used to put in new subdivisions— And we'd sit on an old blue and green plaid blanket that our mom got from our grandma. We'd drink Kool-Aid and eat devilled ham sandwiches with mayo and relish, and we'd feed the crusts to the ducks. We didn't like the crusts. Do you like crusts? Oh, and Mom would tuck some soft, chewy cookies in the picnic basket for dessert. Chocolate chip or peanut butter. But I know that you love Oreo cookies.

VICKY brings out a plate of Oreos.

And we'd tell jokes, of course.

Knock, knock. Who's there? Ben. Ben who? Ben waiting an hour so open up!

VICKY tries to pop an Oreo in GRACE's mouth when she smiles, but she turns her head away. VICKY pulls out the bubble-blower wand.

Knock, knock.

She blows some bubbles.

Video plays of girls blowing bubbles from the backseat of a moving car on the main panel, bubbles floating through water on the side panels. From the video, we hear girls giggling. Bubbles drop down from the catwalk to cover the audience and the stage. GRACE giggles and eagerly pokes at the bubbles and then takes over the job herself, blowing bubbles into the audience.

Who's there? A door. A door who? Adorable.

The video and practical bubbles fade out.

VICKY tidies but leaves the plate of cookies downstage while GRACE blows bubbles. She tries to sing quietly but gets a little louder as she enjoys the song.

"They played jump rope, but the rope it broke
So they just sat around telling knock-knock jokes
The ladybugs twelve
At the ladybugs' picnic
One, two, three
Four, five, six
Seven, eight, nine . . . "

VICKY exits with the tray.

Video of VICKY and the DOCTOR plays, vignette 5.

After initially cowering, GRACE *moves upstage to listen more closely to the conversation.*

DOCTOR: Nurse! I asked you to remove all remnants of music from this room!

VICKY: I did. I took her cello.

DOCTOR: I distinctly heard singing! Yet her chart says she is still not eating. Explain!

VICKY: That wasn't her singing, that was me. She responds so well to music, Doctor, give me more time to work with her. Please. I don't know why she isn't eating yet, but I do know that music is her lifeline right now. Please don't take that away from her.

DOCTOR: Tomorrow morning at 9:00 a.m. this place will be crawling with bureaucrats from the health department. Do you understand? I am on a very short leash, and I have no intention of losing my job. Now, I don't care what you feed her, but I want her eating by the end of the day, and I won't have her disrupting the whole floor with her noise! Get her to eat. Today. Until then, no eating, no music. Of any kind, in any form, from anyone. Period!

VICKY: Dr. McDougall, please, I don't see how this is going to—

DOCTOR: Are you questioning me, Nurse? If you cannot keep your patient under control and following my protocol, then I shall be forced to remove her from your care. Is that clear? No music!

The word "music" echoes loudly, fading into ice cracking during GRACE*'s monologue. We see glaciers calving on all panels.*

GRACE: No. No no no no no! We want Madeline! We want Madeline now!

GRACE *completely trashes her room in a fit of frustration, pulling off the sheets, pillow, and mattress of her bed and throwing it all on the floor.*

We want to go to McDonald's and up on the roof and play music with the stars and eat cinnamon buns and blow bubbles and buy pillows and paint pictures and go to the lake and sing songs and and and . . .

She collapses on top of the mattress. VICKY *runs in during her freak out.*

VICKY: What the—Grace, no! He'll hear you! It's okay. It's okay. Shhh . . . you're all right now.

The video and sound slowly fade out as VICKY *calms* GRACE. VICKY *leads her to the front of the stage, straightens the room, then goes back downstage to sit with her.*

This is it, Grace. You either eat these cookies, or things are about to get much more difficult than you are prepared to handle. All right? Here we go. Eat. Please.

GRACE *doesn't eat.*

Grace, eat. Eat. Eat! Just eat it! Eat it, Grace! Open up your mouth and . . . eat!

They get in a food fight with the cookies. It dissolves into laugher.

(sings very quietly) Ladybugs Two, at the Ladybug picnic!

GRACE *laughs and finally eats a cookie.*

I think I get it. It's all about music, isn't it? That's how you communicate. I'm still not quite sure about the numbers, but I'd bet they have something to do with notes?

(quietly singing the joke) "Knock, knock. Who's there?"

GRACE: Interrupting cow.

Pause.

VICKY: *(singing)* "Interrupting c—"

GRACE: Moo.

VICKY *laughs.*

VICKY: So you can talk. If you want to. Come on, let's get you cleaned up.

She takes GRACE *into the bathroom.*

(singing quietly) "C is for cookie"

GRACE: That's good enough for me.

From the offstage bathroom we hear GRACE *fussing and being difficult while* VICKY *is trying to clean her face and hands.*

VICKY: All right, all right, you do it, then.

VICKY *enters from the bathroom and goes to clean up the cookies on the blanket. She finds the lyrics and numbers written on the floor.*

What's this? "It's here today, nothing for me to say . . . " Grace! You can write words! Poetry? No, this is the song I heard you singing the other day! It's so beautiful. So sad.

Oh god, if he sees this, we'll both be in such trouble.

She searches her pocket for a pen and finds the notebook. She quickly writes down everything she sees on the floor, saying the words as she records them.

"This is the world I've built, inside me. I'm sad that you think this way . . . "

Once done, she begins erasing the lyrics on the floor. GRACE *comes out from the bathroom and sees* VICKY *wiping away her song.*

GRACE: No! No no no no no noooooo!

She screams and throws her body on the floor, protecting her work.

Video of DOCTOR *McDougall, distorted and loud, is projected on the main and side panels.*

DOCTOR: What the hell is going on in here? Nurse! Get your patient under control!

VICKY: It's okay, Grace, it's okay.

GRACE continues to scream and cry.

DOCTOR: I'll get a sedative. And you, Ms. Shelbourne, are fired!

The video cross-fades to underwater from the pre-show on all panels. GRACE speaks her monologue as VICKY tidies the room.

GRACE: It's so quiet, so still. Dark. Blue blue blue and white above. I like it so quiet. I like it. The bubbles are all around, in my hair, under the white, floating and dancing and playing leapfrog. Pretty. So pretty. They can't get out through the crack, it's too small. It's too small. They tumble and slide and run into each other and get bigger or pop into nothing or run away fast fast fast. But there's more. More and more. So pretty. So quiet. So still.

VICKY gently takes GRACE to bed. She tucks the notebook into GRACE's hands, cracks open the window, turns to the door, and exits.

But there's a crack. There's always a crack.

The video fades out. Lights fade to black. We hear water dripping like a loud IV.

SCENE 10: LATER THAT NIGHT

The room is clean. The lyrics are gone. GRACE is on the bed, being tube-fed.

Video of IV dripping is projected on the side panels as the sound of the dripping IV continues at a lower volume.

GRACE: I want to see the sky. Not this cold block, not this nothing. Where are the bubbles? I want to look up, out, into forever and see blue blue blue and white above. Quiet. Still. Floating.

I'm all alone. I'm lonely. They're different. Maybe I am crazy.

VICKY shows up in the window and climbs in.

VICKY: Grace! Grace, I'm so sorry. These past two weeks haven't turned out at all like I'd planned. I wanted to make things better for you, and I know I made them so much worse.

Here, let's get that awful tube out. Take a big breath. Hold it. Hold it.

She pulls out the tube. GRACE *coughs.* VICKY *hugs her and they rock.*

I remember meeting you the day you were born. I was so happy that you were a girl! I wanted a little sister so badly! When Dad left and Mom married Steve, I didn't know how I would fit in, or even if I would. But then you came along. I adored you. All that dark brown hair and big brown eyes. You were so different from me. I was all chubby and round. And you, you were all lean and gangly, even as a baby. How come I got the short, beefy dad and you got the tall, lean one? Hardly seems fair.

You loved music even then. Even when you were a baby, Mom would make up songs to sing for you. There was a lullaby she wrote that you loved most of all. It would always calm you down when you were upset or crying. Do you remember?

(sings) "When the night settles warm
And the moon's on the rise"

GRACE *joins in.*

BOTH: *(sing)* "There's a blanket of love
Glowing stars in your eyes
Mama rock you to sleep"

GRACE *stops, not knowing the rest of the words.*

VICKY: "Keep you safe in her arms
And the moon lights your way
Floating free from all harm."

You used to love that song. I just wish I'd had the chance to hear you sing it. We had no idea, did we? The future has its own agenda, its own sociopathic plans.

GRACE *starts to squirm. She gets out of bed and goes downstage.*

I was just a kid, Grace. Thirteen! What does anybody know at thirteen? That boy I had a crush on, he called to invite me to the dance he was playing at, at the high school. I thought I'd died and gone to heaven! I was dancing around the kitchen. He wanted to see me! Me! Then I realized that the door was open and you weren't there. You'd gone outside. Why would you do that? Out in the cold in your pyjamas? What were you thinking?

Little footprints in the snow all the way to the creek.

You weren't in very deep under the ice but I couldn't get to you. You'd floated away from the hole that you'd made. So I pounded and I pounded on the ice until it finally cracked and I pulled you out. You were cold. So cold. Oh god, I was scared! It felt like I couldn't breathe, but I had to. My mouth covered half of your little face and I put my hands on your tiny chest and pushed and blew and pushed and blew and I pushed . . .

Then you threw up all over me. I guess I deserved that.

And everything changed. No more baby words. No more peekaboo. You were different. I didn't tell anyone. Not Mom, not Steve, no one.

I can't even remember that boy's name.

I wasn't quite an adult when Mom and Steve died, and social services came. They told me they were taking you away. Taking away my baby sister! I was only seventeen, Grace, they wouldn't let me look after you. Foster care, they said. It would be better if I just left you alone for a while so you could adjust to your new family. Your new family! They never told me where you were. I couldn't find you. I tried, but I couldn't find you. What right did they have to keep us apart? To tear us up like that? I called and called, and no one would listen to me. No one would help.

Bastards.

Eventually, I moved away and went to university. Got married. Got divorced. Tried to live my life. But whenever I let my guard down, when my eyes were closed or I'd just be daydreaming, I'd see you. My little sister, all messed up and reaching out to me, crying. Just reaching out to me, screaming as they took you away. I couldn't do anything. I couldn't stop it. I tried, Grace, I yelled and ran to you and they grabbed me and held me back until you were gone.

And it's all my fault. All of it.

But I finally found you. And I know how to look after you, now. I really am a nurse. I had to take a bit more training, but . . . I've worked so hard to get here, Grace, to you, to make things right. I've applied for adult guardianship. It will probably take weeks for the paperwork to go through all the government BS, but then we can start over. We can go home, together. Just you and me. We'll go for walks and grow things in the garden, and make cinnamon buns, and blow bubbles . . .

GRACE has gone back to working on her song with the audience while VICKY is still talking. VICKY stops talking and watches. GRACE and the audience do the whole song together.

Video of the colours and numbers light up the stage in a beautiful display—the full flower of GRACE's creative spirit—as she sings her song.

GRACE: It's here today
Nothing for me to say
It flows through me
Can't stop no way
In simple ways
We learn to play
It fills me up
It's such a rush

'Cause I can prove to you
I'm just me
They try to tell you
That I'm crazy
This is the world I've built
Inside me
I'm sad that you think this way
But I found peace

The video fades out.

VICKY: That's beautiful. You're amazing, Grace.

Pause.

Peace. Here? In this place? Or in your heart, maybe?

You don't want me to come charging in to rescue you. This is your home now. But maybe we can both find that peace. Together. Maybe someday?

I've always wanted to learn how to play something. Something simple, though; I'm obviously not very accomplished on the keyboard. Recorder. Triangle maybe. I suddenly have a lot of time on my hands. I can visit you until the paperwork comes through and then . . . we'll see. We'll see how you feel. But I'll come to see you every day, Grace. Every day. I'm never going away again.

Can you ever forgive me?

GRACE: *(sings)* "Mama rock you to sleep"

VICKY joins in. GRACE adds harmony.

BOTH: "Keep you safe in her arms
And the moon lights your way
Floating free from all harm."

VICKY pulls out her cellphone, looks something up, and dials.

GRACE: She speaks, Madeline!

VICKY: Let's get your cello back, shall we?

Hello, Department of Health? I understand you're sending inspectors to the Ocean Parks Care Home tomorrow. I'm a former employee of that facility. Yes. I was let go only yesterday, in fact. That's right. And my sister is actually a resident there. Well, it's complicated. I have serious concerns about how patients are being treated under this new management, and I would like to talk to someone about that. Yes, I'll hold.

VICKY winks at GRACE as she walks toward the window and climbs out. Lights begin to fade to a special on GRACE.

GRACE: Remember that day my sister and I went to the lake? And all the ducks started coming toward our blanket 'cause they wanted our sandwiches—we didn't know that ducks liked peanut butter sandwiches—and they all came at us and started snapping at our food and pooping all over our blanket and we screamed and ran but the blanket was tucked into the front of my shirt so all the ducks and the food and the Kool-Aid and the blanket went flying and the ducks started chasing us and ducks are pretty fast when they want to chase you especially when there's peanut butter sandwiches with the crusts cut off and we ran down the hill and across the grass to the playground and . . .

Lights and GRACE*'s monologue slowly fade out.*

End of play.

YOU ARE VERY STAR

A TRANSMEDIA EXPLORATION

ELECTRIC COMPANY THEATRE

INTRODUCTION

Electric Company is a creation-based company that builds new works of theatre in a range of collaborative models and has a long history of creating site-specific theatre as well as plays that explore technology's impact on human perception, identity, relationships, and culture.

You Are Very Star was created in a partnership with the H.R. MacMillan Space Centre in Vancouver, whose leadership at the time was looking for ways in which their venue might be utilized as a more versatile cultural space for alternative programming and draw a wider audience through its doors.

When the Space Centre approached us with the offer of sharing their venue with us, I was immediately intrigued by the opportunity to make a show inside their building.

The Space Centre is an iconic piece of architecture in Vancouver. It's perched overlooking Vanier Park on the south shore of English Bay across from Vancouver's downtown core. The building's design, with its eye-catching circular shape and gently sloping conical roof is modelled after a Coast Salish woven cedar hat, but is often mistaken as being a stylized representation of a flying saucer—an alien space craft that has landed on the city's shore after escaping a vintage science-fiction movie.

When I first returned to the building, I was hit by a wave of nostalgia and, in a moment, the thematic core of the project was revealed. The Space Centre was built in 1968 (the same year that I and co-author Craig Erickson were born) at the peak of the space age as the Apollo missions were nearing their ultimate goal of reaching the moon the following year. It was a monument to the dream of the future.

In 2013, however, the building felt like a trip to the past. How could it not? Much of the decor hadn't been changed since the building opened. And beyond the vintage aesthetic, most people's relationship with the building was most commonly established during school field trips, or maybe as a teenager staying out late for a laser light show set to Pink Floyd, after getting high in the parking lot. It was hard to enter the space without thinking of the past.

I became interested in exploring the human tendency to constantly be outside of the present moment, either looking back to the past or dreaming forward to the future; constantly caught between memory and projection.

So as the artistic team assembled and began exploring, we amplified that natural human tendency with the creation of two independent narratives: Act One was set in 1968 with the characters in the newly opened Space Centre, looking ahead with hope to the future. And in Act Two we imagined a future in 2048 where the characters are looking back to the past, unable to fully imagine what it would have been like way back then; and the Space Centre, now an abandoned relic, partially submerged under rising sea levels.

And with this structure, we could make the audience the point of wonder: standing in the future imagined in Act One and at the same time living in the past only hazily remembered by those in Act Two. And there, sandwiched between dream and memory, perhaps we could acknowledge and celebrate our precious fleeting present as both the culmination and the inciting incident. The arrival and departure. How will we fulfill the dreams of those behind us? How will we create a world inhabitable by those ahead of us?

Centring the audience as living in the focal point for the characters in either storyline implicated them directly in the stories. And with the audience now fully within the narrative, we wished to explore what the boundaries of the experience might be. We wanted to create a piece that extended beyond the edges of the stage, the confines of the narrative, and even the time constraints of the show itself.

By attempting to create a transmedia experience—existing via different modes, mediums, and platforms, one that started interacting with the audience at the point you clicked on the show's website (to buy a ticket or even just find out about the play)—we hoped to have the normally hard edges of a play's beginning, middle, and end soften, blur and become permeable. We hoped to let the play slowly draw the audience into its world well before the lights went up on Act One and continue to play with the audience for some time after the curtain call.

The play began with an online experience that started to plant the seeds of the thematic exploration in the minds of the future audience members. Images, stylized and abstracted, of the interior and exterior of the Space Centre were shown throughout the interactive experience of the prologue, further inserting sensory elements about the future experience into the participant's consciousness.

And if the audience member texted a number provided, they would be engaged in a text conversation with a fictional character from the show, Hafa Sharifi, a teenaged girl working with her friends on an interactive exhibit at the planetarium as part of their school project. Audiences were free to carry on the conversation with Hafa for as long as they wished and they could even friend her on Facebook, post on her wall, and observe her mounting anticipation for the project she was fabricating with her friends.

Although she and her classmates never appear during the performance, evidence of their presence is found within the stations throughout the Space Centre with which the audience is invited to engage during the interlude between acts.

The interlude was intended to be a youthful, playful experience. It was designed to appear as if created by teens wishing to provide adults with a flashback to a field-trip experience. But instead of educational displays about astronomy and space exploration, the exhibits were a self-guided scavenger hunt through interactive stations that echoed themes within the storylines: memory, reflection, nostalgia, recovery; and dreaming, flight, technological augmentation, transcendence.

The stations often connected elements presented in one to an aspect of another and frequently created moments of exchange and sharing between strangers.

Subtle hints and clues were left within the stations to give something of a sense of these invisible characters, some of whom would show up in much older and transformed bodies in Act Two.

But for the time being, the protagonists were the audience who were living as player and game-maker; creator and creation.

—Kevin Kerr, 2021

You Are Very Star was first produced by Electric Company Theatre in June of 2013 at the H.R. MacMillan Space Centre with the following cast and creative team:

Earle Birney/Starr: Patti Allan
Rachel/Ava: Dalal Badr
Winnie Martins/Noa Martins: Kathleen Duborg
Frank/Lan: Chirag Naik
Esther/Chichi: Marsha Regis
Professor/Neil: Michael Rinaldi
Rusty Ford:* Rusty Ford
Hafa Sharifi:* Emma Lindsay

Playwrights: Craig Erickson (Act One) and Kevin Kerr (Act Two)
Story Development: Kevin Kerr, Craig Erickson, David Hudgins, Adrienne Wong, Sarah Sharkey, and Mitch Anderson
Prologue: Kevin Kerr and Blake William Turner
Interlude: Georgina Beaty, with Naomi Sider, Veronique West, and Kevin Kerr
Rusty Ford: Earthbound documentary: Mitch Anderson

Director: David Hudgins
Stage Manager: Jan Hodgson
Set and Costume Design: Naomi Sider
Light and Special Effects Design: Adrian Muir
Projection Design: Parjad Sharifi
Sound Design: Troy Slocum
Original Composition: Peter Allen
Web Design: Blake William Turner
Videography: Ryan Alexander McDonald and Michael Sider
Transmedia Coordinator: Lauren Tuvell
Producer: Jessie van Rijn

---

* Appears only on screen in documentary *Rusty Ford: Earthbound* embedded within Act Two.

CHARACTERS

(1968)
Professor
Earl Birney
Rachel
Winnie Martins
Esther
Frank

(2048)
Ava
Chichi
Lan
Noa Martins
Neil

(2013)
Rusty Ford
Hafa Sharifi

PROLOGUE

You Are Very Star *began with an online, interactive experience. If an audience member purchased a ticket online or if they visited the show page on the Electric Company website, they were provided a link so that they could register with the show. The link takes the user to a website, which opens onto . . .*

A black screen.

From out of the void walks a mysterious country-music singer wearing a fancy custom suit replete with large black musical notes on the white panels of his jacket and piping down the trousers. This is RUSTY *Ford.*

As he draws near, he removes his cowboy hat and reveals to us the inside of the crown, which turns out to be a portal to the cosmos. The camera zooms into the hat and now we are floating in . . .

A field of stars.

Text appears:

Are You Ready?

Beneath the floating words there are two clickable choices: "Yes, I'm ready," "No, but I want to be."

On either choice, the star field pans to a new location and new text appears:

You Are Ready

Then:

You Are Already There

Then:

You Are Very Star

The text fades and new text appears:

Let's get to know each other.
Please enter your name.

A cursor blinks at a blank field. When the participant enters their name:

Hello [*their name*]. *You Are Very Star* is a transmedia event that begins as soon as you are aware of it.

Stars flicker in the night sky.

The Future is happening Now The Past is happening Now The Now is happening Now The Play is happening Now.

Pan down to reveal the Space Centre—a faint outline among the stars.

[*Their name*], help us locate you. Take the following survey. The answers you give will form a unique constellation and will determine your path within the show. When you are ready, click "begin."

Upon clicking "begin," a multiple-choice survey is initiated. The questions are subjective and the answers are a choice between four abstracted photographs (close-up details of textures; architectural shapes that have been treated) from within the venue. There is no right answer.

Upon completion, a six-star constellation is formed in an image of the night sky, constructed based on the user's answers to the questions. The images might provide a sense of mood and theme while planting nearly subliminal references to the space in which the show takes place, creating an associative and near dream-like encounter—familiar and strange.

The questions appear, with four abstract images to choose from as answers for each:

Where does fear live?

In which is there longing?

Your first love was a little like this:

Hope will be found here:

In which is there regret?

Which will be a good thing in the end?

Upon completion, a short film plays. The camera zooms into the void. Again, the show speaks to us purely as text on the screen.

EXT. SPACE CENTRE—NIGHT.

Approaching the outside of the Space Centre; the building glows in the darkness. Not a soul to be seen.

This is a memory . . .

An ominous, enormous, metallic-crab fountain stands guard outside the Space Centre.

Close on the claws.

This is something that has happened . . .

The camera presses toward the entrance, through the doors.

INT. SPACE CENTRE STAIRWELL—NIGHT.

A concrete and empty stairwell. The camera ascends the stairs, which are sparsely lit and seem unintended for the public.

To you . . .

INT. SPACE CENTRE STAR DECK—NIGHT.

A curving hallway. Images of galaxies along the wall. Deep red carpet.

Extreme low angle: feet approach to Star Theatre.

In the Future.

INT. SPACE CENTRE VOMITORY—NIGHT.

Tracking down the darkened vomitory we're now looking over the shoulder of a teenaged girl who is walking toward the Star Theatre. The domed ceiling is visible, glowing pink like the sky before dawn. Except for the girl the space seems empty.

Recognize it?

INT. STAR THEATRE—NIGHT.

We're now inside the Star Theatre under the artificial sky. The teenaged girl is sitting in one of the reclining seats looking skyward. The black, metal, insect-like star projector rises from the ringed pit in the centre of the theatre and towers above us.

You will.

The theatre darkens. The stars come out above us and we're under the night sky as we were at the beginning of the prologue.

Text floats in the sky beneath a ten-digit phone number:

This is my number. Text me a message. Just say "Hi." If you can . . . do it right now.

If the user texts the number, they receive a reply from HAFA *Sharifi, a teenaged girl working on a project at the Space Centre that will be on display when the user sees the show.*

After a while, the onscreen text dissolves. Replaced by the show title and dates:

You Are Very Star

PART ONE: ORBITING THE CUSP OF GREATNESS

SCENE 1

December 21, 1968. 4:55 a.m. A basement auditorium at the local, newly constructed planetarium.

As houselights dim, an overhead projector casts a handwritten title upon a vintage screen, which reads "Part One: Orbiting the Cusp of Greatness."

Hypnotic, pulsating space music. There are sirens. An overhead projector. A television sits centre stage, a white cloth and bird feathers strewn around it.

The PROFESSOR *and* EARLE *Birney are breathing heavily near the* TV *set, which is on, but has no signal.* EARLE *is rubbing his jaw. The* PROFESSOR *holds the* TV *antenna, which is broken in half.*

The PROFESSOR *sighs.*

PROFESSOR: There are times when failure is an indistinct murmur. And there are times it pierces the air as clear and vulnerable as Art Garfunkel's high C.

EARLE: You wanted this day to be memorable, and it is!

SCENE 2

December 21, 1968. 4:45 a.m. Ten minutes earlier. The planetarium.

The television is covered by a white sheet. The PROFESSOR *sits on a stool "backstage." He is dimly lit with his back to us. He wears a cloak.*

RACHEL *moves about the room, handing out brightly decorated "mail-art" envelopes to audience members. The envelopes have the phrase "Invitation to Soar!" written on them. There is also a picture of a rocket with a dove on the fuselage.*

Eventually, she respectfully approaches the PROFESSOR.

RACHEL: Our mail-out really worked. They're here . . . to be inspired.

The PROFESSOR *continues his meditation.*

Whenever you're ready, we're set.

RACHEL *checks her watch and adjusts some feathers around the television.*

FRANK *enters from the back, handing out more invitations.*

FRANK: Gate crashers, eh? Even if you weren't on the list, here you go. Hey, are you Bobby Goldsboro?

RACHEL *sees him.*

RACHEL: Frank, where were you?!

FRANK: There's a new guy at the south checkpoint.

RACHEL: What new guy?

FRANK: Old man, twinkle in his eye.

RACHEL: There's not supposed to be a new guy.

FRANK: Don't worry, I explained. He's cool. Trust Frank.

They look at the PROFESSOR.

RACHEL: He hasn't moved since I got here.

FRANK: He's riding his "own vibe"?

They approach the PROFESSOR. *He collapses slightly.* RACHEL *looks at* FRANK, *then checks her watch again.*

RACHEL: It's T minus three, Professor. There's no room for resignation.

Suddenly, the PROFESSOR *rises, stepping up onto his stool. His cloaked arms spread like wings as he rises.*

He slowly wheels around on the stool as he removes the hood of his cloak. We can see his determined face and his closely shaved head.

PROFESSOR: Your father would be proud of you, Rachel. Did . . . Esther respond?

RACHEL: She actually called me, wanted to know more.

PROFESSOR: Really?

RACHEL: But I don't see her out there.

PROFESSOR: And Winnie? I wish I had her poem for this launch.

RACHEL: I've heard she's in labour, Professor.

PROFESSOR: Good excuse.

RACHEL: Guess it'll be early.

The PROFESSOR *steps down and removes his cloak, revealing a white robe. He smiles.*

PROFESSOR: Oh, I don't think so, Rachel. That baby is right on time.

(whispers to her) I am fully flooded with ideas.

He steps out onto the stage, meeting the crowd's gaze. He takes them in.

What better place to explore the frontier of the spirit? This new temple of the future—the *planetarium*. Yes, you're in the right place.

He laughs.

But isn't it a gift of spirit—we get to be here together in this moment. It's okay to be afraid, to feel as exposed as, say . . .

He points to his head.

. . . my *newly-preened locks*!

An underwhelming response. The PROFESSOR *shifts.*

Let's talk about birds briefly.

RACHEL *and* FRANK *look at each other. He has gone off script.*

RACHEL: Professor, remember—

PROFESSOR: The dove, in particular. Common, pedestrian. It does not conquer with strength. It will never be any school's mascot. Go Doves! I doubt it.

He points at an invitation.

On a symbol of war, this symbol of peace. Any Vietnamese people here? We will not vilify; we will not polarize. Maybe later, we can sneak upstairs to behold technology's newest unifying wonder—the Star Theatre! I don't know what's playing at this hour but . . . but in this moment, let's feel free to lament the abandonment of our *connectedness here on earth*. Did you know, the dove's soft drawn-out calls sound like laments?

RACHEL *moves closer to him.*

RACHEL: We have less than a minute.

PROFESSOR: Frank, Rachel: the stimuli!

FRANK scrambles to put on a Sun Ra record. It is dreamy, wild, spacey music. The PROFESSOR takes in the music, then opens his eyes.

The inaugural meeting of the Soar Dove Movement! Like it? Soar Dove!

FRANK comes to life and leads a chant.

FRANK: Everybody! Soar Dove! Soar Dove!

PROFESSOR: *(speaking overtop of the chant)* Thank you, Frank! It's a real movement of the spirit! Can you feel it? Louder!

FRANK & RACHEL: Soar Dove! Soar Dove!

PROFESSOR: Can you envision yourself committed?!

ALL: Soar Dove! Soar Dove. Soar Dove.

The chant peters out as FRANK and RACHEL realize they are also chanting "Sort of! Sort of!"

RACHEL: Professor, it's starting!

PROFESSOR: A significant moment in history begins now. I hear the booster rockets of the spirit. The search for new worlds beckon! Board me! Frank, hit it!

FRANK scurries to the television.

This is our own *Apollo 8* mission!

FRANK removes the sheet. He hits the power button on the TV. Nothing happens. He tries repeatedly.

FRANK: I don't understand.

PROFESSOR: What's the matter?

FRANK: It was working before.

FRANK is checking the power cords.

RACHEL: Four-fifty-one on the nose.

FRANK: Everything looks good.

PROFESSOR: Is't possible?

A voice comes from the back. A security guard (a disguised EARLE Birney) enters.

EARLE: Electrical power is notoriously finicky in new buildings.

PROFESSOR: A Space Centre worker!

FRANK: You're the new guard at the south checkpoint.

The PROFESSOR gestures to the television. EARLE Birney begins removing his hat and coat.

PROFESSOR: Could you check the breaker? Quickly!

EARLE: Oh, it works. I'm the one who turned it off.

EARLE Birney is now fully revealed.

FRANK: What?

PROFESSOR: You!

RACHEL: *(to EARLE)* Can you please turn the power on?

EARLE: I'll let the police deal with it.

RACHEL: You called the police?

EARLE: The invitation says "open to all," little girl.

FRANK: *(to EARLE)* Don't call her that. Frank is off!

FRANK runs off.

EARLE: Ladies and gentlemen. My name is Earle Birney. I am here to do a public service. It's time this law-breaking fraud was exposed for what he is.

PROFESSOR: That's what I've been trying to do—expose myself!

RACHEL: He's just jealous.

EARLE laughs uproariously as he gathers up some feathers.

EARLE: *(calmly)* I simply can't risk you contaminating what I've built with this illegal off-campus gathering. All you seekers, look for meaning somewhere else!

He tosses the feathers into the air.

The PROFESSOR, enraged, speeds down the aisle and tackles EARLE Birney.

PROFESSOR: You ass! Ahhhhhh!!!

The two men wrestle.

RACHEL: Professor! Earle! Stop it! Stop it!!

EARLE: Fool!

An elbow from the PROFESSOR connects. The antenna gets hit/squashed. They are breathing heavily and EARLE is rubbing his jaw.

PROFESSOR: There are times when failure is an indistinct murmur. And there are times it pierces the air as clear and vulnerable as Art Garfunkel's high C.

EARLE: A peaceful movement. Ha!

FRANK comes running back in.

FRANK: Power should be back on!

FRANK runs down the aisle excitedly and turns the TV on. There is no signal, only snow. The PROFESSOR, on the ground, pulls something out from underneath him. It is the TV antenna, now broken.

RACHEL: Professor, I hate to say this but . . .

PROFESSOR: No.

RACHEL: *Apollo 8* is . . .

EARLE: Long gone.

Beat.

PROFESSOR: At least we're here together.

EARLE: There is no "we."

The PROFESSOR closes his eyes and lets out the lamenting cry of the dove.

What is that?

FRANK: It's a dove, obviously.

PROFESSOR: Earle is right. I am a fraud. Thanks, everyone. Go back to your homes.

The PROFESSOR begins to remove his white robe. ESTHER appears, and walks down the aisle, envelope in hand. RACHEL sees her first.

RACHEL: Esther?

PROFESSOR: Esther.

EARLE: Esther!!

ESTHER: *(to EARLE)* I can guess why you're here, Earle.

EARLE: Yes, exposing a fraud. Defeating your oppressor.

ESTHER: You're an angry person.

EARLE: That's our bond.

ESTHER: Not anymore.

PROFESSOR: Esther, I want to apologize publicly.

ESTHER: I know you do. I accept it.

PROFESSOR: Thank you.

EARLE leaves.

RACHEL: You know, Professor, this is part of what you came to do.

RACHEL, FRANK, and the PROFESSOR start to pack up. ESTHER produces an envelope.

ESTHER: Wait. I have something for you.

PROFESSOR: A gift. For me?

ESTHER: I know part of any movement needs to envision possibility.

The PROFESSOR pulls out the collage/transparencies. They are representations of the Apollo 8 *Earthrise photos from December 28. She places the first one on the overhead projector.*

RACHEL: One visionary to another.

There are sounds of the December 28 recording of the Apollo 8 *astronauts seeing the earth from just above the lunar surface.*

The PROFESSOR shudders. He elevates. He astral-projects.

PROFESSOR: Oh. Oh. Is this the future? I have no words. We're part of something so precious.

Blackout.

SCENE 3

December 11, 1968. Ten days earlier. Vancouver Art Gallery.

RACHEL, in a raincoat, stands with some mail-art envelopes in her hand. ESTHER is drawing.

RACHEL: Mail. Art.

ESTHER: It democratizes things. The galleries have no propriety on the creative impulse.

RACHEL: You mail these out to other artists?

ESTHER: *(playful)* Yeah. Anyone. Take off your jacket, stop hovering.

RACHEL: I can't stay. I've—

ESTHER: Well, you're dripping on me.

RACHEL: You're the first real artist I've met.

Beat.

ESTHER: Is that why you're here—to compliment me?

RACHEL: This is odd, even to me, but I'm here on behalf of the professor.

ESTHER: What?

RACHEL: He wants to say sorry.

ESTHER: Rachel, I've read his needy letters.

RACHEL: I know but—

ESTHER: I've already thrown them into a collage I'm making.

RACHEL: Esther, he'd like to meet with you and apologize in person.

ESTHER: No, no. His arrogance, his systemic racist attitudes . . . He is who he is.

RACHEL: He's made mistakes, he wants change.

ESTHER: What are you—his spokesman?

RACHEL: I guess . . .

ESTHER: Why?

RACHEL: He was a friend of my dad's . . . Well . . . he's my friend, too.

ESTHER: I don't want him coming around here.

Beat.

RACHEL: Not here. At the launch of his new "underground happening."

ESTHER: Is that a joke?

RACHEL shakes her head.

RACHEL: In ten days. In Kitsilano. At the new planetarium.

ESTHER: It's open?

RACHEL: Exciting idea, right?

She clears her throat.

To be clear, though, the building itself will not officially be open at the time of the launch.

ESTHER: I don't understand.

RACHEL: Well, it's at four in the morning.

ESTHER: Why so early?

RACHEL: Part of the surprise.

ESTHER: Wait a sec. Isn't that the time of the—

RACHEL: Shhh.

ESTHER: Isn't that illegal?

Beat.

RACHEL: Yes, it is.

ESTHER: He wants me there?

RACHEL: He wants to start off this movement with an egoless act. He wants to demonstrate that differences are resolvable if we embrace the unknown.

ESTHER: I don't know. Who would come to this?

RACHEL: Actually, there's excitement building at the school. Not everyone was happy he was fired. And I'm getting a covert mail-out ready.

Beat.

ESTHER: You're gassed up.

RACHEL: I can't let him be alone.

ESTHER: Are you lovers?

RACHEL laughs.

RACHEL: Lovers? Whaaat? No. Noooo.

ESTHER: Just wondering.

EARLE Birney enters. ESTHER sees him. RACHEL does not.

RACHEL: Him? He's old, scattered, prone to self-absorption—

EARLE: And those are just my good qualities.

RACHEL: Oh!

ESTHER: You're early.

EARLE crosses to ESTHER.

EARLE: The body's anticipatory reflexes keep to their own schedule.

ESTHER and EARLE kiss.

RACHEL: Oh!

ESTHER: You remember Earle Birney.

RACHEL: Of course. Uhh . . . excuse me.

ESTHER: It's all right, baby. It's 1968. Earle, this is my friend Rachel.

EARLE: I remember.

ESTHER: Of course, you do.

EARLE: Creative writing, or whatever the class ended up being called. Of whom were you just speaking, lovely girl?

RACHEL: A friend of mine.

EARLE: Didn't sound like a friend.

RACHEL: I should go.

(to ESTHER) Please consider what I said.

RACHEL backs away.

Enjoy . . . each other. I mean, enjoy your evening.

EARLE: *(smiling)* It's likely we'll do both.

RACHEL bends down to pick up a mail-art envelope.

RACHEL: May I borrow one of these?

She grabs one and goes.

Goodbye.

RACHEL leaves. ESTHER moves away, thinking.

EARLE: Well, don't make me ask.

ESTHER: I barely even know her. She's a Mennonite, helps the draft dodgers. I helped her draw a sign once.

EARLE: Who was she talking about?

ESTHER: Believe it or not, a certain writing professor is starting a new spiritual movement. Rachel's helping him.

EARLE: Ahh, he needs to go away.

ESTHER: No one's seen him for months.

EARLE: And this is his comeback? Interesting.

ESTHER: Yes.

EARLE: You're intrigued?

ESTHER: Not really.

EARLE: What else do you know?

ESTHER: Nothing.

Beat.

EARLE: You're protecting her.

ESTHER: No, I'm not.

EARLE: Actually, I've heard he's got a groundswell of support.

ESTHER: Oh?

EARLE: Some people you can't bury deep enough.

The overhead. The PROFESSOR *inspired in nature. "Bleecker Street" (Simon and Garfunkel) plays. Via overhead projector, transparencies show the* PROFESSOR *inspired by nature.*

Possible images: a) the planetarium from the distance; b) the PROFESSOR *happy in the woods, wide-eyed as he sees the planetarium in the distance; c) the* PROFESSOR *beside his tent, smelling the air, grabbing the branches of two trees as if holding hands; d) the* PROFESSOR *sees an eagle in the woods; it morphs into a dove and lands on his shoulder; he pets it; it grows larger and larger and carries the* PROFESSOR *in its beak.*

SCENE 4

December 1, 1968. Ten days earlier. Evening. The PROFESSOR*'s house.*

The PROFESSOR *sits slumped in his chair reading a book. He has hair and it is dishevelled. He has a bandage on his hand. The book is* Fearless Death: Buddhist Wisdom on the Art of Dying *by Lama Ole Nydahl.*

There is a knock at the door. He shuffles apprehensively to the door, and peers out through the peephole. He sees it is WINNIE*, and his whole body activates. He instinctively moves to clean up.*

PROFESSOR: One moment!

He opens the front door. The PROFESSOR *extends his arm in welcome.*

Winnie! Welcome. You found me.

WINNIE: This is just for one moment.

PROFESSOR: Ha, ha. I just said that.

WINNIE: What?

PROFESSOR: "One moment." That's funny. I saw you through the peephole, and I yelled it. "One moment!" Isn't that funny?

Silence.

(realizing) It's been a while since I talked.

WINNIE: Professor.

PROFESSOR: Am I?

Beat.

I can offer you a glass of Freshie.

He turns to leave.

Not sure how old the packet is.

WINNIE: No. My ride is waiting . . .

The PROFESSOR *turns back.*

PROFESSOR: Places to go. People to ride with.

WINNIE: My husband and I have an appointment.

She touches her stomach.

PROFESSOR: Your marriage is . . . ?

WINNIE: We want to make sure everything's all right. I don't want to disturb you, but—

PROFESSOR: *(defensive)* I'm not disturbed.

WINNIE: I need you to stop writing me.

PROFESSOR: Caring for others has consequences, Winnie.

WINNIE: Please. I'm trying to do the right thing. I'm trying to start clean. You're making it difficult.

PROFESSOR: Well, while we're being honest, admit that you were falling in love with me.

WINNIE: No.

PROFESSOR: No, you won't admit it?

Beat.

WINNIE: I also would like to get my poem back.

PROFESSOR: Uhhhh . . .

WINNIE: Early in the semester, I wrote a poem . . .

Beat.

PROFESSOR: I don't . . . I'm not . . .

WINNIE: Can I have it?

PROFESSOR: I'm not done with it.

WINNIE: Not done with it?

Beat.

PROFESSOR: Where did we go wrong?

WINNIE: There is no "we." It was my only copy, it just poured out of me, and I want my family to be able—

PROFESSOR: *(muttering)* Your family.

WINNIE: Yes, I want to share it with them.

PROFESSOR: You did that already. With me.

WINNIE: I shared it with the class.

PROFESSOR: Well, I burned everything.

WINNIE: What?

PROFESSOR: I burned your poem. This hand. Other things. It's been *Apollo 1* around here.

WINNIE: Why would you do that?

PROFESSOR: A new beginning? Winnie, I keep thinking your baby knew something.

WINNIE goes to leave.

On our date, remember?

WINNIE: That wasn't a date.

PROFESSOR: In this very house! Your baby, it was kicking, it was excited!

WINNIE: Douglas, it didn't even have legs, how could—

PROFESSOR: Yes, it was! It did! It knew! It knew there's too much life between us to have nothing come of it!

WINNIE leaves.

It knew!

He walks slowly over to his chair and decides to turn the radio on.

RADIO: . . . *Apollo 8* will be the second manned mission in the Apollo space program, and the first for the Saturn V rocket. Launch time is in three weeks, December 21. It is anticipated the broadcast of this mission—

There is another knock at the door. The PROFESSOR *turns the radio off, but continues looking at it, thinking about the report. He goes to the door and opens it. It is* RACHEL.

PROFESSOR: Rachel! Hello. I thought you were Winnie. Two visitors in one day. Odd.

RACHEL *looks around.*

RACHEL: Sparse.

PROFESSOR: That's the style. I haven't heard from you.

RACHEL: I haven't heard from you.

PROFESSOR: We cleared that up.

RACHEL *bows her head.*

RACHEL: My dad died.

PROFESSOR: What? Peter? He died?

RACHEL: I thought you'd want to know. Heart attack.

PROFESSOR: Of course. I mean, of course I'd want to know. We were . . . at one time . . . very close.

RACHEL: He was on the road a lot, as you know, so I . . . I don't know how I should feel.

PROFESSOR: I'm so glad you're here.

RACHEL: I didn't know where else to go.

The PROFESSOR *smiles. He hugs her.*

PROFESSOR: I have Freshie.

RACHEL: Yes.

The PROFESSOR *disappears into his kitchen.*

PROFESSOR: *(off-stage)* What about your GI friend, Todd?

RACHEL *walks over to his chair and picks up the book on death he was reading.*

RACHEL: He got a job. He's staying in BC.

She examines a ring on her finger.

PROFESSOR: *(off-stage)* Oh? Glad it worked out.

The PROFESSOR *returns with two packets and two waters and prepares the drinks.*

I'll always remember your father with his coonskin cap long before the Davy Crockett show made it a popular accessory. We both loved hats.

RACHEL: I guess every travelling salesman is a frontiersman of sorts. Just like you are.

PROFESSOR: He was humble. And he didn't live with fear.

RACHEL: Everyone looks a little better from the outside.

He sees the drink is clumpy.

PROFESSOR: Clumpy. I should've added the water after.

RACHEL: I'm sorry Earle Birney wasn't ready for your bold vision, Professor.

PROFESSOR: Pushing the boundaries of academia was bound to feel limiting.

RACHEL: What have you been doing?

PROFESSOR: *(smiling absently)* Preparing? I can't help feeling there's something on the horizon.

RACHEL: Always another rocket to be launched, it seems.

PROFESSOR: I like how you put that.

The PROFESSOR *takes her hand. He hears sounds of space, astronauts talking to one another. He's moved.*

RACHEL: Your whole face is lit up.

PROFESSOR: Would you help me, Rachel? Maybe you're looking for a new start, too?

RACHEL: Help you with what?

PROFESSOR: Oh, I don't know. Just . . . I believe you might be looking into the vulnerable eyes of Vancouver's newest spiritual guru.

SCENE 5

A series of overheads/real-time images that go back in time.

At the same time, the actual PROFESSOR *in his house lies down.*

Overhead: the PROFESSOR *takes his school keys and throws them in a back-alley fire. He takes pieces of his Russian hat and tosses them in the fire as well. Then, he dumps in a whole briefcase full of papers and assignments. He looks closely at one particular piece of paper. His eyes widen, and he tries desperately to rescue it. He tries to blow out the burgeoning flame curling the sides of the paper. It's too late. We see the title at the top of the page as it is engulfed. It is* WINNIE*'s poem, "Unknown." The* PROFESSOR *burns his hand and lets out a pain-induced scream.*

Overhead: time shift. Image of the phone. We hear the PROFESSOR*'s phone ring.*

The actual PROFESSOR *gets up with a start. Pieces of Russian hat fur go flying off his stomach. He scrambles to his feet and answers the phone. The operator of the overhead could turn faster, revealing the same frantic action. Both the* PROFESSOR *in real time and on the overhead transparency hold the phone over their ear. At this point, the animation on the overhead could bend toward the surreal.*

PROFESSOR: Yes, hello?
Oh.
Why?
They're mine—
Oh, I hadn't heard that.
Yes, fine.
I just said I'll return the keys soon enough!

The PROFESSOR *hangs up and lets out a frustrated scream.*

Overhead: the PROFESSOR *walks out of the school building and promptly cuts up his Russian hat.*

SCENE 6

October 15, 1968. Lecture hall.

The PROFESSOR*, dressed in a golden muumuu, stands in front of his class. He looks toward the back of the class, anxious. Some moments pass. The* PROFESSOR *counts his students.*

PROFESSOR: Winnie absent. Rachel absent. I expected that. Our numbers here today are discouraging.

I will try hard, apprentices, to put any slight negativity I've ingested into the work.

FRANK *puts his hand up.*

Yes . . . uh . . .

FRANK: Frank. Is this, sir, what you would call irony?

PROFESSOR: I'm not following.

FRANK: In the three weeks since you've combined all your classes, you have even fewer students than you had at the beginning.

Silence.

PROFESSOR: Just so you know, Earle Birney, the originator of our creative writing program, has asked to stop by today to bear witness to the "new imagining" he requested. So. We're just waiting for that. Has anyone heard from Winnie?

Silence.

FRANK: My mom has a muumuu.

PROFESSOR: They're comfortable.

FRANK: She wears it for health reasons.

PROFESSOR: We'll just wait a couple more minutes.

The PROFESSOR does a half-stretch and plucks absently at his garment.

FRANK: My mom's is tight on her.

PROFESSOR: *(sharply)* That's the chance you take though, isn't it? Perhaps your mother feels, as I do, that her heart is so big it pushes in on the ribs.

FRANK: *(quietly)* That's not it.

EARLE Birney enters from the back of the class.

PROFESSOR: Aha! Professor Birney. You're late!

EARLE: My loss. I had meetings. And, clearly . . .

EARLE looks around at the small gathering/muumuu.

I will have more meetings.

PROFESSOR: That's a shame. I recommend you put your feet up. Enjoy "the informal creative"! Look at them, look at their faces!

EARLE: Hmmm . . .

The PROFESSOR *takes in a large breath.*

PROFESSOR: Life pupils.

*He walks to the lectern, never taking his eyes off the students/*EARLE.

Continuing my recent efforts to push the boundaries of the collective mind, I have procured a consciousness-raising conduit. Some of you are soooooo sleeeeepyyyyyy.

He pulls out some ground leaves and a mug. He dumps the leaves into the mug and looks around the lectern.

Eventually, he sticks his finger into the drink.

I forgot the stir stick. Anyway, these boiled ayahuasca vine leaves will allow you to observe me as I "see with fresh eyes." I doubt your minds are being blown like this in other classes! Hey, Earle?

EARLE: Ayahuasca. *(bemused)* Right here, right now?

PROFESSOR: That's right!

FRANK: Are we all taking it, sir?

PROFESSOR: No, just me.

The PROFESSOR *downs the drink with aplomb, but gags slightly.*

First time.

The PROFESSOR *looks toward the back entrance.*

Get out your writing instruments! Whoa. It's already working.

Unsteady, the PROFESSOR *walks to the turntable. He takes out the John Coltrane record* Interstellar Space *(1967), and places it on the turntable.*

Use this auditory fusion to wake up your poetic soul! I, or some form of "my self," will return directly.

The PROFESSOR *disappears behind the stage. They wait.*

FRANK: *(to anyone)* Didn't he say last class that now we have no grades?

The PROFESSOR *reappears, adorned with a space helmet and carrying a silver astronaut's umbilical cord.*

PROFESSOR: Behold! The call to adventure!

EARLE: God help us.

Grandly, the PROFESSOR *attaches one end of the cord to his midsection, and he begins physically "floating out to space." He moves slowly in and among the students.*

PROFESSOR: Poetic Impressions. Let them flow out of you. No censor, just impulse! And if it helps you, I believe I'll make this your MIDTERM!! But, as I said, you will heretofore be grading yourself.

FRANK: That's what it was.

PROFESSOR: Ignite, dear ones!

He sees FRANK *moving to the beat.*

Yes, dance if you want to! Wow. Am I ever soaring! Consciousness exported into the ether! I can fully recommend this, class! Fully!

FRANK *is writing furiously.*

FRANK: I'm writing some wild shit, Professor!

PROFESSOR: Professor? Who is that? I am a projection of this program's best of what could be! Hey, Earle?

The PROFESSOR *stands on the chairs. He grandly unhinges the silver cord and throws it to the side.*

Unhinge your minds! We can all be Ed Whites! Stepping out into unfamiliar atmospheres.

He walks from armrest to armrest. EARLE, *less euphoric, has moved up on stage and inspects the mug. The* PROFESSOR *does not see him.*

EARLE: *(examining mug)* I don't detect any active ingredient in here.

FRANK: Professor.

EARLE: There should be no hallucinogenic effect whatsoever.

PROFESSOR: The naked soul needs to drift. I wish I had a rope swing in here.

EARLE *takes the needle off the record abruptly. The* PROFESSOR *whirls around.*

EARLE: I think that's enough drifting for one day.

The PROFESSOR, *breathing heavily, moves closer to* EARLE.

Give me your stupid space helmet.

EARLE *grabs at the helmet brusquely and then places it on the ground.*

I can't recommend you stay on with us.

PROFESSOR: What? You're deciding now? You need me creating in this laboratory!

EARLE: You're not an artist. You're a clown.

PROFESSOR: A what?

FRANK: That's not true.

PROFESSOR: Frank gets me. I have plans. Winnie and I have strategized . . .

EARLE: Who's Winnie?

PROFESSOR: She wrote this poem. In my class. I galvanized her!

EARLE: It's over.

PROFESSOR: You're wrong! About all of it! Today's classroom exploration is inspired! And also, I'm high, Birney! I'm high!

EARLE: Not true.

PROFESSOR: I am high as the Seattle Space Needle!

EARLE: Oh, Douglas.

EARLE walks back up the aisle.

Silence.

In your misguided rebellion, you merely enjoyed a mild cup of tea. I'll notify the dean.

PROFESSOR: Our class. It seems. Is over.

SCENE 7

October 12, 1968. Three days earlier. The PROFESSOR's office.

The PROFESSOR is listening to Burl Ives's version of "The Times, They Are A-Changin'" (1968) while following a yogi's instructions trying to see out of his third eye.

He looks like he may implode. He breathes out heavily. RACHEL comes to his door.

RACHEL: Professor.

PROFESSOR: Let it be known. The third eye is . . . tricky to access.

RACHEL: That's why the kids just take drugs.

PROFESSOR: I like it when you stop by. Sometimes I still see your seven-year-old face. I just want to squeeze it.

RACHEL: Professor, I need that intent-to-hire letter.

PROFESSOR: Yes. The letter. Of course.

RACHEL: Immigration is sniffing around—

PROFESSOR: Of course. Of course.

He looks over at a stack of papers.

When exactly is Ted's deadline to—

RACHEL: Todd's.

PROFESSOR: Yes, the deadline for Todd to . . . to . . . do you like this tune?

RACHEL: It's different.

PROFESSOR: It's Burl Ives. It's a cover!

RACHEL stands back and looks at him.

RACHEL: You did write the employment letter, right?

The PROFESSOR starts shuffling through a stack of papers.

PROFESSOR: You said university letterhead, I believe.

RACHEL: Professor, did you write it or . . .

He stops shuffling.

PROFESSOR: No, I didn't.

RACHEL: You didn't.

PROFESSOR: My schedule is in such flux!

RACHEL: You said you would! Todd's counting on this. We're both counting on this!

PROFESSOR: Sounds like you feel pressured?

RACHEL: Yes, and you're not helping.

PROFESSOR: Well, did you think that maybe I might feel a little pressure too? I have things going on . . . I wish I had time to play at being revolutionaries.

RACHEL: Play at? This is life and death. Soldiers are dying, women and children are dying. It's an unjust war waged by imperialist oppressors!

PROFESSOR: You're spouting rhetoric with no understanding.

RACHEL: I understand that if I don't do something, he'll face prison or worse.

PROFESSOR: Why you?

RACHEL: Because change happens one person at a time.

PROFESSOR: And why him?

> *Pause. He sees something in her eyes. The* PROFESSOR *picks up a beat-up ring box and pulls out a ring.*

Here. Give him this to give to you.

RACHEL: What?

PROFESSOR: Marry him. He'll be able to stay then.

> *She takes the ring and examines it.*

RACHEL: You're giving this to me?

PROFESSOR: I . . . I don't need it. You use it.

RACHEL: I don't think I want to get married . . . yet.

PROFESSOR: Oh? So, you want me to gamble away my job writing a fake letter for some coward, but you're not willing to take a risk yourself.

RACHEL: Coward? I know a coward when I see one, but it's not Todd. My dad was wrong about you.

She takes the ring and storms out.

SCENE 8

October 7, 1968. Five days earlier. Evening. The PROFESSOR*'s house.*

The PROFESSOR *is entertaining* WINNIE *in his home. Some dishes around. He enters holding a half full wine glass and a bottle.*

WINNIE: Poets can be creepy until you get to know them.

PROFESSOR: Winnie, I had had it. I looked him straight in his angular newly drenched face . . .

WINNIE: I can't believe you—

PROFESSOR: . . . and said without hesitation, "Let's talk about assumptions. I, for instance, now assume you won't ever refer to me as a poor man's W. D. Snodgrass!"

WINNIE: *(laughing)* I guess that's an insult!?

The PROFESSOR *laughs.*

PROFESSOR: I told Birney that story in my second interview.

A moment.

I had just been published, so much confidence then . . .

WINNIE: Confidence can come and go. And come again! Lovely evening, lovely meal.

She gets up to clear some plates.

PROFESSOR: My mother's recipe.

The PROFESSOR *interrupts her action.*

Please, I want you to be comfortable.

She sits back down. He smiles, relaxing in a pose that makes WINNIE *want to change the subject.*

WINNIE: Professor, I'm a little confused.

PROFESSOR: Douglas. Go on.

He pours WINNIE *a glass of wine.*

WINNIE: Why am I here?

PROFESSOR: You need to hear more of my stream-of-consciousness journaling.

He goes for his book.

WINNIE: Douglas, I've got three exams next week.

PROFESSOR: *(looking up)* Sometimes I forget . . . You seem to me a colleague. Or a comrade.

He goes to take her hand. She lets him. But just for a moment.

The PROFESSOR *laughs in anticipation and disappears.* WINNIE *produces a letter and reviews it as she speaks.*

WINNIE: You wrote me that you were worried about Birney, and what he wants for the program—this "committee to re-imagine"? Can students participate? I mean, could I? And what do you think he means by "suboptimal performers in faculty"?

PROFESSOR: *(off-stage)* All I know is: One has to take leaps of faith in this life . . .

The PROFESSOR *returns with a guitar and his Russian hat.*

Relax. Read over my "Syllabus of Love."

He strums.

It's called "Syllabus of Love."

The PROFESSOR *sings.*

"Booster Rocket takes me skyward
I see the pillowy clouds ahead
I blast through, beyond the ozone
There's no time to rest my head"

WINNIE: Ummm . . .

She gets up.

PROFESSOR: Wait! Imagine for a moment. Together, we move with freedom, class to class, unlocking the inhibited through poetry in a kind of ecstatic spirit release. Zero Gravity Soul Happenings.

WINNIE: Zero gravity . . .

PROFESSOR: Soul Happenings.

WINNIE: Uhhh . . .

PROFESSOR: *(agreeing)* Too hard to chant?

WINNIE: Douglas, perhaps—

PROFESSOR: This might be why you're here! To burst this institution, this city wide open. Into the firmament we go!

WINNIE: I'm a student.

PROFESSOR: I see no label on you.

He goes to take her hand again. She retreats.

WINNIE: I'm still married, Douglas!

PROFESSOR: Happily?

WINNIE: Married.

He's my husband and I'm pregnant!

They both look at WINNIE's stomach. He smiles broadly at her.

Slowly, he moves his hand toward her stomach. He touches it before asking.

PROFESSOR: Darling. May I feel . . . ?

WINNIE: I suppose—

PROFESSOR: . . . with my whole being?

He does a slow, twisty dive and ends up on his back in her lap, his head resting against her stomach. He looks up at her.

Winnie. You don't have to carry the weight of expectation yourself! Ha! Puns! Always a surprise. Hey!

He moves his head sharply, and he rolls off WINNIE's lap onto the floor, shaking his head.

I . . . I just got kicked in the head, right in my ear!

WINNIE: You mean the—

PROFESSOR: That was remarkable! My entire head is ringing!

WINNIE: I don't think—

PROFESSOR: It sensed me. An awakening.

WINNIE retreats slightly. Impulsively, the PROFESSOR grabs her head and kisses her. She allows it. A tender gesture.

I'm seeing a glimmer of what could be . . .

WINNIE: You're a strange, wonderful man. But . . .

They kiss again and he produces a ring box from his pocket. WINNIE *recoils.*

WINNIE: Douglas . . .

PROFESSOR: Your baby sensed a creative life force outside itself! It doesn't matter to me that it belongs to another man.

She pushes him and his ring away.

WINNIE: Stop it! This baby is mine!

WINNIE runs out.

PROFESSOR: Winnie!

SCENE 9

September 25, 1968. Twelve days earlier. University art room.

WINNIE and RACHEL are colouring posters. FRANK enters.

FRANK: Hello, ladies. A pleasant surprise. Sorry for the perspiration.

RACHEL: Where did you just come from, Frank?

FRANK: Ballroom dancing with Mr. Vincent.

RACHEL: I've heard he's tough.

FRANK: It's worth it. The gentlemen-to-ladies ratio definitely falls in my favour.

(to RACHEL) But there's still room for others to join.

RACHEL: My schedule's full.

FRANK: Yeah. Anyways, I've got news. Our creative writing professor has decided to—I want to get this right—"cross-pollinate," allowing all his students to all his classes.

WINNIE: Can he do that?

RACHEL: Adventurous.

FRANK: Of course. He's the man!

Beat.

WINNIE: A lot of change. He's also heading up a new committee as well, right? First meeting—next Monday at his house.

FRANK: I do not recall that.

WINNIE: I have the letter here.

WINNIE pulls out a letter.

FRANK: What I said just went up on a poster in Buchanan Lounge. There was nothing about a meeting at his house.

A moment. FRANK looks at their signs.

Are these for the Hastings march on Saturday?

RACHEL: Yeah. Wanna help?

FRANK: I'll swing by later; I don't like perspiring in front of others.

FRANK leaves.

WINNIE: He's so sweet. What about Frank?

RACHEL: I'm already involved.

WINNIE: Oh yeah?

RACHEL: With a conscientious objector.

WINNIE: Is it serious?

RACHEL: No.

WINNIE: Good.

RACHEL: Not yet.

WINNIE: Has he casually mentioned marriage might help him stay in the country?

RACHEL: I conscientiously object to telling you.

WINNIE: Oh gosh, you're so young, you don't know how free you are. Promise me you'll keep an open mind?

RACHEL: I do promise that.

WINNIE: Y'know, this is strange but . . . with this creative writing class I finally feel like a window has opened up. For me. Now. And the air is invigorating!

Beat.

You love him, don't you?

RACHEL: I think so.

WINNIE: Listen, it's just an idea, you should get the professor, to write a nice letter to the US government saying his department simply cannot thrive without hiring your precious conscientious objector. He might be open to it. He certainly loves writing letters.

She raises her poster.

In the meantime, let's raise a little hell!

RACHEL: Winnie!

They laugh.

Black power!

WINNIE: Mexico City!

RACHEL: American sprinters!

WINNIE: Good-looking American sprinters!

TOGETHER: Love is all you need!

SCENE 10

September 23, 1968. Two days earlier. The chancellor's lobby.

A sit-in. Sounds of students milling about, clamouring.

ESTHER: I stand today to protest this university's overwhelmingly high male-to-female ratio in academia. Today we women, and this one courageous male fraternity over here, flash more potential for real change with our inner thighs than most boys will in a lifetime. Get ready! To be free from small-minded patriarchy, masculine assumptions, and covert sexism.

A cheer. EARLE *Birney enters, stepping around students.*

EARLE: Keep up the fight, young people.

ESTHER: You're the one we're fighting.

EARLE *stops in his tracks.*

EARLE: Oh, I don't think so.

ESTHER: You look like establishment to me.

EARLE: No, no. I'm from creative writing. The arts. That's where revolution begins.

ESTHER: Funny. I just quit creative writing, so I know this is where the revolution begins.

EARLE: Why would you do that? Words can be your weapons.

ESTHER: I have words.

EARLE: Oh?

ESTHER raps in a 60s style, free-flowing beat-type poetry.

ESTHER: Imagine your social identity,
your personal serenity
called into question
at a poetry session,
and publicly lynched.
That's right, I said it.
The message I'll spread it round.
True character assassination
Through cultural abomination can be found
Here
Like a cardboard cutout creation

She cuts a piece of cardboard and it falls.

Unjust and unsound.
Are we of one nation?
I thought so!! But feel the separation
Taste humiliation
When a certain anemic academic
From the Creative Writing Epidemic
Projects the pandemic of latent racism
Up in the sky for all to see.

She turns on the overhead projector.

Why, massa, I done reckon I do the same!!
Glory be!!
Play a similar game!!
Assimilate him.
Capture his image!!
Humiliate him
On my line of scrimmage!!

She completes a tiny cut-out of the PROFESSOR *that she holds out for all to see.*

As transparent as tranparencies
On an overhead world
Dance, my little voodoo chile
Dance for your dream girl.

She takes the paper image of the PROFESSOR *and places it on her overhead projector.*

Little man . . . you are now my little puppet
You got a groin? You better cup it
'Cause I'm comin' out kickin'
Your fate's paper thin
Prepare to take your lickin'
Esther Maddox checking in.

EARLE: Well. It sounds like you learned something in class.

ESTHER: I learned if I want change, I won't find it there.

EARLE: I hired Douglas for a reason. It escapes me at the moment but . . . Generally, my vocation is to reimagine the future, so thank you, beautiful poetess, for your feedback. The program is ignited by the talent of tomorrow.

ESTHER: And yet it's taught by the mediocre of today.

He holds out his hand. She takes it.

EARLE: I'm Earle Birney.

SCENE 11

September 23, 1968. Same day. Lecture hall.

The PROFESSOR *sits deep in thought. The room is dim. The melancholic strains of the Beatles's "A Day in the Life" play on the turntable. He sits on the edge of the stage with a globe, which he spins with one hand. His other hand slowly orbits the spinning globe, tracing an imaginary flight path.*

He notices RACHEL *enter.*

PROFESSOR: Rachel?

RACHEL: I went home on the weekend. My dad gave me this to give to you.

She produces a large Russian hat.

He said you'd appreciate it. Maybe it's a joke.

PROFESSOR: No . . . it's . . . it's . . .

RACHEL: Are you all right?

He puts it on. Tries to stop himself from emotion.

PROFESSOR: It's so elusive. So elusive.

RACHEL: What is?

The final bars of the song are stuck on repeat. He gets up and turns off the music.

PROFESSOR: Sit up front. Stay close by. I could use a friendly face.

The PROFESSOR *notices the rest of the class filing in.*

The PROFESSOR *motions for her to sit down and speaks abruptly. Perhaps not everyone has sat down fully.*

The PROFESSOR *begins reciting the poem "My Little Messenger" by Joe Rosenblatt. Not perfectly, with some omissions here and there.*

The janitor starts cleaning next door. The drone of an industrial vacuum. The PROFESSOR *looks angrily toward the back of the room.*

He ends the poem, strangely moved but unsure.

I wish I'd written that.

The PROFESSOR *strides to his lectern, muttering and sneering.*

Any members of the "common crowd"? Any "poseurs" slinking about who aren't quite sure who they are?

ESTHER *is getting restless in her seat.*

ESTHER: I can think of one.

PROFESSOR: What's that?

Silence.

You can bet the Apollo space program is breeding confidence! Tear up your picture books, kiddos! By the end of this year, a man is going to the moon. Meanwhile, the rest of us "travellers" lick our wounds in the dirt, stuck in the most earthy of earth orbits!

ESTHER: I'm sorry. Can we stop?!

PROFESSOR: What's the matter, Miss Mattocks?

ESTHER: Why, why are we here?

PROFESSOR: Why are we here . . . ?

ESTHER: Yeah, what's the point? I mean—

PROFESSOR: Ahhh. I apologize. The contagion that is existential angst. So sorry.

ESTHER: No. That's not what I—

PROFESSOR: If it's any comfort, these feelings are undeniably a soul stimulant for artistic growth—

ESTHER: No!

She stands.

I literally want to know. What's the point, what's the goal of this class?

PROFESSOR: Did you receive a syllabus . . . ?

ESTHER: What? No—

PROFESSOR: Why are you *standing*?

ESTHER: I've got the syllabus.

She holds it up.

The one that's completely irrelevant.

PROFESSOR: Everyone gets the same syllabus.

ESTHER: A lot of quotes about finding greatness through "the creative impulse." But three weeks into the semester . . . When do we work on this?

PROFESSOR: You want more "exercises and assignments." That may be a lovely theoretical discussion, but it's not . . . for today. Schedule an appointment during office hours.

ESTHER: You cancelled them.

PROFESSOR: Fine! Let's talk. But know that today begins seven years ago in 1961, when most of you were playing with your butterfly yo-yos. We in the West looked on, suspicious. For *Yuri Gagarin*, the Russian cosmonaut, had already stuffed his wee body into *Vostok 1*!

ESTHER: *(muttering)* I can't believe this.

PROFESSOR: The first man to experience that breadth of flight, April 12, 1961. His spirit passed this morning. So think! In the scope of things, we have no time at all.

The PROFESSOR *gets distracted by the industrial vacuum.*

(trying to be patient) Can someone tell them these rooms are clean enough?

FRANK *raises his hand.*

FRANK: Frank is off.

FRANK *exits eagerly.*

PROFESSOR: Thank you.

The vacuum shuts off.

This morning Yuri Gagarin spoke to me: "For what are you born on the earth . . . for? How," he whispered, "do you dare to dream?

FRANK *bursts back into the room.*

FRANK: Do you want *us* to answer?

PROFESSOR: No! Use your imagination!

The PROFESSOR *thrusts a paper up, now in the shape of an airplane.*

I wanted to write transcendence into the sky.

The PROFESSOR *paces wildly, squeezing his airplane. He begins a slow descent to the floor, out of sync with his rapid-fire thoughts.*

Am I a Vostok booster rocket crashing, predictably, into the middle of the Siberian Sea!? Bent out of shape, mangled . . . craving authentic Gagarin back at my side? Or am I Gherman Titov, Gagarin's backup, ready to go in principle, sure, but ultimately stuck in a holding pattern. Nobody's building statues of Titov!

ESTHER: I can appreciate, Professor, how bad you're feeling.

But your tangents about exploration and Russian space capsules don't belong here.

PROFESSOR: Listen everyone, a pioneer's death is a tangent now!

ESTHER: In the art world, you make a mess, you work it out to expand the self. This is a creative writing class, but you seem to go out of your way to avoid the topic.

RACHEL: Whoa.

PROFESSOR: Oh, the art world. Please. Work it out right now, then. In front of us. What—no canvas?

ESTHER: I'm a graphic artist.

The PROFESSOR shrugs. ESTHER packs up her things.

This city is onto something! You're throwing it away.

PROFESSOR: I'm doing the opposite.

ESTHER: Not in this class! Today, for instance, we're supposed to present our poems—

PROFESSOR: Wait, wait. I'm not . . . you think that's today?

ESTHER: I know it is. I—

PROFESSOR: Whoa. One at a time. Let's check . . . umm . . . Rachel?

He finds RACHEL.

Yes. Go ahead.

RACHEL: And do what?

PROFESSOR: Is there a presentation of some sort due today?

She checks her notes.

RACHEL: Yes. The response-to-nature poems—

PROFESSOR: Ah, ah. What do your notes say?

RACHEL: It says they're quote "due next class." Unquote.

PROFESSOR: Correct. And what is the special caveat to that reminder?

RACHEL: I don't know.

PROFESSOR: The special . . . don't know?! Is that the semester should be viewed as one long, continual class.

ESTHER: It's starting to feel like that.

PROFESSOR: So that—keep up now—"next class" could be today or two weeks from today.

(to RACHEL) You don't have any of this?

ESTHER: Esther Jean Mattocks. Cross me off your list. I've got better things to do.

FRANK: You going to the sit-in, Esther?

ESTHER: I'm leading it, baby.

PROFESSOR: Better things to do, heh?

ESTHER smiles at FRANK.

ESTHER: See you there, then.

(to RACHEL) What about you?

The PROFESSOR turns back to his lectern.

PROFESSOR: Bah.

RACHEL: I didn't know about it.

The PROFESSOR *angrily sorts through a clump of papers.*

PROFESSOR: That's fine. I'll cross you off. Easily done, easily . . . where is that sheet . . . ?

ESTHER: Make your time count. Chancellor's lobby at one.

PROFESSOR: Go about your day!

She begins to head out.

ESTHER: Come to the Johnny Neon installation at the gallery this week. He's sponsoring me.

FRANK: Vancouver Art Gallery.

ESTHER: Right.

PROFESSOR: Such a narcissistic generation.

WINNIE *has entered from the back. She looks through her oversized bag for a pen.*

You're late, Mrs. Martins!

WINNIE: Sorry, Professor.

PROFESSOR: Every protest around here comes drenched in self-importance—

ESTHER: That's complete bullshit.

WINNIE: Oh.

PROFESSOR: Oh. Is it?

ESTHER: Yes. And we're not "a generation!" I'm so sick of that—

PROFESSOR: You know, you may want to consider the journalism department.

Apparently—

ESTHER: This is the generation that actually cares about something other than themselves!

PROFESSOR: —the *Georgia Straight*, I've read, needs reporters comfortable with obscenity!

ESTHER: So, in closing, it's been a fucking waste of time.

She goes to leave. Shock. The PROFESSOR *steps off the stage and closes in on* ESTHER.

PROFESSOR: You disrespect me and this institution like that?

ESTHER: You're right. My adjective was misplaced. A waste of fucking time. 'Cause that's what's "of the essence," Professor. Who has time to sit here watching you in front of us masturbating!

Silence. Everyone is taken aback.

FRANK: *(to anyone)* What did she say?

WINNIE: That's too far, Esther . . . even for an artist.

PROFESSOR: *(steaming)* Should've saved my *Georgia Straight* insult . . . Who else thinks I'm up here . . . doing *that*—M-word–ing?

FRANK *puts his hand up.*

FRANK: Question.

PROFESSOR: Figuratively, obviously.

FRANK *puts his hand down. The* PROFESSOR *surveys the rest of the room.*

See? No one. Ambusher.

He begins to return to the lectern.

I guess that's how the rude girls speak in Hogan's Alley, is it, missy?

ESTHER: Pardon me?

PROFESSOR: Forget it.

ESTHER looks right through the PROFESSOR, who's between the front of the stage and the lectern. ESTHER moves powerfully and sensually close to him as she responds.

ESTHER: Yeah, Professa, that be where I learned some cuss words. If you're likin' what I say, way down inside your dirty child-heart, make sure you partake in our nigga brothels. We'll show *you* a good time 'specially.

She walks back up the aisle. And out.

The PROFESSOR laughs weakly. He checks his watch. He looks up in the air . . . It's awkward.

WINNIE: Professor. You need to apologize.

At the back of the room, EARLE enters, whistles like a theremin.

EARLE: The silent supplication to the muse. I could smell the inspiration from the hall.

FRANK: Earle Birney.

EARLE: Sorry, Dougie, I saw a student leave and assumed class was over.

PROFESSOR: No, it's not a . . . This is uh . . . I'm sure you all know . . . Earle Mister Professor Birney is the, uh . . . well, he's a, he's a—

EARLE: Dinosaur.

PROFESSOR: He's the originator of the program.

EARLE: Interrupting a great class, no doubt. I'm just a wandering hallway fool in his dotage.

PROFESSOR: No, oh no. Don't you believe it. This man's a . . . genius. Are you . . . uh, did you just get back? Sorry I'm . . .

EARLE: *(to class)* You're witness to a surprise reunion.

(to PROFESSOR) Yes, I'm back,

(to students) Looks like I'll be "acting" chair of the department.

PROFESSOR: Oh. Lucky us.

EARLE: I'll try to stay out of the way. Do my little tinkering. "Reimagining," I'm calling it. I just got back from San Francisco; ears are still a little—

PROFESSOR: Oh, that must have been exciting.

EARLE: What? No, nothing special, but I did meditate with Ginsberg at the Tosca Cafe.

PROFESSOR: Allen Ginsberg is an American—

EARLE: Dougie, they've been in your class for three weeks; they know who Allen Ginsberg is, yes?

PROFESSOR: Uh, probably. The class is more writing than read—

EARLE: Doesn't matter. The point is: I had a vision of an equally unparalleled scene here in Vancouver.

PROFESSOR: See, everyone? Looking ahead.

EARLE: And there's no reason why not! We've got bissett, we've got Purdy, we've got . . .

PROFESSOR: Joe Rosenblatt.

EARLE: Hmm?

PROFESSOR: Joe . . . He wrote a great poem about cats. Just read it.

Beat.

Now that you're here, though—

EARLE: Forget me, widen your vision! The future is sitting right in front of you!

EARLE looks to the students, pats the PROFESSOR.

I'll let you continue. Oh, I love the spirit of this age!

He winks and leaves.

The PROFESSOR takes his time crossing to his stool and opens his bag lunch. He looks at his plain sandwich before biting into it. He looks up at the class.

PROFESSOR: You can be dismissed. You can go.

WINNIE: What do you mean?

PROFESSOR: You're dismissed. Leave.

RACHEL: Now?

PROFESSOR: Now.

Beat.

FRANK: He's tricking us.

PROFESSOR: No, I'm not. I . . . I have nothing to offer you.

Beat.

FRANK: He's still tricking us—

PROFESSOR: Stop saying I'm tricking you.

This class is over.

WINNIE: We're here now.

The PROFESSOR shakes his head.

Quit wallowing and get back to "transcendence in the sky."

PROFESSOR: The younger me . . .

WINNIE: No! You have a gift; you inspire with your words. But you need to relax.

PROFESSOR: Sure.

WINNIE: Did you know that—upon re-entry to Earth's atmosphere, Gagarin was whistling?

PROFESSOR: Whistling? Is that true?

WINNIE: Yes.

PROFESSOR: And what do you suppose compelled him, Mrs. Martins?

WINNIE: Call me Winnie.

A connection. He smiles at WINNIE.

PROFESSOR: Winnie.

WINNIE: Perhaps he got high enough above the earth to feel how much it held him . . . and how much he held it.

PROFESSOR: Affinity.

WINNIE: Love.

Beat.

Working on this poem was the high point of my week! Unlike Esther . . . everything you've talked about in here—space, escape, longing—hasn't seemed out of bounds to me. I'm . . . I'm going through some changes myself and . . . Well, I hope you'll hear the gratitude.

PROFESSOR: Are you saying, you incorporated my words, Mrs. Martins?

WINNIE *nods.*

WINNIE: In a matter of speaking.

PROFESSOR: I have allowed these walls to be altars of mediocrity! They have been the confines of my broken capsule! But no more weakness. It's time to soar my way!

Wild-eyed and delirious, the PROFESSOR *has made it back to where he started.*

Ha! Ha! Who's M-word–ing now?

FRANK: Is this still a writing class, Professor?

The PROFESSOR *takes* FRANK*'s head in his hands.*

PROFESSOR: All that, and more, Frank! And who knows where it will lead?

FRANK: *(joining in)* I have no idea!

PROFESSOR: Rhetorical questions, Frank. We'll work on that.

The PROFESSOR *laughs and bounds up on stage.*

He gleefully grabs the paper airplane lying on the floor. Maybe he picks it up and throws it again with abandon.

You all look so beautiful. I see myself in you! And I have, class, just in this moment, revived my office hours!

WINNIE: Professor. Can I present my poem?

Everyone looks at WINNIE.

PROFESSOR: Yes. Of course. Go ahead, my dove.

The PROFESSOR *retreats and gives the floor to* WINNIE.

WINNIE: This class has been part—

PROFESSOR: Please. Call me Douglas.

WINNIE: Douglas. Part of my flight into the unknown.

She reads.

We all need to fly.
It's just the launch pads that are different.
Do we float unguarded
Hoping to bump up against the unknown?
Can we hope for New Life Forms, new Surfaces to Imprint?
Reminding us of home . . .
Leaving the Earth doesn't mean I won't care for it
Doesn't mean I won't coddle the fear stuck in my throat
Doesn't mean I won't dream of an earlier time
Doesn't mean I don't have my loved ones' best interests
In my heart to stay.

WINNIE's poem is taken over by sound. Countdown to liftoff. "T minus fifteen seconds. Ignition of remaining rocket boosters. Liftoff thrust stable," and so on.

Sound: T minus ten seconds, nine, eight, seven, six, five, four, three—

The PROFESSOR looks at WINNIE. His lectern begins to shake and rumble.

Two, one . . . Liftoff. Engine explosions. Possible projection of rocket ship.

PROFESSOR: *(shouting, ecstatic)* I can rise again! There's room in the void! What are the limits of this age?! The end can be the beginning! Class dismissed!

He grabs his Russian hat, comes down off the stage, and starts out the back. We hear the sounds of the Apollo 8 *mission.*

INTERLUDE

At the end of Act One, the audience is asked to refer to their programs for instructions to the Interlude, an interactive treasure hunt that takes place in the public spaces of the Space Centre (lobby, gallery, washrooms, outside, etc.)

A map printed on the program leads audience members to various locations throughout the building where they can find quirky "exhibits" that require some form of interaction and often participation between individuals.

Often one exhibit has a connection to another elsewhere in the building and it's up to the audience to discover these different callbacks.

The premise: a group of high school students on the cusp of graduation have created an interactive experience for the grown-ups that have come to see a play. These characters connect the two acts.

The students are doing this as an assignment for their teacher, NOA *Martins.* NOA *is* Winnie's *unborn baby from Act One. She shows up as the elderly keeper of the Star Theatre in Act Two, set eighty years after Act One. Two of the three students credited for this exhibit, though present only through their playful installations, are also in Act Two.* NEIL *is a transhumanist pioneer in the future, and Oliver is a transgender woman named* STARR.

The third student responsible for this installation, HAFA, *has passed away in the future at the time of Act Two; but her daughter is our protagonist in 2048.* HAFA *is already familiar to us as she's been texting with us since before the show and perhaps has friended us on Facebook. She's also an aspiring filmmaker and environmental activist. She's making a documentary that is alluded to in the Interlude. We see some of the documentary in Act Two as a lost relic recovered.*

The instructions to the treasure hunt of the Interlude read:

Intermission: Interlude (2013) invitation to the last night of analogue

For: You

Where: MacMillan Space Centre

Date: Tonight

From: Neil, Hafa, and Oliver—graduating class 2013

Throughout the building there are hidden experiences for you to discover. The path you choose is the right one. How will you spend your time?

Game Instructions

When Act One ends, you have twenty minutes to visit as many stations as you can.

Find your icon (rocket or bird) on your map and go to your unique starting place.

At each station, you'll see your icon and instructions on how to engage. On the back of your map, there is a list of ten things for you to gather.

The Interlude ends when you've completed all ten stations or the intermission time is up. At that point, head immediately to the star marked "Win" on your map and you'll be led into the future!

You have exactly twenty minutes! Go!

There are two paths: Rocket Route and Bird Route

The map has stations marked on it numbered one to twenty. Programs indicate which station to start at, with each program having a different starting station.

At each station there's a set of instructions teaching the audience how to interact. Below are the instructions.

ROCKET ROUTE

STATION 1: SOAR DOVE

Put a bird into the cannon

Let it fly!

Take a bird-splatter from the nest.

Take it to the cork board straight ahead and to your left.

Pin it up.

> *Taxidermized birds are perched inside a large glass enclosed space resembling some sort of walk-in atrium. Audience members take shots at the birds with slingshots and then pick up feathered "remains" from the floor which they can add to a cooperatively built collage on the wall.*

STATION 2: OUR CAMPING SPOT

We're sleeping over here tonight. The Space Centre is okay with it.

Go into the tent and take one of our stuffed animals to keep you company.

> *In the lower level there's a forgotten courtyard—an outdoor space completely surrounded on four sides by the building's structure, but open to the sky. It's quite dream-like—both indoors and outdoors at the same time. We set up a tent where the present-day characters were camping out for the night, but only their stuffed animals are there when the audience arrives. A recording of their voices played from within the tent providing three monologues from each character—each confessing a secret and their fears and trepidations for the future.*

STATION 3: AUGMENTATION PASSPORT

Position yourself in the lines

Add something to augment yourself from the selection

Put a mole on your face

Take a picture and text it to this number

When you leave the washroom pin your bird splatter to the bulletin board

> *In this station in both the women's and men's washrooms, two-dimensional paper props such as cartoonish fake moustaches, crowns, glasses, exaggerated lips, etc., are available for the audience to add to their face as they take a selfie, which they then text to the number on the bathroom wall. The number belongs to a cellphone that lived with the jukebox in station #17.*

STATION 4: GOODBYE CHILDHOOD

Attach your mascot to the top of the string.

Let it go on a ride into the past.

Yell "incoming!"

> *This station encourages you to take the stuffed animal you adopted from the tent in station #2 and send it flying down a zip line that runs from the lobby to the lower level. Stuffies accumulate in a pile of lost innocence.*

STATION 5: SOCIAL EXPERIMENT

Stand on the X.

Call this number using your cellphone.

Listen to the person on the other end, as you normally would. They might ask you to do something. Maybe you'll do it.

Put an X on your clothes with tape.

> *The phone number provided belongs to an operational pay phone that is tucked away in the lower level near the mysterious courtyard. The voice on the other end would be another audience member who is at station #12.*

STATION 6: ROCKET

Go outside (!)

Choose a rocket.

Pump it up.

Let it go.

See whose goes higher.

Take a rocket.

Outside the building an usher helps audience members launch bottle rockets—a classic childhood science project.

STATION 7: PERSONAL PLANETARIUM

Go inside the planetarium.

See what you see.

Find meaning in the stars.

A giant papier-mâché dome structure is perched atop a stand in the public gallery and there is room for one person to crawl under and stand up with their head inside the dome.

Pinholes allow light in, creating a lo-fi planetarium with constellations visible. Initials of the creators are visible within a heart of stars—a teenaged profession of love.

STATION 8: SKYPE WITH A SENIOR

Sit down and say hello to someone interesting.

Let them know how old you are.

They'll let you know what they expected from the future when they were your age. You're two people talking! Who knows what will happen?

Give other people a chance.

> *There is a laptop open with the video conference application Skype providing a link to a volunteer in distant location.*
>
> *The volunteer is an elder in their 70s who is there to chat with any audience members who sit down and engage. If the audience member tells the elder how old they are, the volunteer reflects on what their life was like at that age.*

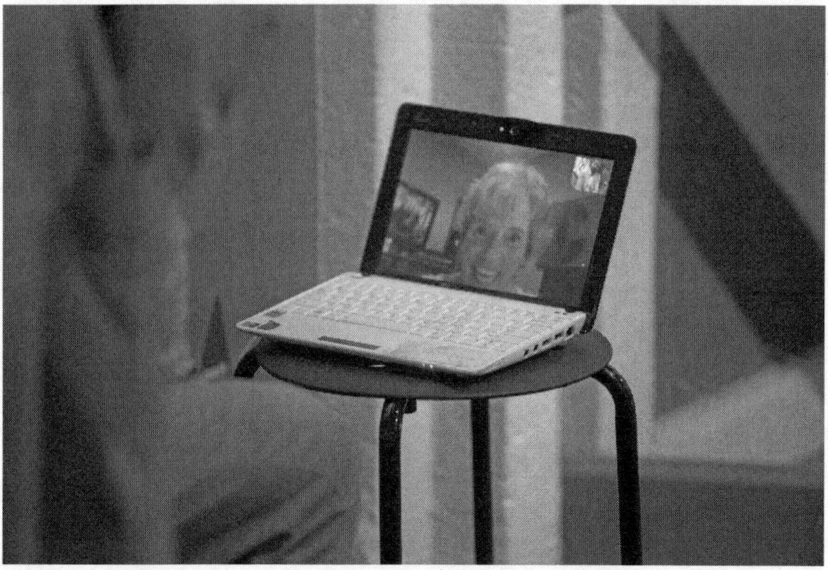

STATION 9: SENSATION STATION

Feel/taste/smell inside the box.

Guess what it is.

Check if you're right (and then hide it for the next person).

Take a sample pouch.

> *This is a whimsical adaptation of the Halloween haunted house activity where, blindfolded, you stick your hands into bowls of grapes and are told they're eyeballs, or cooked macaroni suggested as brains. In this station the audience reaches into boxes marked with titles like "memory," "insight," "hope," and "regret" and the objects felt would be things like feathers, magnetic audio tape, wooden match sticks, and dice.*

STATION 10: THE VIEW FROM ABOVE

One person gets in the spacesuit. Put on the headphones you find there.

There are two iPods.

Press go on both of them at exactly the same time.

Take a picture.

Using an existing display of a hollowed out backless spacesuit used by visitors for taking silly photos of themselves, the station asks people to work in pairs. One person gets in the spacesuit, looking out through the helmet while wearing headphones provided, which offer instructions to make facial gestures and look left, right, up, and down. The other person wears a second set of headphones while watching their partner and listening to a monologue that syncs up to the facial expressions, transforming their partner into a character in a story about a spacewalk.

BIRD ROUTE

STATION 11: COMFORT ANIMAL

Take a mascot.

Name it.

Bond.

> *Audience members find stuffed animals on the lower level at the end of the zip line of station #4.*

STATION 12: A PAYPHONE THAT STILL WORKS

When the phone rings, pick it up.

Open a letter and read the instructions in it to the person on the other end of the line.

When you're done, say goodbye.

Will you ever again speak on a payphone?

Take a "token" from the coin return.

> *The caller is the audience member in station #5. The token can be used in the jukebox at station #17.*

STATION 13: OBSOLETE DREAMS

Take a piece of paper from a person outside of the washroom or the tray beside the washroom door.

Look at this visual representation of your dream. Open your flower and find the interpretation of your dream.

Tack it up on the wall.

I hope you keep dreaming.

> *This station is a blend of origami, fortune cookie wisdom, and a collaborative collage.*

STATION 14: FLOWERS

Go into the tent and tuck your mascot in.

Take the time you need to say goodbye, and then leave it there.

Take a flower from the box in front of the tent, and keep it with you.

> *This completes the journey of the stuffed animal that travelled between the tent in station #2, to the zip line in station #4, down to the comfort animals of station #11, and then back to the tent.*

STATION 15: EIGHT DAYS A WEEK

Put on the pin that says "Space Centre Employee."

Pick up the walkie-talkie.

Say the name on your tag, and "Over."

Listen to what the boss asks you to do. You care about space, so you do your job well.

> *This is a playful improv led by one of the show's staff who watches the audience member with the walkie-talkie from their position at the front desk.*

STATION 16: LETTERS

One person sits at the typewriter.

Another dictates a letter and fills in the blanks as they go with the appropriate words.

The person at the typewriter types what they hear, and then folds up the letter, puts it in an envelope, and then into the mailbox.

> *In a cross between Mad Libs and broken telephone, visitors clack out transcriptions of semi-improvised letters on a manual typewriter set up inside the main gallery. It might become a spectator sport.*

STATION 17: JUKEBOXES ARE MAGIC

Don't press anything yet.

Wait until you get an incoming photo on the cellphone.

This is your dance partner for the last dance of high school prom.

Pick a song specifically for them and them alone.

Text back, "This one's for you."

> *A dedicated cellphone is perched upon the vintage jukebox set up in the lobby. The texts (and selfies) come from audience members at the Augmentation Passport Station (#3). Music played in response can be heard throughout the building.*

STATION 18: STAR GATE

We're watching *2001: A Space Odyssey.*

Take some seeds and hold on to them.

Stay as long as you like, but don't miss your future.

> *A circular room, like a little escape pod, is tucked near the back of the public gallery. It's a small* AV *room for showing videos and we've turned it into a slumber party space. Sleeping bags are laid out and on the screen plays the climax of* 2001: A Space Odyssey, *which is a sort of psychedelic light show representing the transcendence of human consciousness—a prelude to Act Two. As one of the collectable souvenirs, audience members pick up popcorn kernels labelled "seeds"—an image with a payoff in Act Two.*

STATION 19: WHAT HAPPENS NEXT

Add an element to the story or change the path of the story.

Go with your first choice.

A wordless series of simple black and white images, like a panel comic strip, tells the story of a journey to the stars. Audience members can change the order, add or remove images, or crop the images to change the journey.

STATION 20: SECRET PROJECTIONS

Click through the projections.

Someone stands behind the screen on the X.

Make the image that feels right.

Dual carousel slide projectors cast images on a semi-translucent screen, one from behind and one in front, creating surreal composites out of random nature shots. One subject stands in the light of the rear projector, becoming a silhouette on the screen. Another audience member uses remotes to move through slides from either projector to create a satisfying composition.

Interlude's end.

When players have collected the various souvenirs at the various stations, they bring them to the Win Station and pin their own star onto an image of a nebula—a birthing ground for young stars.

From there, they are led up a back stairwell, not normally accessed by the public, to the upper level and the entrance to the Star Theatre.

PART TWO: 2048 TRANSCENDENCE IS NEAR

SCENE 1: PRE-SHOW

Entering the Star Theatre below a projection of a pinky-blue sky with clouds, we find CHICHI, *an augmented human, a caregiver, and a transhumanist disciple caring for a man,* NEIL, *who is sitting up in bed wearing a bathrobe, facing upstage.* AVA, *his daughter, sits with her legs dangling over the circular stage, which is in the centre of the Star Theatre, encircled by the audience.*

The set is composed of modular blocks of varying sizes that can be arranged as furniture. Their surfaces are clean, white, and flat. Video mapping allows them to be animated as individual screens or to be "wrapped" in projected colour and texture to take on the appearance of furniture, appliances, or other devices. Small, abstractly shaped screens perch atop slender rods, like large futuristic flowers which also animate with projections.

CHICHI *repeatedly mops* NEIL'*s forehead. She occasionally wrings her cloth out into a bowl. A couple of times she waters the plant in a nearby flower pot with the contents of the bowl.*

Other cast members sit on the small stage. Very faintly the sound of rain can be heard.

CHICHI *lifts an object (a balloon or small set fragment) and blesses it with a flick of the holy sweat. It suddenly radiates light and reveals an image of the earth from space.*

Shift to:

SCENE 2: THE PILLARS OF CREATION

CHICHI claps her hands once and the sky changes to pulsing green lasers. The opening, swelling strains of Pink Floyd's "Comfortably Numb," play very loudly, fill the space. She claps again.

The lasers and music grind down pathetically to a halt. Now all we hear is the rain. Scanning the vast control panel that only she can see, she curses.

CHICHI: Crudge. Who changed my settings?

She claps twice more and the sky shifts to a view of deep space Pillars of Creation. Soft "modern" music (i.e., adult easy listening in 2048) plays.

CHICHI adjusts the settings and turns the volume up enough to cover the sound of the rain as the scene shifts.

A title card appears: "Part Two: Transcendence (is Near)"

SCENE 3: AVA'S STUDY

Projected images on the dome suggest a lavish personal library.

AVA: I try to think like a human. But it's hard. It keeps slipping away.

Lines echo as we toggle between live speech and voice-over.

I try to think like a human. But it's hard. We've changed so much, so fast.

Images flash on the set pieces. A suggestion of the multiverse.

I try to think like a human. But it's hard. We've changed so much, so fast, and now to slow the thoughts down, to stretch ideas out, one word at a time . . . that's very, very hard.

Visions of her teenaged parents appear.

I imagine travelling back in time. That seems human. To want to go back. So, I imagine going back. To the year I was born. Tell my human teenage mother—never knew her, because she died— Tell my human teenage father—never knew him, because he changed, no longer human, but augmented, like me—and tell them . . .

She stands.

Hello, my name is Ava, I'm your daughter, from the future, from 2048, and you will not believe what it's like. What would you think of us? How can I describe what happens?

The scenes shift seamlessly as AVA *is experiencing these thoughts while at the same time interacting with* CHICHI *and her dad in the physical space, as well as with her friend* LAN *in a virtual environment.*

SCENE 4: SANCTUARY

AVA *is working with* CHICHI, *who is clipping* NEIL'*s toenails as he sits crossing and uncrossing his fingers.*

AVA: Hi, Dad; how are you Chichi? How is he?

CHICHI: He's running a little fever.

AVA: A fever?

CHICHI: I know, right? It's not good, is it? Or maybe it's okay?

AVA: Well, it's a symptom of being sick.

CHICHI: I don't know. Is it? I've never seen it happen to anyone except the obsoletes.

Silence.

AVA: Well, you think we'd know if it was a problem. You're looking good, Dad.

Do you think he knows I'm here?

CHICHI: Oh, sure. In ways you can't imagine.

Shift:

SCENE 5: A LUNAR LANDSCAPE

AVA *observes a projection of Earth from the surface of the moon.*

AVA: It's so hard to think like this. To tell a story instead of just know a story. But I practice . . .

Today, through a virtual reality that is for all intents and purposes exactly the same as physical reality, our brains can be partitioned into one thousand points of view. So, I can be thinking these thoughts at the same time as I—

Shift:

SCENE 6: SANCTUARY

AVA *and* CHICHI *care for her dad.*

AVA: *(voice-over)* Am physically present in this environment. And at the same time as I am in this conversation.

Shift:

SCENE 7: THINK TANK

LAN: Do you see this?

AVA: Yes, Lan, and I'm ignoring it.

LAN: You don't want to hold me?

AVA: It gets complicated.

LAN: That's good complication though.

Shift:

SCENE 8: AVA'S STUDY

AVA: And meanwhile I can be hundreds of other places. See all the sights, read all the books, enjoy all the company I could desire.

Shift:

SCENE 9: THINK TANK

LAN: Make me something fun.

AVA: *(voice-over)* We now exist almost entirely as creators.

LAN: I love your work.

AVA: And with all these selves available to us, there's always an audience. Still, I often feel stretched.

AVA: I'm supposed to catalogue DNA.

LAN: Can't it wait?

AVA: We've lost starlings. Species are dropping like flies.

LAN: Flies are rocking though. Some really great new housefly mutations.

AVA: They're everywhere.

LAN: This is a busy time.

AVA: I'm rushing to get it all done before we transcend.

LAN: Do you really think we will.

AVA: Don't you?

LAN: Nope.

AVA: I envy your conviction.

LAN: *(noticing that* AVA *is sobbing)* You're crying, let me hold you.

AVA: Huh, I'm not—oh that, that's an emotional response to—part of me's watching an old movie and it's such good acting from such another time. Embarrassing.

LAN: Let's see.

She shows him.

Oh, that's a good one. Yeah, I've been getting a bit of experiential leakage as well. The other night I screamed in the middle of giving a friend a lyrical massage, because another me was attacked by a godawful spider in the Australian outback.

AVA: Maybe the system can't support everyone having a thousand selves.

LAN: It's a bandwidth issue.

AVA: It's buggy.

LAN: It's buggy because we need more bandwidth.

AVA: You know, I have an idea, a way to solve that.

The sound of rain pouring down as the scene shifts.

SCENE 10: AVA'S STUDY

AVA: Okay, here's what happened. We are the product of accelerating changes in a few different branches of science: genetics, nanotechnology, artificial intelligence, computer science, and playwriting. It was that fifth one that no one expected to figure in to the equation, but what can you say? Life has so many surprises.

Now we think with the speed of a computer. The quest for a conscious machine was solved when you, Neil, came up with a program that contained one important organic element: your brain. Your human intuition is the element that allows the machine to think for itself. You are the server, and through you we are connected to all human knowledge and to each other.

Does that make sense? How would a human describe this? Am I making it harder than it should be?

Meanwhile:

SCENE 11: THINK TANK

LAN: It's just a thought experiment. Don't stress about it.

AVA: I want to be able to do this though; to think like them.

LAN: Why?

AVA: To relate to them.

LAN: To the obsoletes?

AVA: I don't like that term.

LAN: Again, why?

AVA: Don't they deserve our consideration?

SCENE 12: FAN MAIL FROM A STARR

Rain. Shitty, endless rain.

STARR: I'm responding to your request for interviews with pre-augmented humans that aren't D-forty positive. I actually am D-forty positive, you probably can tell that somehow, but I thought I'd write anyway, because I happen to personally know Neil Gaze. I went to high school with him when he was pre-augmented. I lost track of him after. But if you are interested, I have an old notebook of Neil's. Maybe it's valuable. Maybe not. It's got written on it "Transcendence notes." But it also has "Pink Floyd rules" and "4:20" with a doodle of a stoned pelican smoking a doob. So, I don't want to oversell the thing. I don't walk so great anymore, but I think I could come to you if you gave me an address. Your message gave me the impression that Neil was around? That he lived in Burnaby. Though I thought he was in Geneva. Or dead. Anyway, I don't expect to hear back. I don't really know anything about you types, augmented or whatever you are. So, I'll sign off by saying not all of us regular people hate all of you. But I probably do a little. Joking. Not totally. Starr.

SCENE 13: SANCTUARY

In the sanctuary, CHICHI is grinding NEIL's toenails with a mortar and pestle as AVA comes in.

AVA: I got a letter.

CHICHI: A letter?

AVA: A piece of paper, with writing, from a human.

CHICHI: Let's see.

Zap, indicating a thought transfer.

Hm. Oh—no, no. Why would you want her to come over?

AVA: Well—it might be nice?

CHICHI: For who?

AVA: For her.

CHICHI: You can't presume to know what they need.

Zaps.

AVA: It doesn't seem fair.

CHICHI: Species go extinct. It's sad because we're up close, awkward because we're coexisting—old species and new species side by side—but wait four hundred million years and see what has risen from the ashes.

So much more beauty, more than we can imagine. We're playing the long game here, Ava.

AVA: Yeah, that's fine for us to say, we've got options. They're the ones that will be stuck on a dying planet.

CHICHI: Maybe. Maybe not. But here, look: I'm adding him to the soil in the garden and . . . there is consciousness emerging in the plants. Can you sense that? It's starting to spread, we're very close now. Don't stand in the way, Ava.

CHICHI sprinkles the ground-up toenails into a planter box. Suddenly they begin to radiate energy, colour, light, and music.

Let's tuck him in.

They ease NEIL back onto the bed.

CHICHI sings to NEIL. If she knew its origins the song may sound like "You Are Very Star" by the Rheostatics.

AVA: Where did you get that?

CHICHI: I just woke up one day and it was in my head. He's inside us all.

AVA: Why doesn't he leave anything for me?

CHICHI: You're not listening.

CHICHI exits, leaving AVA alone with NEIL.

AVA stands and looks at the flower box with the glowing flowers. Flies buzz gloriously around—it sounds like music.

AVA: I don't know. I'm just not at your level.

She doesn't notice that NEIL has struggled to his feet. He reaches out toward her as he takes a shuffling step in her direction.

The doorbell rings.

Oh my god. She's really here.

AVA leaves the sanctuary without ever seeing her father reaching for her.

The scene shifts to the living space of this apartment. The doorbell rings again.

Shift:

SCENE 14: WORLD'S COLLIDE

As the doorbell's chime resonates in a long, slow decay, AVA opens the door and finds herself face to face with STARR.

Neither is quite prepared for what she sees.

AVA: Hello.

STARR: Hello.

AVA: Hello.

STARR: Hello?

AVA: Hello.

STARR: Hello.

AVA: Hello, hello.

STARR: Hello.

AVA: I love you.

STARR: Oh, what? Um—

AVA: *(to self)* Shoot, this is hard.

Hello. Am I baking consensus?

STARR: Um?

AVA: Am I baking consensus?

STARR: Are you . . . ?

AVA: Am. Am. Am. Am I . . . Am. A.—M. —A.M.—A.M. Radio, tuning in to your channel. A.M. Am. I.—Am. I. Making. Am I making sense to. To. T. O. T.O. Toronto. Toronto Maple Leafs. To. Am. I. Making. Sense. To. You.

(suddenly clear) Am I making sense to you?

STARR: No.

AVA: Is that a yes?

STARR: No.

Beat.

AVA: I'll take that as a no.

STARR: I'm . . . I'm probably doing something wrong.

AVA: *(to self)* Sheez, this is hard. I had it earlier.

Beat.

STARR: Am I supposed to be . . . ? Is there a thingy that I need . . . a . . . ? I don't know what you're doing.

AVA: Okay. I have a prepared text. I will read to . . . you from a prepared . . . text. Okay?

STARR: Sure.

AVA: Did you get that?

STARR: Get what?

AVA: The text.

STARR: No. You haven't said anything.

AVA: I'll say it again.

STARR: Okay.

AVA: Okay?

STARR: Okay.

AVA: You understand?

STARR: Understand what?

AVA: The text.

STARR: What text? There's no text.

AVA: Wait. Let me . . . decompress it.

STARR: You know I'm not online, yes? I get dial-up at my co-op, but I'm . . .

AVA: Here's the text:

She's suddenly strangely convivial; everything is said with a sort of chummy and overly familiar air.

Hello, my name is Ava, that's right, that's right, and I'm Neil Gaze's daughter, and like him, I'm augmented. I recognize that puts me at an immediate advantage. If that sounds threatening, offensive, the fault is entirely mine. I am at an advantage, but I will not take advantage. If you do not have augmented people in your lives, you may have acquired opinions about augmented people that cast us in an unfavourable light, but I would like to establish that I take seriously a position of non-interference. I will state that I personally believe in augmentation for all; even though that's not available right now, that's what I believe in and you are welcome here.

Beat.

STARR: Well, thank you.

AVA: I'm sorry, that didn't sound as good as I expected.

STARR: That's all right.

AVA: Is it?

STARR: Sure.

AVA: Sure?

STARR: Sure.

AVA: Can you hear me?

STARR: Yes.

AVA: The words.

STARR: Yes.

AVA: And anything else?

STARR: Um . . .

Meanwhile AVA *is chatting with* LAN.

AVA: *(to* LAN*)* I did not realize how sparse, how little information flows in a conversation with one of them.

LAN: Yeah, I know they just sort of do one thing at a time regardless of how insignificant. Checkmate. And also I came.

AVA: *(to* LAN*)* But when she touched me, I found I could focus, I could hear, and slow down.

STARR: Give us a hug.

STARR *embraces* AVA. AVA *is surprised.* STARR *pulls back and begins to speak. As she does, she touches* AVA*'s arm, her hair, squeezes her hands. The contact is mesmerizing to* AVA.

Pause.

SCENE 15: BRIDGING THE GAP

STARR: You're Ava? Little Ava? The last time I saw you, you were a baby. A Facebook update. But now, suddenly I feel like I've always known you.

AVA *snaps to.*

AVA: Come in, please.

STARR: Thank you so much, I—

Beat.

Where exactly are we, by the way.

AVA: Where are we?

STARR: This building.

AVA: This is . . . I'm not sure what you mean.

STARR: I thought this might be . . . I wasn't sure where I was going. I thought maybe it's a business address.

AVA: Right.

STARR: Or a laboratory, maybe.

AVA: Sure.

STARR: Or an outreach centre.

AVA: Okay. All those work.

STARR: But it looks like a crappy one-bedroom apartment.

AVA: Oh?

Beat.

STARR: Oh my goodness, no offence.

AVA: Oh! This place. My dad lives here. And you can't offend me.

STARR: I wouldn't want to. How's your dad?

AVA: Hard to describe. Have a seat if you'd like.

STARR: Just . . . Where? Here?

AVA: If you'd like.

STARR sits.

I'll turn the heat up.

The seat glows.

STARR: Oh, that's nice.

Awkward silence.

AVA: You're hungry.

STARR: I'm—

AVA: Let's see what we have, we have popcorn. And water.

STARR: That doesn't look like water.

AVA: You don't have a filter, do you? Internally. No? No, then you shouldn't drink that. Just have the popcorn.

STARR: You seem to have a lot of popcorn.

AVA: I live on it.

STARR: Oh, you really like it, do you?

AVA: No. I live on it.

Whirring sound of hot-air popper.

STARR: So, I was hoping to see Neil.

AVA: Yes. And I was hoping to get to know him.

STARR: You're his daughter.

AVA: I don't want to come off as entitled, but . . .

STARR: You want get to know him?

AVA: Please.

STARR: Through me, love?

AVA: Yes. Tell me.

STARR: I haven't seen Neil in thirty-five years.

AVA: Exactly. That's the Neil I'm interested in.

STARR: Oh, well . . . and I was kind of curious about the one that's living right now.

CHICHI enters, grabs a handful of popcorn; she winks.

AVA: You mentioned a journal.

STARR: Uh—

CHICHI: Nice day.

STARR: Uh.

AVA: Great day.

AVA: *(to STARR)* Uh . . . journal.

STARR: Yes. This was his journal.

AVA: This?

She takes it reverently. Opens it.

CHICHI: You look good.

AVA: You look good.

CHICHI winks.

STARR: What is she doing?

AVA: You ask the hardest questions. Metabolizing?

STARR: With her eye.

AVA: Oh, winking.

STARR: Yes. Why?

AVA: Why?

CHICHI winks.

STARR: Am I supposed to do something?

AVA: Not unless you want to.

STARR: *(to CHICHI)* You look good.

STARR winks back to CHICHI, who suddenly stands.

CHICHI: Go to hell!

She storms out.

STARR: I offended her?

AVA: Again, you can't actually offend. But Chichi is concerned for Dad's safety. So we better move. I'll trade you your memories for a chance to see him in person.

STARR: You want my stories of Neil?

AVA: No, stories take too long. We don't have the time.

She finds a DVD in the journal.

What's this? *Rusty Ford: Earthbound.*

STARR: Oh, that's a documentary your mother made. I haven't seen it since high school.

Zap! She tries to find information on it.

AVA: I wish I could see it. DVD. Obsolete format. Lost.

STARR: It's okay.

STARR touches AVA gently.

Beat.

AVA: He's in there.

SCENE 16: AT THE THRESHOLD

STARR stands at the threshold of the sanctuary.

STARR: I'm nervous.

AVA: I could maybe synthesize a sedative.

STARR: No, I kind of like it. Feelings are fun. Oh god, I'm going to be sick.

AVA: Not a problem.

STARR: The way he's been described makes him sound like a god.

AVA: A pioneer is my preferred image.

STARR: He'll live forever?

AVA: If things go as planned.

STARR: You'll all live forever?

AVA: It looks like it might be an option. But we don't completely know.

STARR: Could he make me live forever?

AVA: It would be just the augmented population, but again . . .

STARR: I wouldn't want it anyway. Weather being what it is.

AVA: I do believe in augmentation for all. It's just, not available yet.

STARR: I'm not looking to be saved. I just want to see if what I remember is real, to see if I can find— Sometimes my eyes water when I'm nervous.

AVA: I'm worried you'll be disappointed.

STARR: I'm worried he'll be disappointed.

AVA: I don't think that's possible.

STARR: Just a quick hello. Do you have a mirror?

SCENE 17: REUNION

AVA: I usually just look at someone looking at me, but you don't have that, um . . . "app" do you?

STARR: I have no apps.

AVA: I know, I just can't . . . it's amazing. Once upon a time that's how we were, and in there is the guy that changed everything.

> *STARR enters the sanctuary and approaches NEIL, who sits staring out into space. Occasionally he gestures very subtly as he manipulates unfathomable quantities of data. She's overcome when she sees him.*

STARR: Oh.

> *She gathers herself.*

Hello . . . Neil. It's good to . . . meet you, I suppose. That we are meeting for the first time. A person that I used to be once knew a person that you used to be. I don't know if you remember.

> *She holds out a high school yearbook.*

I was a boy, or in a boy's body at least, my name was Oliver. And you, you were just a person, not an almost-god. Though you were an almost-god to me. And now you're the inventor of a new type of person or so I hear.

The buzzing of a fly catches her attention. STARR *moves a little closer.*

Your daughter is beautiful. I'm sorry that I never met her; I'm sorry that I never told you that I was sorry about missing her arrival, about her mother's death, Hafa's death, about never saying goodbye. I think about her as often as I think about you. And I think of you every day.

She moves a little closer.

Do you remember? When we were all in grade twelve, we did that thing at the planetarium. It stuck with me, I guess. It's funny how a time and space might do that.

And I would go back there from time to time as it drifted closer and closer to the shore; well, of course the shore was drifting closer and closer to it, we know that, but it was like it was just pushing off, heading off to sea, to sail off across the ocean, off the edge, past the turtles, somewhere maybe a little darker, but also maybe a little less painful than this old place.

She moves a little closer.

Do you remember me? If you did, would there be any way that you could tell me?

She sits by him.

She opens the yearbook.

I've been gathering from what your daughter has been saying that you don't forget anything anymore. That every moment lived is always available. That's amazing. I don't remember much. I do remember the time we kissed. I can still taste that. I've kissed a thousand times after that, and most of them don't register. But that one, though, I still taste it. And I love that it stands out like that.

She rubs her legs.

Gosh, you look so good. You've aged so little, I guess that's how it works for you folks. I've got a few things that are catching up with me. But I'm not here for a miracle, I don't need to be healed, I just wanted to say hello; an old friend.

She moves closer.

Can I touch you?

She strokes his hair. The flowers in the planter react.

Why is it so satisfying to see you again? What is it about a memory that calls us? What is it that connects us? Maybe without those memories we become untethered.

STARR *falls asleep leaning on* NEIL. CHICHI *passes quietly through the space.*

SCENE 18: WAKING

NEIL *stirs and seems to become aware of his surroundings. He looks at* STARR. *After a while, he sings:*

NEIL: I missed you baby,
But my aim's improving
I've drawn my bead on you
But you keep on moving
I've been hunting high and low
Oh, my darling, where did you go
I missed you baby,
But my aim's improving.

He starts to unplug himself. A little attachment on his head comes free and he pulls out a long thread from his skull. It requires a little forceful tug at the end to free it from his brain.

As the thread comes free, it unleashes an explosive cue. Something like the beginning of Pink Floyd's "In the Flesh" blasts with light and fury.

NEIL *is gone.*

Meanwhile:

SCENE 19: AVA'S STUDY

AVA is rolling a twenty-sided die.

CHICHI: What's that?

AVA: A die. I've been rolling it and trying to predict the outcome.

CHICHI: Oh yeah? What's your accuracy?

AVA: 100 percent

CHICHI: It's only twenty sides, pretty easy to calculate. Throw it.

AVA does.

Nine.

AVA: Yep.

CHICHI: It's crazy that thirty years ago that would be a mystery. "Oh my, what number will it be?" I like my uncertainty to reside at the quantum level. That's more interesting.

AVA: What's more interesting to me is that this was his. This actual object was something that held his attention for a time. It feels like the most concrete thing I know about him from then, and I still don't understand.

CHICHI: Give it. I'll roll an eleven from here.

AVA: I feel so far away from him. Chichi, I think it's me, isn't it? I'm holding us back from transcendence. Something I haven't done for him, I haven't been there for him; and now he's so far gone, he's so far away, and I can't reach him. How do I solve this?

CHICHI: That's weird, I got a three.

AVA has drifted off.

What's that smell?

LAN appears.

LAN: Hello!

CHICHI: Who are you?

LAN: Friend of Ava's—profile!

Flash!

CHICHI: Oh, him. I mean you.

LAN: Yeah. Don't judge. We were just in the middle of a conversation when she disappeared.

CHICHI: I don't know anything about that. She's got a lot going on right now.

LAN: I see, but I've been working on something she started and I've got . . . I wanted her to know before anyone else.

AVA wakes up.

AVA: What's that smell? Lan?

LAN: Sorry, did I wake you?

AVA: Wait? What? Are you *physically* here?

LAN: Uh . . .

She touches him.

CHICHI: He just walked in.

AVA: I thought your body was in Johannesburg.

LAN: Did you? Oh, no—uh . . .

CHICHI: Profile.

Flash.

LAN: Right, I had the old . . . of course. No, I'm, uh, just over on Boundary now.

AVA: You live in Burnaby? Since when?

LAN: Not too long.

AVA: Are you stalking me?

LAN: No!

CHICHI: Are you creeping?

LAN: No, no . . . I didn't want to make a big deal out of it, but it's a short-term stay. A little work trip. I'm doing an on-the-ground, real-world archeological dig at Electronic Arts and, uh, the principal investigator is very hush-hush. I had to keep privacy settings really tight, but anyway, ta-da! Here we are, it's me, Lan, in the flesh!

AVA: I have to sit down.

LAN: No, but listen . . .

CHICHI: You have a lot of weird things going on in you—you're very wound up.

LAN: I'm excited.

CHICHI: We're very near a sacred space. You need to calm down.

LAN: No, I don't. Wound up is kind of my thing.

CHICHI: Not here it's not. Drink this.

LAN: No, I won't and here's why:

Zap, indicating a thought transfer.

CHICHI: Ah, good point, but:

Zap.

LAN: No, I know, but:

Zap.

CHICHI: But:

Zap.

LAN: But:

Zap.

CHICHI: But:

Zap.

LAN: But:

CHICHI: But:

LAN: But:

CHICHI: But:

Zap. Zap. Zap. Zap.

LAN: But: And: And: And: And: AND: Finally:

Zap, zip, zop, zop, zap, zip, Zing!

CHICHI: Well, I suppose that's definitive. Except:

Zwish.

LAN: Shard! Very good. Touché. I see what you did there. Fine, I'll drink your sedative.

He does.

Okay. I have news. Ava, please, this is critical.

AVA: Okay.

LAN: While you were gone, I thought about what you said and then suddenly I realized—on my own, mind you—it could, in fact, be done. The rain algorithm is possible.

CHICHI: What?

AVA: Using the rain as increased processing power—a steady data stream.

LAN: I've got the equation.

AVA: You know calculus?

LAN: Of course, I know calculus, I know kung fu.

AVA: Yes, of course, everybody knows everything, but not everybody is *good* at everything.

LAN: True. My kung fu is weak, but I'm not bad at math.

AVA: You've figured it out.

LAN: I think so. The main principle at least. The collective will solve the rest.

AVA: You haven't uploaded it?

LAN: I wanted you to know before I did, so you could see it happen. When I give it over to the collective, and if the theory holds up, it could change everything.

CHICHI: Do it.

LAN: Yes?

AVA: Yes.

He releases the information.

Wait! What about her?

LAN: Who?

CHICHI: What about her?

AVA: I wanted to give her the chance to augment.

CHICHI: Too late.

AVA: But my father . . .

LAN: Look!

Flash! His ideas are open source now. They collectively gasp.

TOGETHER: Oh!

The vision grows.

Oh!

It's picked up by the group mind and expanded.

Wow!

Theories are tested and proven.

Yes!

More.

Yes!

More!

Yes!

Something unexpected.

Huh?

A problem.

Uh . . .

It's bigger than expected.

Oh no.

It's now clear.

Oh.

AVA: Come on. You forgot to carry the one.

LAN: Oops.

CHICHI: But hey . . .

LAN: It doesn't matter—still works!

AVA: It works. It's working.

Rain thunders down.

CHICHI: It's actually happening, I can't believe it.

LAN: We're using nature as a processor. This is amazing!

AVA: Everything's going so much faster now.

CHICHI: The acceleration is accelerating! It's happening. We're on the verge. The singularity is now!

The distant sound of bombastic Pink Floyd. Everything comes to a halt.

SCENE 20: SANCTUARY

AVA, CHICHI, and LAN are instantly bursting into the sanctuary.

AVA: He's gone!

CHICHI: No! We're almost there.

LAN: He's unplugged.

CHICHI: But . . . then . . .

LAN: Why is the collective still functional?

AVA: It shouldn't run without him.

LAN: And yet I'm still / connected . . . uhhhhhhhhhhhh.

AVA: What's happening?

CHICHI: He's crashing. His identities are all shutting down. He's going offline. It's all arrrrrrhhhhhhh.

AVA: Chichi! The world's coming apart!

LAN and CHICHI collapse.

Dad! Daddy! Daddy!

Blackout.

SCENE 21: SANCTUARY-STARR AND AVA

Darkness. There is a grinding sound of someone operating a small, hand-cranked flashlight.

AVA: *(waking)* Help.

STARR: Just a moment.

Wind, wind, wind.

AVA: What is that?

STARR: I think the power's out, but that's normal for us folks. I always carry my little cranky.

She turns on the flashlight.

AVA: Daddy?

STARR: Oh, love . . .

AVA: Where are you?

STARR: I've messed things up.

AVA: I wish I had never—

STARR: I wish *I* had never—

AVA has found an origami bird.

What is that?

STARR holds it.

An origami bird. A clue.

AVA: Where is he?

STARR: If I know Neil and, really, I don't know if I do anymore, but if I did—

AVA: If you know where he is, please get him!

STARR: My legs . . . I don't think I can make it . . .

AVA: Where?

STARR: Kitsilano. But if I told you, though, where to go . . .

AVA: I have no memory. No map. No GPS. Nothing in me to give direction.

STARR: Be my legs, I'll be your compass.

AVA lifts STARR onto her back. Rain is heard beyond the dome and behind that the sound of someone whistling.

SCENE 22: OUTSIDE THE DOME

The sound of whistling draws our attention up to the dome.

On the dome appears the image of the Space Centre from Vanier Park.

Lightning. A thunderclap.

SCENE 23: NOA'S ARC

On stage, NOA, a woman in her eighties, has entered carrying a model of the Space Centre. She places it on a table as she sets up for a presentation. Above is blue sky; clouds drift lazily by. Rain pounds loudly on the roof.

STARR and AVA enter from behind the stage as if entering the Star Theatre.

SCENE 24: IN THE STAR THEATRE

AVA: Dad?

NOA gasps.

STARR: Neil?

NOA: Welcome!

STARR: Oh my god!

NOA: Are you space travellers?

AVA: No, we're—

NOA: In fact, you are! And the rocket leaves tonight!

AVA: Is there a rocket?

NOA: Maybe. Have a seat I'll be starting the show in just a minute.

AVA: No, we're sorry. We're— Have you seen / a man?

STARR: Oh my god, Ms. Martins!

NOA: What? Hello?

STARR: Ms. Martins. You were my teacher.

NOA: Was I? I guess you didn't make much of an impression. Joking. No, but who are you?

STARR: You wouldn't remember me; I've changed a lot. But you're still *here*—you don't know how happy that makes me.

NOA: Makes me pretty happy too.

AVA: We're looking for someone. We think he's here. Do you know—

NOA: I typically notice when visitors come in.

STARR: We think he's playing hide and seek.

NOA: Hide and seek. How old is he?

STARR: Fifty-three.

NOA: Oh, so he could be quite good. Probably more sophisticated than just crouching in the seats.

STARR: Could he be downstairs?

NOA: No, that's all sealed off. Ocean levels flooded it out. Just this level is open.

Now if you'll just take your seats, I'll begin the presentation.

AVA: We're not here for a presentation.

NOA: Well, it's a function of the space, so you'll have to accept it.

Whistling is heard.

AVA: I hear him!

STARR: He's under here!

NOA: I don't think so. This was put in when the place went digital. It's been like this since 2013?

STARR: That's the last time I was here.

NOA: Oh. *That's* the last time? You should consider an annual membership. It motivates you!

STARR: I was with a boy named Neil. And a girl named Hafa.

NOA: Are you Oliver?

STARR: No, but I was.

Whistling.

AVA: Can we open it up?

NOA: Not while I have a show to do. So, sit down or get out because it's going to get very dark.

AVA: How long are the shows because we need to find him. Humanity is dying without him.

NOA: Humanity is always dying. The universe is always dying. Things fall apart. But it's in the decay that true creation comes!

Whistling. NOA *stomps her foot.*

Shut up, ghosts! And listen!

NOA *points to the model.*

You are here. Now, this is supposed to be a show about stars, but the system has fallen into disrepair.

So instead of looking up at the stars, let's imagine we're the stars looking up at earth. Eh? Change the perspective. Besides, since this endless rain began, the stars have been very lonely and unobserved. So, let's join them.

NOA *peers in through the top of the model as if looking into the Star Theatre. A giant eye appears on the dome. It's* NOA *looking at us.*

There you go, my little dreamers. You're leaning back, imagine yourself. You've bought a ticket, you're warm and dry. And you're leaning back. Reclining. Do you like that? It's a "we'll take care of you" position. Like you're getting your hair washed, your teeth cleaned. Like you're lying down for a little midday nap.

It's an imagining posture. A hopeful position. A place to ask questions. What if? What will happen? What's next? If you could fly, where would you go?

She picks up the model of the Space Centre and "flies" it around the space.

Okay, comfy? Welcome to the H.R. MacMillan Space Centre and compassion shelter. Tonight's show: Behind the Clouds.

The eyeball continues to gaze down. The stage transforms back to the sanctuary.

SCENE 25: SANCTUARY—CHICHI AND LAN

LAN and CHICHI awake. Voice-overs, spoken by NEIL, drift in.

VOICE: *(or projected text)* Their Minds. Are untethered. They have no connection. And the space between them seems vast and inconsiderate. Yes. Cruel Space. Alone, in the vacuum.

CHICHI: So much space around me. What is this feeling?

VOICE: They had long forgotten what it was like to be alone with their thoughts.

LAN: Lonely. I'm so lonely.

CHICHI: Where are you?

LAN is shaking his head, desperately trying to reboot.

LAN: I don't know . . . it's all a blank . . . No information. Locate! Locate!

CHICHI: Here, come here, let me—

They try to grab each other but miss despite being only inches apart.

LAN: Where are—

CHICHI: Hold still—

She grasps him. It's clumsy and awkward.

Got your nose.

VOICE: They had long forgotten what it was like to be so connected.

LAN: What is that?

CHICHI: That's me, holding you.

LAN: Oh. Good?

CHICHI: Just don't get any . . .

LAN: Get any what?

CHICHI: Didn't I just say?

LAN: Not that I . . .

CHICHI: Not that you what?

LAN: Didn't I just say?

CHICHI: Hm. I wonder if we should have . . .

LAN: What? Should have what? You just sort of . . .

CHICHI: Huh? Sort of what? Just sort of . . .

LAN: What? Don't let go!

CHICHI: This is so strange . . . everything is kind of flat—

LAN: And . . . slow and linear and . . .

CHICHI: And hard to connect— I keep forgetting what I was . . .

LAN: What were you?

CHICHI: What was I what?

LAN: I . . . don't . . .

CHICHI: We've got to try to carry through to the end of a . . .

LAN: Thought?

CHICHI: Yeah, that's . . .

LAN: It?

CHICHI: Yes, good. Keep it—

LAN: Real.

CHICHI: No, keep it . . .

LAN: Coming.

CHICHI: Better.

LAN: We've got . . .

CHICHI: To do this . . .

LAN: Better?

CHICHI: No. / Together.

LAN: Together. High five.

They kiss.

CHICHI: That wasn't . . .

LAN: A five.

CHICHI: No . . . calibration is—

LAN: —off . . .

CHICHI: I think that's—

LAN: It.

CHICHI: This . . .

LAN: Can work?

CHICHI: Can it? No.

Beat.

Oh, we were stupid to let a . . . an

LAN: An obsolete

CHICHI: An obsolete human into our space . . .

LAN: Nothing but / trouble . . .

CHICHI: Trouble. We've got to . . .

LAN: Get him—

CHICHI: Neil

LAN: Get Neil

CHICHI: Back. I can't believe / he unplugged

LAN: He unplugged. Why? / Why!

CHICHI: Why. I don't . . .

LAN: Know. Where did we . . .

CHICHI: Go wrong? / Maybe we . . .

LAN: Maybe we should / never have

CHICHI: Never have had a—

LAN: White guy?

Pause.

CHICHI: White guy?

LAN: You know. Running the thing.

CHICHI: Huh?

LAN: You know? Just to point out the—

CHICHI: Elephant?

LAN: In the room.

CHICHI: It doesn't matter that / he was . . .

LAN: He was white?

CHICHI: Yeah, augmentation erased the—

LAN: Idea of privilege.

CHICHI: Right.

LAN: Still, look at what—

CHICHI: —happened . . . just when—

LAN: We're just about to go somewhere—

TOGETHER: Singularity!

LAN: He just ups and—

CHICHI: Fracks off.

LAN: Intentionally?

CHICHI: No, probably not.

LAN: Never intentionally. But that might have been / the problem.

CHICHI: That Problem.

LAN: A trend with well-meaning guys like him.

CHICHI: General cluelessness.

LAN: Head a little bit up

CHICHI: The proverbial

LAN: Ass.

CHICHI: Right. Should have seen it

LAN: Coming

CHICHI: And now look at us—

LAN: There's a hundred

CHICHI: Thousand augmented

LAN: People around the world

CHICHI: And they are now

LAN: Entirely,

CHICHI: Entirely,

LAN: Entirely,

CHICHI: Alone.

LAN: Squeeze me.

CHICHI: Okay.

Pause.

LAN: Could you . . . plug in? In his place?

CHICHI: What? No; gross. And it's all organized around Neil's biology, his brain patterns, his chemical makeup.

LAN: Look at you go with the thought flow! Maybe, maybe . . . If you could find a way to fly in under the radar . . . subvert the system. Mess with the patterns, occupy the chemistry.

CHICHI: I don't know.

LAN: But

CHICHI: We need to get online soon.

LAN: Yes.

CHICHI: Because if we're offline—

LAN: Yes.

CHICHI: Our bodies aren't safe.

LAN: Yes.

CHICHI: Nanobots don't work.

LAN: Yes.

CHICHI: And the world is toxic!

LAN: Yes.

CHICHI: Shard.

LAN: Exactly.

CHICHI: But how can I make the system change from his chemistry to . . .

LAN: Yours?

CHICHI notes music in the room.

CHICHI: Do you hear that? Singing . . .

CHICHI picks up a plant, pulls a leaf off it, nibbles. Music grows. Images of microscopic drones appear on the screens.

Oh, something's happening.

LAN: What?

CHICHI: A tingling in the top of my head.

LAN: Are you—

CHICHI: I can see them. Can you see them? The robots inside us! They're going to work. They're taking us all apart! Hang on, Lan. You better hang on.

LAN: This evening is getting stranger and stranger.

SCENE 26: MUSIC BREAK

The beginning of a spacey love song; the pieces of the stage start to detach and fly off into space.

SCENE 27: BEHIND THE DOOR

AVA, NOA, and STARR are revealed on a walkway behind the dome, which, like a scrim, becomes translucent when lit from behind.

AVA: What *is* this place?

NOA: We're in the firmament now! Metaphorically. In a more literal sense, it's a crawl space. Storage.

STARR: Look at all this!

NOA: Slide projectors. Lasers. DVD players. Lava lamp. All the old systems.

It's part of my past. I was born in 1968 on the night *Apollo 8* was looking back to earth from the dark side of the moon. My mom later told me there was a spiritual movement launched the night I was born. It was a short-lived one mind you, but she knew the guru, a teacher, who helped her find her voice as a poet.

STARR: I remember when you told us that and you also said:

NOA: Everyone can use a guide from time to time.

STARR: That was the last night of analogue.

AVA: What's the last night of analogue.

NOA: A little party that was being hosted at the Space Centre. They were finally upgrading their analogue system for doing shows—everything was going digital! I invited these three high school kids to make a presentation for it.

STARR: That night is the reason I thought we'd find Neil here. It's where he lives in my memory.

NOA: I said, make a science project for the Space Centre.

STARR: They were tearing the place apart. We watched the workers dismantle the old and make way for the new. We watched and thought about what we would do, and late that night we got high out by the crab sculpture, and then it came to us: a treasure hunt. A field trip for grown-ups. Filled with ideas about past and future. Analogue and digital. Invented by your mom and Neil and me. It was an excuse to get into the Space Centre after hours, while they were closed, to work late, and stay overnight.

NOA: Bad judgment call on my part. But you had impressed me with your work. Like that space cowboy documentary.

AVA: This documentary? Rusty Ford?

NOA: Let me see.

STARR: We were weirdos.

NOA: Potential!

STARR: Outcasts.

NOA: Potential!

STARR: Aliens in our school, in our skin.

NOA: To me, you were future stars.

STARR: Oh well, I've been a star for years. Fat lot of good it's done me.

AVA: Hey, wait, look, I'm a star too.

NOA: Me too.

> *Three pinpoints of light emerge in the sky. Flashlights are being held behind the dome, which appears solid again as the rest of the lights behind the dome fade.*

Ever wonder what we would have been if we couldn't have seen the stars?

STARR: You mean long ago?

> *Constellations emerge, formed by the cast behind the dome.*

NOA: Yes, back thousands and thousands of years, when we were growing our big brains, there was a constant backdrop of the night sky to be observed at the end of a long day's work surviving.

The crew looks up.

How do you sleep at night?

AVA: I don't very much.

NOA: That's right. And those early insomniacs saw this recurring pattern every night. Vast, but consistently recognizable. The same shapes floating across the sky with enough minor variation to draw attention to themselves.

STARR: Stars.

NOA: I think this is where we learned to imagine—to project our ideas into stories, possible futures and possible pasts. On this canvas of the night sky was drawn the first legends, myths, the heroes and villains that could provide a way for them to figure out how to live. Where else was there something so consistent—a writing so permanent—and yet in motion. It is the structure in which we find our own stories . . . It is the motion that suggests a beginning, a middle, and an end. The night sky: a projection machine for us to fill in the blanks and shape the stories that make sense of our individual lives. We need that. It's been gone a long, long, time . . . before this rain even, the stars were replaced with facts and data and very little room left for us to connect our own dots, draw our own pictures.

SCENE 28: DOCUMENTARY

An establishing shot of RUSTY's apartment building.

A red door in the centre of the frame flickers into existence out of black.

Traffic sounds.

Jump cut to exterior of RUSTY's apartment.

Closer to the door, HAFA runs up and knocks.

Over black, music plays: "I Miss You (But My Aim's Improving)"

Title card fades in: Rusty Ford: Earthbound

Exterior of RUSTY*'s apartment.*

RUSTY *opens the door and greets the camera with a smile.*

Fast forward through following edits.

Interior of RUSTY*'s apartment—stairwell.*

The song continues.

RUSTY *walks up the stairs to his apartment.*

Jump cut to interior of RUSTY*'s apartment—external hallway.*

The song continues.

RUSTY *walks down the hall of his apartment.*

A series of shots:

>> Rusty Ford concert poster

>> Bones and antlers

>> Rusty Ford CD

>> Bathroom squid.

Interior of RUSTY*'s suite—kitchen.*

A stuffed-animal bear head. Tilt down to reveal suite hallway.

Interior of RUSTY*'s apartment—external hallway.*

Song continues.

RUSTY *arrives at his door and opens it, enters.*

Interior of RUSTY*'s suite—hallway.*

Song continues.

Walks down the hall to his kitchen.

A series of shots:

>> Stompin' Tom Connors eight-track tape

>> Light switch

>> Radiator

Interior of RUSTY*'s suite—kitchen.*

RUSTY *is laughing in conversation.*

HAFA *can be (barely) seen at the edge of the frame, shot over the shoulder as she interviews* RUSTY*.*

Jump cut to interior of RUSTY*'s suite—kitchen.*

RUSTY *is finishing the song on his guitar.*

Over black, a title card reads: A film by Hafa Sharifi.

Sound of applause from the crew.

RUSTY: Now that's country music.

Interior of RUSTY*'s suite—kitchen.*

RUSTY *begins putting down his guitar.*

Now. The meaning of life.

Interior of RUSTY*'s suite—kitchen.*

Slate in frame claps down with authority. RUSTY*'s guitar is down.*

Jump cut to interior of RUSTY*'s suite—kitchen.*

RUSTY *is talking about consciousness.*

STARR: *(voice-over)* Hafa discovered Rusty Ford, a country singer . . .

RUSTY: I think it's really kind of exhausting to be alive and experience consciousness. I think that's why we have to take a break and go on a little brain vacation every evening.

STARR: *(voice-over)* . . . who seemed to know a lot about science.

Jump cut to interior of RUSTY*'s suite—kitchen.*

RUSTY *puts an ice pack under his hat.*

RUSTY: Does the hat look okay? Is it riding a little high?

Cut to interior of RUSTY*'s suite—kitchen.*

STARR: *(voice-over)* And space travel.

RUSTY: Mars kind of sucks.

RUSTY *continues talking as we hear the voice-over.*

STARR: *(voice-over)* She wanted to make a documentary about him. He was an undiscovered star that Hafa could claim as her own.

RUSTY: And if you remember— Well, you probably don't remember; you're a youngster and I'm old.

But the first pictures that they beamed back from Mars . . .

Insert of images of Martian landscape.

Are the same pictures we're seeing today, which is like 100 percent pure boring . . .

Jump cut to interior of RUSTY*'s suite—kitchen.*

RUSTY *continues to talk. Voice-over continues.*

In comparison to anything on the planet earth. Like, imagine if Martians sent a probe to earth.

STARR: *(voice-over)* He seemed so impossible. A beautiful accident of evolution.

A series of shots:

>> RUSTY *eats ice cream*

>> RUSTY *shops for veggies*

>> RUSTY *plays guitar in the park*

RUSTY: If Martians sent something to Earth it could be hit in traffic; it could be swallowed by a whale; it would drown in the ocean probably . . .

Exterior of Grandview Park.

RUSTY *walks amid the people in the park.*

Well, I don't mean to be prejudiced or anything but, man, this is the best planet going. I mean, like, my god . . .

Interior of RUSTY*'s suite—kitchen.*

. . . if this was real estate, if this was the game of Monopoly, this would be Park Place.

Fade out.

Insert of HAFA*'s eye up close.*

It would be the most primo place in the entire universe.

STARR: *(voice-over)* And I watched her watching him.

Interior of RUSTY*'s suite—kitchen.*

Plants grow on the deck. More wisdom from RUSTY.

RUSTY: I think that when we first left our atmosphere was the first time we realized how incredibly special this place was.

Insert of a teenage boy's eyes.

STARR: *(voice-over)* And I watched Neil watching her.

Insert of an image of Earth from behind the moon.

RUSTY: The people that went to the moon—there was only about twenty-four of them—they experienced a view that almost no one in the history of humanity has had the privilege of seeing . . .

Interior of RUSTY*'s suite—kitchen.*

Which is our tiny little planet in the vast, completely empty, fuck-all of space, and to see that perspective . . .

Interior of Space Centre—cosmic courtyard.

We pull back to reveal the footage in the kitchen is actually being projected on the cosmic courtyard.

And just to realize what an unbelievably important oasis of creation and life our planet is in the middle of really fuck-all is incredibly important.

A series of shots:

>> *Typewriter*

>> *Spacesuit*

>> *Jukebox*

>> *Pay phone*

>> *Map*

>> 2001: A Space Odyssey *playing on TV*

>> *Garden and tent*

STARR: *(voice-over)* So we included parts of the documentary in our treasure hunt. And that night she watched as people played with the things we made. I watched her watching in delight. A cosmic miracle.

An insert investigating HAFA*: close-ups on her.*

A slow-motion running toward the door and never quite revealing her face as she turns back to the camera.

Her hand reaching up and touching a shoulder.

(voice-over) And then I realized it was like I was viewing my planet from space. She was living in the body that I should have, the planet where I belonged, while I was stuck in some alien vessel. And then suddenly, he disappeared into the night. Hafa and I searched and searched, but we couldn't find him.

Exterior, atrium—night.

The tent is lit from within.

(voice-over) And after everyone left for home, we spent the night in the tent . . . We waited and waited for him to return.

I did something wrong, and Neil had disappeared. And there was no going back.

Exterior of Santa Barbara market.

RUSTY *shops for fruit.*

HAFA: Do you think the earth would be better off without humans?

RUSTY: Sometimes I think, god, we're so stupid. Why don't we just go away?

Exterior Space Centre—launch pad.

A bottle rocket is primed, pointing to the sky. Someone pumps the rocket. Pressure builds.

STARR: *(voice-over)* I needed to break free, to find my own planet. And I did, came whistling down like Gagarin, all risk and joy, and found my home. My true celestial body and have been living in it since . . . with only the regret of finding it too late . . .

Interior of RUSTY*'s suite—kitchen.*

(voice-over) For when we three were in love and awkward and incomplete.

HAFA: Where do you want humans to be in one hundred years?

RUSTY: Well, I think humans are kind of like adolescents that have stolen their mom's car keys, and they've gone for a spin and they've thrown some beer bottles out the window and they're having a great time . . .

Exterior industrial alley.

RUSTY *plays guitar in a back alley. Music quietly in the background.*

But they're making a hell of a racket and mess, and I kind of hope we come home, apologize to Mom, gas up the car, and get some sleep and a hundred years from now maybe realize that—

A series of shots:

>> *Jukebox playing records: close-up*

We don't have to tear the crap out of the place to have a good time.

AVA: Maybe it wasn't you that made him drift away. Maybe it was him.

I can see him on that night.

On that night . . . he watched the people playing with what you made.

>> *Stuffy riding zip line*

>> *Fake bird flying into glass*

>> *Popcorn popping*

>> *Mirror*

And he realized that this, this night in 2013, was just a future memory and that its value was to be determined at some time ahead.

Someone would deem it as beautiful, or worthless, or offensive, or pointless, but he had no way to know if what he was living was to be condemned or celebrated or just forgotten.

>> *Slide shows*

He couldn't go on; he became paralyzed by indecision, as he couldn't determine if who he was or what he did would be reviled or loved. So he began imagining a time when there would be no time . . .

>> *Tent in garden*

But maybe he wasn't big enough, or whole enough, or strong enough to do it . . . and he's still waiting there in the past to be released.

Exterior Commercial Drive.

RUSTY *walks toward the camera.*

RUSTY: What makes people special? If you look at it through the lens of being able to perceive creation we may have the most sophisticated view of creation of anything in the entire universe, and that makes us special.

Exterior Grandview Park.

RUSTY *plays guitar in the park.*

I think the important thing to focus on is just accepting that we have, uh, perhaps the simplest and most important job in the entire universe . . .

Insert of HAFA*'s eye watching* RUSTY*.*

It's almost as though we're seeing the world through the eye of an insect.

HAFA's eye watches.

And if you look at the eye of an insect through a microscope, it's got all these little facets that point in slightly different directions. And each one of us is one of those facets.

Interior of RUSTY's suite—kitchen.

And sometimes when people see something different than someone else, they think that they must be crazy or they're lying or you're stupid or something else, and I think that the important thing is that we do see the universe from a slightly different perspective.

Star Theatre—live.

The cast starts to emerge into the theatre. They watch the final lines of the documentary.

Conscious life? How weird is that? That is literally a cosmic miracle. And I think that's one of the things that makes people special and it also makes everything else on the planet special. Like a dog, or whale or fish or birds, imagine how they're experiencing creation. And I think if we're put on this earth to do anything, the best answer I can think of is that we're here to enjoy the view; because nothing else can enjoy the view.

Fade to black.

SCENE 29: UNCOVERING NEIL

NOA: Listen, the rain has stopped. The sky is clearing.

AVA: Look!

The star projector is beginning to rise out of the pit. NEIL is under the projector playing guitar.

CHICHI: A robot!

LAN: A spaceship!

STARR: A dream machine.

AVA: A time machine.

NOA: A time capsule.

AVA: We found him. It's the beginning. It's where we started.

NOA: The last night of analogue.

STARR: It's where we ended. The night I lost him.

AVA: But it's also the moment you began to find him again! It was the perfect moment, because it led us to right now.

STARR stands close to NEIL as he plays his guitar. She reaches out to him.

CHICHI: Ava, it's happening. We've done it. Transcendence is now.

LAN: Singularity is now.

CHICHI: Are you coming?

AVA: Just a moment.

CHICHI: There's no time.

AVA: But there's still a little time.

LAN: Oh, not much.

AVA: But just a little, and for now I just want to stay right here. With them.

CHICHI: With who?

AVA: With them.

NEIL stops playing as music begins to fill the space from elsewhere.

SCENE 30: FINALE. TIME CAPSULE UNEARTHED/HAROLD'S RETURN

Light fades away in the space. Slowly the cast extinguish their lanterns. The stars appear in the night sky growing more and more brilliant.

AVA: We're lying on our backs, face out to the universe. We are projections of a distant dream, a distant memory. We are projections, recurring points of light on which to build a story. And the space between us is just possibility untold.

The stars appear to move. We rotate along through space. Music plays.

ABOUT THE CONTRIBUTORS

Tyler Clarke is an actor, writer, and filmmaker. He played various characters in each of The Virtual Stage's annual *Zombie Syndrome* productions (2012 to 2016) and was also on the writing team for *Alien Contagion: Rise of The Zombie Syndrome* (2015) and *The Zombie Syndrome: Dead in the Water* (2016). Clarke is a graduate of Vancouver's Frames Film Program.

Stan Douglas is a visual artist who lives and works in Vancouver and Los Angeles. His films, videos, and photographs have been seen in exhibitions internationally, including Documenta IX, X, and XI (1992, 1997, 2002) and four Venice Biennales (1990, 2001, 2005, and 2019). A survey of his work, *Stan Douglas: Mise en scène*, toured Europe from 2013 until the end of 2015. From 2014 until 2017, his play *Helen Lawrence* was seen in Vancouver, Toronto, Munich, Antwerp, Edinburgh, Brooklyn, and Los Angeles, and he will represent Canada at the fifty-ninth Venice Biennale in 2021. He received the International Center of Photography's Infinity Award in 2012, the Hasselblad Award in 2016, the Audain Prize for Lifetime Achievement in the Visual Arts in 2019, and was named a Chevalier in French Ordre des Arts et des Lettres in 2020. Between 2004 and 2006 he was a professor at Universität der Künste Berlin and since 2009 has been a member of the core faculty in Graduate Arts at ArtCenter College of Design in Pasadena.

Craig Erickson is an actor and writer based in Vancouver. He has been nominated for nine Jessie Richardson Awards. Other writing includes his one-person fringe show *Jesus Made Me Funny* and *Big Bad* (Boca del Lupo). He is also an independent filmmaker, having written and directed two short films. Over the years, he has traversed the country working as an actor, often in classical theatre (Stratford, Shaw, Bard on the Beach). Acting work with Electric Company includes *Tear the Curtain* (Arts Club/Canadian Stage) and the workshop version of *You Are Very Star.* Craig first met Kevin Kerr upstairs in the drama room at Kamloops Senior Secondary where it was evident to all that Kevin was a theatrical star.

Barbra French is a theatre director, educator, playwright and creator of *Muse*. Her passion for image-based, multidisciplinary approaches to storytelling led to a twenty-year love affair with devised theatre and co-creative art forms. She is an alumnus of Vancouver Island University, the University of British Columbia (BA, Honours) and the University of Alberta (MFA). Barbra was the founding artistic director of the Etcetera Theatre Collective (Edmonton), In Other Words Theatre (Nanaimo), and currently Vita Theatre (Duncan). Additionally, she has taught acting and performance creation at universities, colleges, and private theatres across Western Canada. Her plays include *incoheRANT*, *DOSSIER*, *Shadowplay: curiosities in light and dark*, and *pause*. She is currently writing *Sick*, a full-length, one-woman show, as well as a collection of short plays entitled *SOLO: Performance Pieces for Mature Actors*. Barbra lives on Vancouver Island with her husband, Greg.

Finn Ghosh-Leudke is an actor, playwright, and tap dancer. He came up with the *Alien Contagion* story on the play's writing team when he was only nine years old. At age ten, Ghosh-Leudke co-wrote the story for The Virtual Stage's production of *The Zombie Syndrome: Dead in the Water*.

Chris Haddock's stint as a street musician led him to street theatre, where he first tried his hand at scripting material and writing songs for live performance. He continued lyric writing in a number of club bands and finally stumbled upon screenwriting as an intermittently viable alternative. Chris has since received wide acclaim and awards for his writing and producing. His many credits include creating the international hit *Da Vinci's Inquest* and its spinoff *Da Vinci's City Hall*, the cult favourite *Intelligence* and a stint writing and producing Martin Scorsese's *Boardwalk Empire*, for which he received a Writers Guild of America Award. Most recently he has executive produced his first feature effort, *Small City*, set in London, England. The play included in this collection, *Helen Lawrence*, is his first foray into legit theatre and he is excited and inspired by the experience and thrilled by its international success.

Kevin Kerr is a founding member of Vancouver's Electric Company Theatre with whom he's collaborated on the creation of more than a dozen full-length productions, including *Brilliant!*, *Studies in Motion*, *Tear the Curtain!*, and *You Are Very Star*. A four-time recipient of the Jessie Richardson Award for Outstanding Original Play, Kevin's other plays include *Skydive*, *Spine* (both for Realwheels Theatre), *The Remittance Man* (Sunshine Theatre), *Secret World of Og* (Carousel Theatre for Young People), and *The Night's Mare* (Caravan Farm Theatre). He received the Governor General's Literary Award for *Unity (1918)*, which originally premiered with Touchstone Theatre in 2001. New Media projects include writing the dialogue for Stan Douglas's augmented-reality app and interactive installation, *Circa 1948*, produced by the National Film Board; and in 2019 he wrote and directed *The Virtual Light of Day*, a suite of three virtual reality installations as companion pieces to Electric Company's production of *The Full Light of Day*. He lives with poet Marita Dachsel and their three children on the territory of the lək̓ʷəŋən people (Songhees and Esquimalt First Nations) and teaches playwriting at the University of Victoria's Department of Creative Writing.

Freya Björg Olafson is an intermedia artist who works with video, audio, animation, motion capture, XR, painting, and performance. Her praxis engages with identity and the body, as informed by technology and the Internet. Olafson's work has been exhibited and performed internationally at the Bauhaus Archive (Berlin), SECCA—Southeastern Center for Contemporary Art (North Carolina), Ludwig Museum (Budapest), and the National Arts Centre (Ottawa). Olafson has benefitted from residencies, most notably through EMPAC—Experimental Media and Performing Arts Center (New York), OBORO (Montreal), and CounterPulse (San Francisco). They hold an MFA in New Media from the Transart Institute/ Danube University Krems and joined the Department of Dance at York University as an assistant professor in July 2017. In July 2021 she began a position in Digital Media at the School of Art, University of Manitoba. Olafson was one of the 2020 Sobey Art Award recipients.

David Owen holds a PhD in Performance and Theatre Studies from York University, an MFA in Directing from the University of Calgary, and an MA in Dramatic Theory and Criticism from the University of Alberta. He is an award-winning scholar, a theatre director, and a member of the Playwrights Guild of Canada. His current research focuses on the intersection of performance, game structures, and digital technology. He has written on a range of related topics such as LARP, burlesque, roller derby, and ideology embedded within planned communities. His book *Player and Avatar: The Affective Potential of Videogames* was published in 2017. He resides in Edmonton, Alberta.

Theatre Replacement is an ongoing collaboration between James Long and Maiko Yamamoto. Whether working together or apart, the pair work with a wide range of collaborators and use extended processes to create performances, events, and public art projects from intentionally simple beginnings. Their work is about a genuine attempt to coexist. Conversations, interviews, and arguments collide with Yamamoto and Long's aesthetics, resulting in theatrical experiences that are authentic, immediate, and hopeful. The company continues to build and tour work, and has been presented in forty-three cities and venues across the world.

Andy Thompson (www.andythompson.ca) is a multi-award-winning Vancouver-based producer, director, playwright, teacher, and actor. He is the creator of several acclaimed plays, including *The Birth of Freedom*, the hit musical *Broken Sex Doll*, and the *Zombie Syndrome* theatre series. He is a graduate of Studio 58's professional acting training program and performs regularly in film and television.